ABORIGINAL AFFAIRS
1967–2005
Seeking a Solution

ABORIGINAL AFFAIRS
1967–2005
Seeking a Solution

Max Griffiths

ROSENBERG

First published in Australia in 2006
by Rosenberg Publishing Pty Ltd
PO Box 6125, Dural Delivery Centre NSW 2158
Phone: 61 2 9654 1502 Fax: 61 2 9654 1338
Email: rosenbergpub@smartchat.net.au
Web: www.rosenbergpub.com.au

National Library of Australia Cataloguing-in-Publication data:

Griffiths, Max.
Aboriginal affairs 1967-2005 : seeking a solution

Bibliography.
Includes index.
ISBN 1 877058 45 9.

1. Aboriginal Australians - Government relations - History.
2. Aboriginal Australians - Social conditions - History.
3. Aboriginal Australians - Health and hygiene. 4.
Aboriginal Australians - Land tenure. 5. Aboriginal
Australians - Civil rights. 6. Australia - Politics and
government. 7. Australia - Race relations. I. Title.

305.89915

Cover design: Highway 51, based on the painting *The Voice of the Great Spirit* by
Ainslie Roberts

Set in 12 on 14 point Warnock Pro
Printed in China by Everbest Printing Co Limited
10 9 8 7 6 5 4 3 2 1

Contents

Preface

When the idea was first put to me that I write another book about Aboriginal affairs, I must confess to a lack of enthusiasm at being faced with the prospect of ploughing my way once more through volume after volume of parliamentary *Hansard*. Yet so much had happened since the publication of my first book in 1995 it was difficult to resist the invitation to record what had happened in the so-called 'post-Mabo' period. On a broader canvas I felt there would be value in covering the 40 years since the Australian people, by referendum in 1967, gave to the federal parliament powers to make laws for the Aboriginal people.

Initially I was tempted to call the book '*The Aboriginal Problem*' because that had been an expression frequently used in the federal parliament. Indeed, I had a suspicion that it was also the mental and emotional framework within which many non-indigenous Australians placed the Aboriginal people—in much the same way as we speak of 'problem children'. The problem-solving policies of the various federal governments since 1967 have been labelled with such terms as 'assimilation', 'self-determination', 'separation', 'reconciliation' and, more recently, 'mutual obligation'. In addition to legislative efforts there have been a number of landmark court cases such as the Blackburn judgment and the High Court cases commonly referred to as Mabo and Wik. Those who framed the legislation or made the judgments sincerely believed that they were paving the way for a more enlightened and constructive approach to Aboriginal affairs. In 1995, I believed it was too early to pass judgment on the benefits or otherwise of these attempts. Ten years further down the track, I am now of the opinion that the evidence speaks for itself.

One hard fact which cannot be ignored is that the vast majority of Aboriginal people now live in urban surroundings, either in capital or regional cities and towns. There has been a steady stream of humanity making this move over a number of decades, which, if I can be bold enough to give it a name, I would call 'assimilation by stealth'. In other words, the Aboriginal people have spoken with their feet. Yet it is only in very recent times that federal parliament has recognised the need to devise special policies for urban Aboriginal people.

The thing people fear about assimilation, be they Aborigines or any ethnic group that has come to Australia, is that it means they will lose the right to retain their distinctive group characteristics. Either that, or be subjected to racist treatment from other sections of Australian society. History provides evidence that both these fears are often justified, at least in part. But that which distinguishes the Aboriginal people from migrated ethic groups is their relationship with the land and claims of prior ownership to it. In the past this has led to fears that the recognition of land rights would split the nation apart. It would seem that this is unlikely to happen, and the question now becomes: What do the Aborigines want to do with the land rights they have achieved? Neither legislation nor law case has provided the answer. To put it bluntly, Aborigines themselves will have to decide whether their land assets will be applied to the retention of traditional cultural practices or to the development of economic opportunity. Their decision will be awaited with great interest.

I wish to thank my editor Anne Savage for her professional and sometimes refreshingly provocative comments on the manuscript. I also wish to thank the federal parliamentary authorities who have made *Hansard* available on the Internet, thus saving me the physical burden of carrying its volumes around a public library. In the completion of a book such as this the final and most boring task is the preparation of the index. I thank Wendy Coates for helping me and relieving the monotony with her lively company.

Max Griffiths MBE
Melbourne
December 2005

Introduction
The Rocky Road to Reconciliation

Whatever questions may surround their origins the Aboriginal people certainly were here when, just over 200 years ago, a motley group of British convicts and their military minders became the first representatives of Western civilisation to settle in Australia. What happened to the Aboriginal people prior to that time and the extent to which their lives were affected by changes in climate and the environment generally can be determined only roughly through discoveries of human remains, artefacts, rock paintings and other relics of their occupation of the continent. Anthropologists say that Aboriginal culture has probably remained unchanged for thousands of years, although one cannot speak with absolute confidence about things which might have happened over a period of 40 000 years.

However, the origin of what was once termed the 'Aboriginal problem' can most effectively be identified with the arrival of Europeans on Australia's shores, if for no other reason than that the concept was conceived by the first Europeans and those who followed after them. While this might appear to be stating the obvious, it is important to make the assertion because there are those who believe that the 'problem' lies with the Aboriginal people themselves. They wonder why, after 40 000 years, there is no indication of the cultural developments seen in other parts of the world. Indeed, for a long time after the arrival of the Europeans there was, and maybe there still is among some, an explicit or implicit assumption that the Aborigines were an inferior race. That may not have been a problem for the Europeans but it certainly became a problem for the Aborigines, for the time came when they were no longer prepared to passively accept relegation to the position of second or even third class human beings.

In 1995 David Rosenberg published my book *Aboriginal Affairs 1788–1995: A Brief History*, in which I traced in some detail the relations between Aboriginal people and European settlers. This new book deals more specifically with the period from the referendum of 1967, when Aboriginal people first received national recognition, to 2005, a period during which the problems in Aboriginal society were tackled with a great degree of intensity, by governments of all political persuasions and by Aborigines themselves. Sadly, many of the policies and programmes introduced during this period have been weighed in the balance and found wanting. We appear to have reached a point of impasse where there seems to be no way forward and no unexplored paths to follow. A reflection on this period of nearly 40 years therefore seems a useful exercise to determine how we sought a solution, and how and why all solutions so far have failed.

It's worth noting at this point some of the salient features of Aboriginal affairs, from the time of the arrival of the first Europeans to the time of the referendum of 1967. While the convicts and their military minders were not the most impressive representatives of Western civilisation of the day, the local inhabitants appeared by comparison to belong to the civilisation of the Stone Age. In the words of the *Encyclopaedia Britannica*, they represented 'the prehistoric cultural stage or level of human development characterised by the use of stone implements.'[1]

One hundred and seventy-five years after the first European settlement, Ion Idriess, noted for his detailed works on the Australian outback, wrote *Our Living Stone Age*, based on spending 'half a lifetime and a bit more' in Aboriginal country. It's quite apparent that Idriess believed the lifestyles and practices of the Aboriginal people hadn't changed much for thousands of years: 'I hope there is enough here to give you some inkling of that life, that amazing forgotten life whence you and I also came, the life lived by our own Stone Age mothers and fathers in the vanished past.'[2]

Sadly, the stories of the Aboriginal people that Idriess painted so vividly were only part of a much wider canvas. Other parts of that canvas are occupied with stories of bloody encounters between the new arrivals and the old inhabitants, encounters in which the old inhabitants generally suffered defeat and humiliation, and too often death. This was due substantially to a failure to understand that the Aboriginal people were not as wild and untamed as they appeared, but led a life that was well organised and disciplined. They could not have survived on this continent for 40 000 years had their lifestyle lacked discipline. Moreover, as has only begun to be understood in recent decades, Aboriginal culture was based on a special relationship with the land. The failure to recognise this relationship as significantly different to that of Western cultures has caused untold hardship and misery for the Aboriginal people.

Initially, white settlement in Australia was limited to a number of coastal penal settlements, but as the potential of the country became apparent, colonisation began to occur in the form of land acquisition and development. It was then that the Aboriginal people began to resist, with their knowledge of the land and their capacity to be elusive making them a difficult enemy to combat. Then, with the massive influx of new arrivals following the discovery of gold in 1861, things changed dramatically. So rapidly did the population expand that in a short time the colonists vastly outnumbered the indigenous people, a situation quite different from that in the European colonies in Africa, India and Asia. It wasn't long before the Aborigines began to diminish in number so rapidly it became widely believed that as a race they would vanish altogether.

The plight of the Aborigines led people of charitable disposition to believe that something had to be done to protect them from falling further into wretchedness and possible extinction. So the various colonial governments in Australia adopted a 'protection' policy, with Protectors appointed to administer it. The highly mobile lifestyle of the Aboriginal people made it extremely difficult to deliver 'welfare on the run', however, so another policy was devised, of 'arresting' Aboriginal people and bringing them together in permanent settlements. This meant uprooting them from the places where they had a traditional affinity with the land and herding them together in compounds. Where once they had hunted and gathered their food as they moved around the country, they now lived a sedentary life in a dependency relationship. Those who lived on reserves run by Christian missionaries suffered the additional trauma of being forced to follow the precepts of a religion different to the beliefs they held. They were taught to sing strange songs—and sang them very well, although the meaning of the words often escaped them. Thus, while Australia's new inhabitants prospered, the Aboriginal people's condition remained static at best, but in general deteriorated.

Despite these attempts to adopt a more humane approach, Aborigines were still treated as a race apart. This is demonstrated by the fact that the Constitution which laid the foundation of the Australian nation in 1901 contained only two brief references to the Aborigines. The first excluded them from inclusion in census-taking. The second said that the Commonwealth Government could make laws for people of any race except the Aboriginal people. This, negating the possibility of having any national policy, left the Aborigines completely in the hands of and at the mercy of state governments.

Complicating the situation even more was the growth in the number of people known as 'half-castes', the offspring of relationships between whites and Aborigines. Unwelcome in Aboriginal communities and ill-equipped to enter white society, the half-castes ended up in a cultural and social wasteland. The Great Depression that savaged all levels of Australian society from 1929 until well into the 1930s had its greatest impact on Aboriginal and half-caste people, some of the camps in which they lived turning literally into human rubbish dumps. Once again, people of charitable intent spurred the various state governments into action. The states decided there should be one policy for full-blood Aborigines, who mainly lived traditional lifestyles, and another for the half-castes, who generally lived on the fringes of rural and remote communities. Full-blood Aborigines would be assisted to retain their traditional lifestyle and protected from interference, while it was assumed that half-castes had only one way to go, and that was to be assimilated into white society.

The end of World War II brought with it strong international feeling against racial discrimination which eventually filtered through to have an impact on Australia's treatment of its Aboriginal people. While the Commonwealth Government was still shackled by the limitations placed on it by the Constitution, a growing awareness of the plight of the Aboriginal people brought with it increasing pressure for a referendum which would enable appropriate changes to be made to the Constitution.

By the time the referendum was held in 1967 it had become patently obvious that there were things which needed to be done for the welfare of Aboriginal people that could only be done at the national level. Over 90 per cent of voters said 'yes' to the proposition that the clauses discriminating against the Aborigines should be removed from the Constitution. The referendum not only gave Aborigines the right to be numbered among those who could be counted as Australians, it also recognised their right to have their identity respected. The Commonwealth Government could now make special laws for the Aboriginal people. Finally, it seemed, the Aboriginal people had come out of the Stone Age.

Or had they?

It's a sad but inescapable fact that Aboriginal people still don't fit comfortably into the mainstream of Australian society. By contrast, and despite some painful adjustments on both sides, migrants from all over the world have managed to find their niche and make their mark in the mainstream community, some going from rags to riches—while many Aborigines remain in rags. Contrary to the belief of many politicians, the making of laws is not the final solution to any problem. In the years since the referendum untold numbers of laws, judicial decisions, policies and programmes have been designed and/or passed to preserve and dignify the Aboriginal identity. But all too often they have failed to achieve their objectives.

The history of the Aboriginal people since the referendum of 1967 is not one of a Stone Age people putting the past behind them and beginning a new era. Rather it is a story of a people determined to take their culture into the future and, instead of its being dismissed as primitive, savage and heathen, having it accepted as deserving recognition and respect. The assertion of the Aboriginal people is that the 'whitefella' got it wrong from the very beginning and almost destroyed them and their culture. What the referendum gave them was not the opportunity to step up the ladder into a 'more civilised' status, but the opportunity to assert the quality of their own culture and have it recognised and respected by the whitefella as of equal value to their own. This didn't go down very well with those who believed that their 'yes' vote was opening the door to allow Aboriginal people to share the blessings of Western culture. Thus the determination of Aboriginal people to assert their rights, especially their 'land rights', led to a great deal of tension and confrontation, often ending up in the law courts.

If the Aboriginal people are right in their assertion, where did the newcomers to the country go wrong? The fundamental position of the Aboriginal people is that white people invaded their country, dispossessed them of their land, treated them abominably and almost destroyed their culture. Their claim is that they were the first to occupy this continent, and that they have done so for up to 40 000 years, a time in which they developed a special relationship with the land and created tribal practices and customs that were appropriate to this relationship. Even when white people began to understand these things, it was still believed that the separate identity of the Aboriginal people would gradually fade away. The move to assert the right to retain this separate identity only really gained momentum after the referendum of 1967, and it has to be said that in the years since then, Aboriginal people have experienced some pretty rough times in the pursuit of their goals. So where did things go wrong, and can they be set right?

The plight of the Aboriginal people has been perceived as a problem, a problem which government has striven to resolve—and perhaps that in itself is part of the problem. Aboriginal affairs are now at a watershed, and our collective inability to resolve the situation leaves no alternative but to reassess relationships and responsibilities. Reflecting on the recent history of Aboriginal affairs may provide new guidelines and a new injection of hope for the future.

1

The Origins of the Land Rights Movement

My first encounter with Aboriginal people occurred not long before the referendum of 1967. In 1965 I visited the remote northwest of Australia to observe the momentous events taking place there. I began my journey in the Pilbara, where the discovery of iron ore was seeing the beginnings of a huge new export industry. It was an exciting time to be in an exciting place. Mines and mining towns, ports and port facilities, with railway lines connecting them, and ore container ships of sizes hitherto undreamed of, were being built in record-breaking time. It was breathtaking to watch it happening. But in the midst of this hive of activity I encountered the other side of the Australian outback, where changes were also beginning to take place—but at a snail's pace in comparison.

My first encounter occurred in the small town of Roebourne, which at that time had the only airport in the southern Pilbara. As we drove along the road that took us out into the desert I saw a line of Aboriginal people ambling along, with no apparent sense of purpose. Dressed in shabby clothes, their heads bent, they looked as if they were carrying heavy loads. A short time later we passed the reserve where they lived. The buildings, if you could call them that, were of a kind you might see in a film about refugee camps in Africa, and the people had the same appearance of hopelessness beyond despair. I knew in my mind I was still in Australia but felt in my heart I was in another world.

These fleeting, disturbing impressions were confirmed some years later when my organisation, the Australian Inland Mission, sent a nursing sister to Roebourne to tackle the health problems of its Aboriginal people. Highly experienced in Aboriginal health issues, she discovered conditions worse than she had ever encountered previously. Most of the thousand people she treated were suffering from multiple diseases, such as leprosy, venereal disease, roundworms and trachoma. On the reserve she discovered about 250 Aborigines living in a variety of substandard accommodation: in tin huts, in old car bodies, under tent flies. There was no hot water, no adequate rubbish collection, and the whole place was littered with broken beer bottles. The reserve was a sea of mud in the wet season and a dust bowl in the dry.

After spending several months in the Pilbara I flew further north to the Kimberley. In contrast to the barren desert of the Pilbara, the Kimberley is a tropical region, with a wet season that brings heavy rain, high temperatures and debilitating humidity. Here the Aborigines constituted about half the population, all living in conditions not unlike those I had seen in Roebourne. We (the Australian Inland Mission) conducted three nursing outpost hospitals in the Kimberley, at Fitzroy Crossing, Halls Creek and Kununurra, the only medical services inland from the coastal towns of Wyndham, Derby and Broome. At Fitzroy Crossing and Halls Creek the great majority of the patients were Aborigines. Raging viral epidemics were not uncommon, with the nurses often at their wits' end trying to cope with sudden influxes of seriously ill patients. During my time at Fitzroy Crossing hospital I saw ten Aboriginal babies, suffering from severe respiratory or diarrhoeal problems, bedded down in wooden banana boxes because there was nowhere else to put them. I also had my first contact with a patient suffering from leprosy; for the nurses this was an everyday experience.

I came to learn that these conditions were representative of what Aboriginal people were enduring all over the Australian outback. While politicians seemed convinced that once the referendum gave the Commonwealth powers to make laws for Aboriginal people, the way would be clear to solve their problems, politics are never far removed from economics. The elevation of Aboriginal people to full recognition produced two consequences that had dramatic economic and social impacts on them. The first was the decision in 1969 to grant Aborigines working on cattle stations the full basic wage. Up until that time the stations had provided food and other provisions to all the Aboriginal people who lived on them. Some of the men worked as stockmen or rouseabouts, some of the women were involved in housework. The granting of the basic wage brought an angry reaction from cattle station managers. Faced with the need to pay full wages to their stockmen and housemaids, they retaliated by refusing to give provisions to the non-employed Aborigines living in the station camps. In some cases they were driven from the station properties and in others departed of their own accord. This led to massive social disruption as the displaced Aborigines drifted to the fringes of towns and settlements such as Fitzroy Crossing and Halls Creek, which in turn brought them close to liquor outlets. Full citizenship rights included the right to drink alcohol, and this was the genesis of what became one of their major health problems. Driven from their traditional lands by the establishment of the pastoral industry in the nineteenth century, the Aborigines had found some measure of stability in the cattle station camps. Now once again they were destabilised drifters, easy prey to the vices of Western civilisation.

The second major impact on Aboriginal people was caused by the discovery of huge mineral deposit in the regions where they lived. Two discoveries in particular had far-reaching implications, for both the Aboriginal people and the wider Australian community. The first was the discovery of bauxite. World War II had brought with it many innovations, one of which was the increasing use of aluminium, from building aeroplanes to manufacturing soft drink cans. Australia had been totally dependent on imports of aluminium and was desperately searching for bauxite, the ore from which it is made.

Out of the blue almost simultaneous discoveries of bauxite were made, in Arnhem Land and on Cape York Peninsula. Both sites were located on land held under lease by churches for the conduct of Aboriginal missions. The lease on Cape York Peninsula was held by the Presbyterian Church and contained two Aboriginal communities called Weipa and Aurukun. After protracted negotiations with the government and the mining company concerned, the church agreed to transfer the Weipa lease to the mining company on the understanding that it built a new town for the Aboriginal people. On the other side of the Gulf of Carpentaria the Arnhem Land lease was held by the Methodist Church, which conducted an Aboriginal mission at a place called Yirrkala. Again, after careful negotiations the church agreed to transfer the lease to the mining company. In both cases the churches believed that the mining operations would provide employment and other economic benefits for the Aboriginal people.

The honeymoon period of the Yirrkala agreement didn't last long, for a Methodist missionary posted to Yirrkala discovered that the Aborigines there hadn't been properly consulted about the transfer of the leased land. He went public with his views on the subject, and in retaliation the Methodist authorities dismissed him from his post. Back in Canberra, Kim Beazley senior and Gordon Bryant of the Labor Party seized on the situation as an opportunity to embarrass the government. Beazley visited Yirrkala and, satisfied that the Aborigines hadn't been properly consulted, encouraged them to send a protest to parliament in the form of a traditional bark painting. This unusual method provoked a great deal of media attention. Beazley then moved in parliament for the appointment of a select committee to investigate the complaints of the Yirrkala people. Paul Hasluck, then Minister for Aboriginal Affairs, accepted Beazley's proposal but pointed out that the twelve signatories on the bark painting petition represented only six of the thirteen tribal groups concerned. Hasluck also pointed out that none of the signatories was over 30 and that therefore none of the elders of the tribal groups had signed the petition, both factors making it unrepresentative of the whole community's feelings.

Why hadn't the Methodist authorities consulted with the Aborigines over the transfer of the lease to the mining company? Rev. Cecil Gribble, chairman of the mission board, gave this reply:

> The question was put to me as to why the people were not consulted before the lease was granted. I replied that mining companies had been prospecting in the area since 1956 and the Aborigines had been helping them as paid labour. We had taken it for granted that the people had no strong feelings against the mining project coming there.
>
> When I asked them if they were afraid of this development they assured me that they were not afraid and left me with the impression that they welcomed the coming of this new work which would provide a market for their fish and vegetables and other products of Yirrkala and also give them opportunities for work.[1]

The Yirrkala people may not have been opposed to mining but they were angered that they hadn't been consulted about the transfer of the lease and were afraid that their sacred sites and special places would be damaged. A Grievance Committee appointed by parliament visited Yirrkala in 1963 and confirmed that the Aborigines had not been consulted. Further, the committee said, the land leased to the mining company should be declared a protected area, with Aborigines having exclusive rights of hunting; and there should be consultation on the preservation of sacred sites. With respect to the key issue of the mining of bauxite, however, the Grievance Committee said that it was a national asset which presented a challenge for assimilation, from which 'we should not back away'.

The way was now clear for the mining company to proceed. But no sooner had the contracts been signed than a group of Yirrkala Aborigines stunned everyone by suing the Commonwealth Government and the mining company, Nabalco, claiming that the leases were unlawful and that they, the Aborigines, had been deprived of the 'use and enjoyment of the land'. The case that resulted from this claim was to make history and indeed was the catalyst for a whole chain of events which ultimately led to the legal recognition of land rights. The full name of the law case was *Milirrpum and Others v. Nabalco*

Pty Ltd and the Commonwealth of Australia, and the claim of the Aboriginal plaintiffs was:

> that from an indefinite time in the past—a period which for them began with the deeds of the great spirits who they believe were their ancestors— their predecessors have continuously used the subject land in the manner in which they themselves claim still to be entitled to do without interference.[2]

The central contention of this claim was that, in common law, Aboriginal rights to land within territory acquired by the Crown still persisted and must be respected by the Crown and its subjects unless they were validly terminated. While acknowledging there were 'great and difficult moral issues involved', presiding judge Mr Justice Blackburn said that his powers were limited to legal issues which focused on the question whether there existed in law a doctrine of native title. It was the first time the expression 'native title' had been used in a court of law. Blackburn said:

> There is what might be called the central question, namely does there exist at common law, a doctrine of native title, such as the plaintiffs' counsel propounded, or any such doctrine? If so, is the nature of the plaintiffs' relationship with their land as proved, such as to require the application of the doctrine?[3]

Actually Blackburn had two issues to decide. The first was whether the doctrine of communal native title was a valid part of any law in any part of Australia. The second question was whether the nature of the Aborigines' relationship with the land was such as to confer on them proprietary rights. With respect to this latter issue, Blackburn said:

> Here again it is important to make clear what it is that the plaintiffs are asserting. It is not that the immemorial presence of Aboriginals on the subject land gives the plaintiffs, as Aboriginals, a right to exclude the defendant Nabalco. It is that the plaintiff clan and no others, have in their several ways, occupied the subject land from time immemorial as of right; that the rights of the plaintiff clans are proprietary rights; that these rights are still in existence; and that Nabalco's activities are unlawful in that they are an invasion of such proprietary rights.[4]

In the absence of any written or recorded evidence, the Aboriginal plaintiffs had to depend firstly on the oral evidence of clan members and secondly on the evidence of anthropologists.

The admissibility of the oral evidence was fiercely argued, with counsel for the Commonwealth Government and Nabalco claiming that what had been told to Aboriginal witnesses by others now dead amounted to hearsay. Blackburn rejected this assertion, saying that the law should be applied in a rational and not a mechanical way. The admissibility of the 'expert' evidence of anthropologists was even more fiercely contested by the defendants. Blackburn ruled that it was admissible, saying that anthropology was a valid field of study and knowledge, which included studying the social organisation of primitive people. However, he reminded the parties that 'what is in question at present is merely the admissibility of the evidence. Whether I should make a finding in accordance with the evidence so admitted, is a totally different question.'[5]

The evidence allowed provided a very detailed account of the social organisation of the Aborigines prior to the coming of the Methodist missionaries in 1935. It was claimed that the people believed themselves to be the descendants of 'great spirit' ancestors who had ordained the system of life which the Aborigines practised. However, once the evidence proceeded beyond this stage, the actual nature of the relationship between the people and the land became very complex and confusing. Debate ensued about the boundaries of land attributable to each of the clans involved in the litigation. Rev. Wilbur Chaseling, the Methodist minister who founded the mission at Yirrkala in 1935, gave evidence which conflicted with that of the anthropologists. Despite Chaseling's long service as a missionary and his closeness to the Aborigines, Blackburn was inclined to reject his evidence as less expert than that of the anthropologists, and decided that the Aboriginal clans were related to a whole tract of land and not simply to the sacred sites or special places located on them.

After a lengthy hearing, Blackburn brought down his judgment on 27 April 1971. The most difficult issue which he had to decide was whether the relationship between the Aboriginal clans and specific tracts of land had existed unchanged, since 'time immemorial'. There were no written records offered as evidence and he came to the conclusion that the presence of sacred sites on particular pieces of land was not evidence of title. On the issue of unbroken and unchanged association with the land, the plaintiffs had to rely firstly on the evidence of mythology and secondly on what the anthropologists called 'the relative stability of Aboriginal social organisation'. Evidence presented by the defendants, which included that of Chaseling, claimed that Aboriginal society was more fluid than had been suggested by the plaintiffs and that, in any case, some of the clans had become extinct. The evidence of the anthropologists on these matters was placed under considerable scrutiny by the judge:

> With all respect to Professor Berndt [anthropologist], I was left with the impression that in a sincere attempt to explain to the Court ... a difficult and indeed disputed analysis of the anthropological facts he ... tended to stress the mythological explanation and reduce to relative unimportance as of more doubtful significance, the purely historical explanation. But in fact, the issues before the Court are such that the mere existence of the possibility of a historical explanation, if such a possibility does exist, is of considerable importance.[6]

Faced with a complex issue in which oral tradition and anthropological speculation outweighed matters of fact, Blackburn came to the conclusion that in 1788 the plaintiffs' ancestors had 'the same links to the same areas of land as those which the plaintiffs now claim'. This conclusion, however, was only a preliminary finding to that which he repeatedly referred to as 'the central question':

> The plaintiffs contend that at common law, communal occupation of land by the aboriginal inhabitants of a territory acquired by the Crown is recognised as a legally enforceable right. In order to be so recognised, the aboriginal right must be such as is capable of recognition by the common law. The Court must ascertain what, according to aboriginal law and custom is the identity of the community claiming the land; what are the limits of the land claimed; whether the interest claimed is proprietary; and the incidents of that interest. Once established, the native title owes its validity to the common law. This whole doctrine for which the plaintiffs contended, may be given for convenience, the name of 'the doctrine of communal native title'.[7]

This claim to communal native title was unique in Australian legal history. Indeed, Blackburn commented that such a claim would not have been conceivable before the coming of the anthropologists. In dealing with the question, Blackburn began by referring to some historical perspectives of the British law as it came to be applied in Australia. The first was that the discovery of a new land was in itself grounds for claiming title and possession. In the case of Great Britain, such title and possession was vested in the Crown. One of the benefits of this vesting was to prevent unscrupulous individuals from taking advantage of the Aboriginal people. The application of British law to its colonies was a well-established practice in 1788 and, Blackburn said, by contrast there was no evidence of the existence of the doctrine of communal native title at that time or subsequently.

Blackburn went on to observe that it was not his job to give a balanced historical account of the relations between the Aboriginal and the white races of Australia: 'Everyone knows that the white race has a great deal to be ashamed of'. But he pointed out that right from the beginning of white settlement there had been official concern for the welfare of the Aborigines, and that this concern had increased as successive governments became more aware of their plight. As early as 1837 disregard for the territorial rights of the Aborigines had been acknowledged and subsequently large tracts of land had been set aside as reserves. Nonetheless, Blackburn came to the conclusion that at no stage had there been any suggestion, let alone a legal judgment, which validated the concept of communal native title.

The second major question the judge had to decide was whether the Aboriginal clans' relationship to the land included a 'recognisable and proprietary interest'. While acknowledging that indigenous people the world over had varying degrees of sophistication in their social organisation, Blackburn determined that the Arnhem Land clans, the plaintiffs in this case, constituted definable communities with a recognisable system of law. However, he was not moved by the arguments of counsel for the plaintiffs that the interest of the clans in the land was proprietary:

The evidence seems to me to show that the Aboriginals have a more cogent feeling of obligation to the land than of ownership of it. It is dangerous to attempt to express a matter so subtle and difficult by a mere aphorism, but it seems easier on the evidence, to say that the clan belongs to the land than that the land belongs to the clan.[8]

Blackburn found for the defendants, Nabalco Pty Ltd and the Commonwealth of Australia. The claim of the plaintiffs representing the native clans of Arnhem Land was dismissed. The principal reasons for his decision were that it had not been proved that communal native title was an accepted fact in common law and that it had not been proved that the clans had a recognisable and proprietary interest in the land in question. Blackburn did acknowledge that the evidence of probability suggested that the clans concerned had an unbroken line of succession since 1788 and that their system of social organisation had remained substantially the same. Further, their relationship with the land under consideration had also remained unchanged. But, he remarked, his job was not to give a balanced description of the history of the relations between the Aboriginal and white races of Australia, but to reach a judgment in law, according to the evidence presented to him. Blackburn's judgment was that communal native title didn't exist in common law and the clans didn't have a proprietary interest in the land in question.

One interesting outcome of the case was that the two senior counsel involved, A. E. Woodward, QC, for the plaintiffs and R. J. Ellicott, QC, for the defendants, went on to become prominent figures in Australian legal and political circles. Despite being on opposing sides, both were convinced that whatever the validity of Blackburn's legal decision, the relationship of the Aborigines to the land had not been resolved. Ellicott, Solicitor-General for the Commonwealth and its counsel in the Yirrkala case, wrote a paper which he presented to Prime Minister William McMahon, stating that the Blackburn judgment had clearly demonstrated there was a real relationship between the Aborigines and the land which the government should do something about. Ellicott later became Minister for the Territories in the Fraser government and continued to take an active interest in Aboriginal affairs.

Woodward (later Sir Edward), counsel for the plaintiffs, was later appointed by Prime Minister Gough Whitlam as chair of a Royal Commission to investigate Aboriginal land rights in the Northern Territory.

The Blackburn judgment was by no means the final word on Aboriginal land rights. Rather, it was the beginning of a lengthy judicial and legislative process which, 20 years later, culminated in the High Court case of *Mabo and Others v. State of Queensland*. The historical importance of the judgment is that Blackburn's findings about communal native title differed profoundly from those in the Mabo case. Which of them was correct in law would never be settled because by the time the High Court brought down its judgment in the Mabo case, the right of appeal to the Privy Council in Great Britain had been abolished.

The question of the validity of the doctrine of communal native title remained a hotly contested issue until federal parliament passed the *Native Title Act* in 1993. By that time Aboriginal land rights had become one of the most fiercely debated issues in Australian history.

2

Rural Rebellion and Urban Action

The mining boom that dominated the Australian economy from 1960 onward overshadowed the importance of the pastoral industry that had held sway for the previous hundred years. Yet the pastoral industry also was involved in an uncomfortable relationship with the Aboriginal people. From the early days of the nineteenth century, lured by reports of lush grazing land in the outback, pioneering pastoralists journeyed inland to establish sheep and cattle stations. Some, like the Durack family, drove cattle from Queensland across the top of the continent to the Kimberley, a long and costly expedition which took two years to accomplish with many cattle perishing along the way. But the journey was completed and a cattle industry born in this wild, remote and hitherto inaccessible region. Here the Duracks encountered Aborigines who had never seen a white man before; but they also encountered fevers and diseases which struck down both black and white without discrimination. Wrote Mary Durack:

> All over the country, men rode after stock in an aching daze or lay on the creek banks with their hats pulled over their eyes praying for the night to bring remission from the cruel light and the blazing heat of the sun. 'Was it always like this here?' they asked the blacks but gathered little sense from their reply.[1]

In this grim struggle for survival, there was little time for sensitive behaviour. For many of the new white settlers, the blacks were only one more hazard to be faced, along with harsh climate, debilitating disease and the harrowing task of droving cattle thousands of kilometres to market. Skirmishes between blacks and whites were frequent and the rugged nature of the Kimberley terrain made apprehension of the Aborigines involved extremely difficult. In 1886 John Durack was speared to death by Aborigines as he rode. A huge reprisal hunt was mounted, but the vengeful stockmen were unable to track down the offenders.

The history of Aboriginal and white relationships in the Kimberley is one of the most turbulent and tragic in Australia. Partly this was due to the tempestuous climate and rugged environment, which took their relentless toll of all its inhabitants. But the Kimberley is also a classic case of how the best-intentioned policies of government come to nothing when they have to be implemented in places which are both geographically and culturally divorced from the major population centres and, even worse in those days, from distant Great Britain.

By the early part of the twentieth century the Aboriginal peoples in the Kimberley and elsewhere in the Australian outback had been' subdued' and were living either on government reserves and missions or in camps on cattle stations. A radical change occurred in 1965 when the Arbitration Commission decided that Aborigines working on pastoral stations should receive the basic wage, although it deferred implementing the decision for three years to give the industry time to adjust. Some Aborigines weren't prepared to wait that long, however. In June 1966, about 80 members of the Gurindji tribe employed on Wave Hill cattle station in the Northern Territory walked off the job, declaring that they would no longer work for unjust wages. Encouraged by white advisers they set up camp in the dry bed of the nearby Victoria River and began a unique campaign of industrial protest. They also sent a letter to Labor's spokesman on Aboriginal Affairs, Gordon Bryant, which he read out to parliament. Its contents aroused considerable surprise and concern. The Gurindji wanted:

> to regain tenure of our tribal lands, of which we were forcibly dispossessed

in times past and for which we have received no recompense. This land belonged to our forefathers from time immemorial—we feel that morally if not legally, the land is ours and should be returned to us. We are not a degraded people and if given our rightful heritage, we would show the rest of Australia and the world, that we are capable of working and planning our own destiny as free citizens.[2]

Suddenly what had begun as an industrial dispute turned into a well-articulated campaign for land rights that heralded the beginning of an era of Aboriginal activism. The possibility of Aborigines forming a strong, united and militant organisation had never occurred to anyone before this. In the first place they were few in number and widely scattered across the country. In 1966 an unofficial count established that there were about 80 000 Aborigines in Australia. However, the first official count in the 1971 Census returned a count of 106 000. This was attributable to a change in definition of who was an Aborigine. Prior to 1971 a distinction had been drawn between full-blood Aborigines and those deemed to be of mixed blood or half-caste. As this latter term was now deemed degrading, the 1971 Census adopted the definition of an Aborigine as: 'a person of Aboriginal or Islander descent, who identifies as an Aboriginal or Islander and is accepted as such by the community with which he is associated'.

Under this more embracing definition, the biggest increase recorded in the 1971 Census occurred in New South Wales, where few if any Aborigines lived in tribal or semi-tribal situations. The increased numbers were predominantly in metropolitan or settled rural communities. It's hardly surprising that the militant activism which sprang up in urban areas such as Redfern in Sydney owed its origins to the successful Negro political activism in urban areas of the United States. In his MA thesis at the National University of Australia, titled 'The Aboriginal Embassy 1972', Scott Robinson wrote:

The Black American experience was the most profound exogenous influence on Aboriginal political activism in the 1960s. At this time, the long history of the search for equity and justice by American Blacks had reached a crucial point. Martin Luther King with his tactical preference for non-violence came to personify the ideals of the movement. However the black protest movement in the USA underwent a radical change in the mid-1960s. The peaceful protest model of Martin Luther King was swept aside and more revolutionary, violent methods were promoted by a group called the Black Panthers. Led by Stokely Carmichael, the Black Panthers changed the theme of protest from Black Rights to Black Power. This too had an impact on Australian Aboriginal activists.[3]

Not all Aboriginal activists were proponents of Black Power politics. Others who made outstanding contributions to the cause of their people demonstrated considerable courage and dignity in the process without having to resort to the language or deeds of violence, people like Charles Perkins, who grew up in the post-Depression years and had tasted the bitterness of the appalling life on the reserves. Born in Central Australia, Perkins was taken from his family and tribal surroundings to live in a children's home in Adelaide. Despite this disrupted childhood he became a successful sportsman, graduated from university, and ultimately rose to occupy a senior position in the Commonwealth Public Service. Inspired by the black American freedom riders of the 1960s, Perkins organised freedom rides to rural towns in New South Wales where racial discrimination was rampant. Often facing anger and hostility from the white populations of these towns, he achieved considerable publicity and lifted the nation's awareness of the plight of its Aboriginal people. When the Office of Aboriginal Affairs was formed in 1969, Perkins was employed as a research officer and subsequently rose to considerable prominence, being named head of the renamed Department of Aboriginal Affairs in 1984. Although not aligning himself with the Black Power movement, he continued to speak out on Aboriginal issues and was probably his people's best-known advocate at the time.

It was the post-World War II generation of young Aborigines who grew up in places such as Redfern that came under the influence of the Black Power movement. Garry Foley, Paul Coe and Michael Anderson were some of the leaders who exploded into public prominence. From 1967 onward the urban activists began to exert an increasing influence in Aboriginal welfare organisations, which up to that time had been dominated by whites. Some wore the headbands of the Black Power movement and adopted its clenched-fist salute. In Redfern, relations between Aborigines and police were marked by tension and occasional outbreaks of violence, the Aborigines claiming that the police constantly harassed or assaulted them. The more aggressive members of the Aboriginal Black Panther group dropped hints to the media suggesting that armed Aboriginal guerrilla bands were wandering the streets of Sydney, a tactic which ensured that Aboriginal issues were kept on the front pages. The language of Garry Foley and like-minded activists, though often provocative, carried more threat than reality— but once introduced, the concept of violence became the key theme for describing the treatment of Aborigines. Broadly stated, the 'violence' theme asserted that since the beginning of white settlement, Aborigines had been subjected to excessive bloodshed, degradation, dispossession and humiliation, and the time had come to hit back.[4]

In the escalation of Aboriginal activism, 1971 was a notable year. Appropriately, it was the United Nations Year Against Racism, and also coincided with considerable public interest and support for the anti-apartheid movement in South Africa. Thus Mr Justice Blackburn's judgment in the case of *Milirrpum and Others v. Nabalco Pty Ltd and the Commonwealth of Australia* came at a time when claims of racial discrimination against Aboriginal people were reaching new heights. The adverse judgment, while devastating in that sense, provided Aboriginal activists with a rallying point for future action—and that rallying point was land rights. Though publicly maintaining an air of aloofness, privately the Commonwealth Government was not convinced of the validity of the Aborigines' land rights claims and continued to pursue its policy of assimilation. Ultimately it was forced to declare its position, with Peter Nixon, Minister for the Interior, making this statement in parliament:

> The Government believes it is wholly wrong to encourage Aborigines to think that because their ancestors had a long association with a particular piece of land, the Aborigines of the present day have a right to demand ownership of it. The Government believes that it would be a hindrance and no help. They should receive ownership under the system that applied to the Australian community and not outside it.[5]

However, the government's assimilation goals were not being achieved as speedily as it would have liked. In explaining the failure of the housing programme to meet its objectives, Minister for Aboriginal Affairs W. C. Wentworth sought to excuse it by saying that a death in an Aboriginal family often drove people out of their houses for twelve months and that this, together with their outdoor living style, inhibited the development of housing projects. Wentworth also expressed disappointment at 'the pace and development of Aborigines involved in employment training'.[6] In criticising Wentworth's statement the Opposition said that the failure of the housing programme was due to the grossly inadequate amount of money being directed towards Aboriginal welfare. Manfred Cross, the Labor member for Brisbane, quoted the noted anthropologist C. D. Rowley as saying that Aboriginal housing had 'twice as many persons per dwelling and three times the number of persons per room as other Australians, with 25 to 33 per cent of non-metropolitan Aborigines facing health risks from lack of drainage, plumbing and water'.[7]

More and more investigations were conducted into the conditions under which Aboriginal people lived. Professor Berndt, an eminent anthropologist who had spent a lot of time in Arnhem Land, was quoted in parliament on his reactions to the establishment of a liquor store near the mission at Oenpelli in Arnhem Land:

> Unless action is taken immediately, the 500 or so aborigines on the mission would be destroyed. Fifty per cent of the community's money went to the store. Family life was disrupted and children neglected. The continuation of the present state of affairs spells genocide just as surely as if the people were being massacred.[8]

The land rights cause was further boosted when Mr Justice Blackburn and R. J. Ellicott, QC, jointly proposed to the government that some way should be found to acknowledge and preserve the special relationship between the Aborigines of the Yirrkala area and the land around them to enable them to regain self-respect and dignity, especially after losing the lengthy lawsuit. Prime Minister William McMahon was impressed by this joint approach and requested the Council for Aboriginal Affairs:

> to prepare a submission designed to give Aborigines protection for use and benefit of reserve lands for ceremonial, religious, recreational and productive purposes and to establish a land fund for Aboriginal people outside reserves; to enable them to participate profitably in mining ventures and to be compensated for disturbance to their traditional ways of life.[9]

This request met with strong resistance on two fronts—from the Department of the Interior, and from the administrators in the Northern Territory—both urging the Prime Minister not to deviate from the policy of assimilation. Well aware that his political stocks were waning, McMahon was anxious to promote an image of political leadership and vision. On Australia Day, 26 January 1972, he gave a keynote address to the nation, the substance of which was later repeated in parliament by Peter Howson, Minister for Aboriginal Affairs:

> The Government's aim is to have one Australian society in which all Australians, including Aboriginal Australians, will have equal rights, responsibilities and opportunities. Aborigines will receive effective and respected places in a single Australian society. But at the same time, they will be encouraged to preserve and develop their own culture, languages, tradition and art, which will become living elements in the diverse culture of our society. [They will have] a right to decide for themselves at what pace and to what extent they can come to identify themselves with that society. The thought of separate development of Aborigines as a long-time aim is completely alien to the Government's objectives.
>
> [Addressing the crucial issue of land rights]: Accordingly the Government has decided to create a new form of lease for land on Aboriginal reserves rather than attempt simply to translate the Aboriginal affinity with the land into some form of legal right which could lead to uncertainty and possible legal challenge in relation to land titles in Australia which are presently unchallenged and secure.
>
> [And, regarding mineral leases]: The government has concluded that it was in the national interest as well as in the interest of the Aborigines themselves, for mineral exploration and development on Aboriginal reserves, to continue. [10]

If McMahon expected this policy statement to be heralded as the beginning of a new era in assimilation, he was doomed to bitter disappointment. The next day, the *Canberra Times* reported that a group of Aborigines had set up a camp on the lawns in front of Parliament House. The origins of the Aboriginal Tent Embassy, as it came to be known, are obscured by a wide variety of anecdotal accounts. Whether it was the product of long-term planning or a spontaneous act of demonstration is difficult to assess. What is known is that a group of Aborigines arrived in Canberra the day before McMahon delivered his Australia Day speech and, soon after he delivered it, squatted on the lawn in front of Parliament House with a beach umbrella and a few placards. Though small in size the demonstration quickly attracted media attention. Who coined the term 'Tent Embassy' is also uncertain, but the name was immediately adopted. Gary Foley, a leading activist of the time, said, 'They declared it the Aboriginal Embassy, the rationale being that Aborigines are treated like aliens in their own land.' Others soon joined the small group and several tents were erected. It wasn't long before the link between this protest gathering and McMahon's Australia Day statement became apparent. The issue in contention was land rights. According to Scott Robinson, 'The ideology expressed at this stage [by the Aborigines], was at its most, vague, a slogan rather than a programme. It was some weeks before a more comprehensive set of demands was presented to the public.'[11]

What did become increasingly clear was that urban Aboriginal activists had seized on land rights as a focal point for the prosecution of their cause. It also became clear that the underlying purpose of this new movement was to provide an economic base which would give Aborigines independence and power where previously there had been dependence and powerlessness. The demand for land rights became a burning torch which brought together Aborigines from all over the continent in a way that probably nothing else could have. Whether planned or spontaneous, the establishment of the tent embassy was a brilliant public relations coup. It provided an irresistible attraction for the Australian media, especially television. And since it was set up right outside their front door, the federal politicians could scarcely ignore it.

Soon after it was 'opened', Gough Whitlam, the Leader of the Opposition, visited the embassy and gave the Aborigines a number of assurances, including a promise to legislate for land rights when his party came to power. As a lawyer, Whitlam believed that the principal difficulty facing Aboriginal ownership of land was that the law required property to be vested in an individual or a corporate person, whereas the Aborigines in many cases wanted ownership to be vested in a tribe or clan. Whitlam's solution was to legislate for the incorporation of tribes, thus allowing them to become corporate persons. The protesters at the tent embassy had not formulated their own concepts of land rights, but Whitlam's commitment to the general principle gave them a strong link with the Labor Party and its policy. Members of the Coalition government were refused entry to the embassy tents, while visits by Aborigines from Yirrkala and other remote areas enhanced its status as representing the whole Aboriginal constituency. Almost a month after the tent embassy was established, parliament convened and the presence of the Aborigines on the lawns outside was immediately raised. Howson, the minister responsible for Aboriginal Affairs, continued to assert the government's position that while providing Aborigines with long-term leases over land and guaranteeing safeguards of sacred sites and hunting rights would continue, the policy of assimilation would also continue.

As the weeks passed the tent embassy continued to occupy the lawns of Parliament House and became a gathering point for disciples of the culture of protest, especially university students. In May 1972, four months after the embassy appeared, the government made moves to have it removed. An ordinance authorising its removal was gazetted and on 20 July, after due warning had been given, the police moved in. Accounts of what happened next vary with respect to the amount of violence that occurred. Fewer than 100 Aborigines and their supporters were present at the time, but about 150 police were involved in dismantling the tents. A week later 200 Aborigines and supporters attempted to re-erect the embassy. They were met by a still larger contingent of police, and again there were violent struggles, which led to some injuries and arrests. Negotiators from both sides sought to reach a solution to the impasse in the face of fears that further confrontation could lead to serious violence, perhaps even death. Government ministers sought to find a way of appeasing the Aborigines while standing firm on their determination to put an end to the embassy. The Labor Party vowed to stand with the Aborigines in any further demonstrations.

On Sunday 30 July, a third and final attempt was made to re-establish the tent embassy. This time the number of Aborigines and supporters involved had grown to something over 2000, including busloads of people who had come from other states. The demonstrators gathered at the Australian National University, which had become protest headquarters, and from there marched to Parliament House. The police presence which met them totalled around 300. The tents of the embassy were re-erected and the protesters gathered around them in circles to await an onslaught from the police. But nothing happened. As the hours wore on, the protesters sang songs and listened to addresses while some of the Aborigines performed dances. Still there was no response from the police, except to extend the deadline for dispersal and encourage the protesters to leave. By mid-afternoon, many of the students began to leave. Behind the scenes, the leaders of the demonstration and the police had quietly reached an agreement under which the police would take down the tents and there would be no resistance. Eventually the tents were removed and the demonstration ended peacefully. The saga of the tent embassy ended as quietly as it had begun.

With the removal of the Aboriginal Tent Embassy from the lawns in front of Parliament House, the government had survived an extremely dangerous challenge to its power and its policies. But whatever small sense of triumph it savoured was to be short-lived. Within a few months an election was held in which the government was toppled, and on 3 December 1972, Gough Whitlam succeeded William McMahon as Prime Minister of Australia.

3

Gough Whitlam's Age of Enlightenment

In the months leading up to the 1972 federal election, the Labor Party, confident of defeating the McMahon Coalition government, was already foreshadowing the changes that would be made in Aboriginal Affairs. Any illusion that assimilation still had bipartisan support in parliament was quickly dispelled when Kim Beazley senior condemned it as 'undefined destiny without hope'. When Labor came to power in December 1972, Australia was experiencing an enormous boost to its economy, mainly due to the booming growth of the mining industry. Determined that the benefits of this new 'golden age' would be shared among all Australians, Prime Minister Gough Whitlam introduced a range of welfare programmes, high on the list of which was assistance to Aborigines. According to the *Year Book of Australia* for 1973: 'The underlying principle of the [Whitlam] Government's present approach to Aboriginal Affairs may be briefly described as "self determination", [that is], Aboriginal participation in making policies and in decisions about their progress that affect them and about their future'.

The second plank in Labor's Aboriginal policy was the recognition of land rights. Reservations in the Northern Territory already covered an area of over 243 460 square kilometres, which the new government undertook to vest in the Aboriginal people. In addition it promised to provide funds for the acquisition of further land. More controversially, the new government declared that Aboriginal land ownership would carry with it full rights to mineral and timber resources. In this rapid and remarkable turnaround from the Blackburn judgment of 1971, Aboriginal land rights in the Northern Territory could now be achieved by law, since the Territory was under the direct control of the federal government. Aborigines, who at that time constituted about 1 per cent of the population of Australia, had won an enormous victory. Ironically, Paul Hasluck, the architect of assimilation, who subsequently became Governor-General, was called upon to deliver the government's policy speech at the opening of parliament in 1973. As it included the decision to do away with his policy of assimilation it must have been a very painful experience. Gordon Bryant, Minister for Aboriginal Affairs in the new government, spelled out its objectives in more detail: 'The Government is going to take steps to protect the interests of the Aboriginal people in the land of Australia ... It will not be terribly difficult to define the land rights of the Aboriginal people in regard to existing reserves'.[1]

It's interesting to note that Bryant's 'not terribly difficult' assessment underestimated the difficulties which lay ahead, as had Hasluck's 'small problem' statement of an earlier year. The radical new land rights policy was based on Whitlam's interpretation of the powers given to the Commonwealth in the 1967 referendum. On land rights and related matters, Whitlam frequently spoke as if the referendum had given the Commonwealth power to override the states in matters of Aboriginal Affairs. For example, in answer to a question from Ralph Hunt, now on the Opposition benches, as to whether the terms of the newly created Aboriginal Land Rights Commission was confined to the Northern Territory, Whitlam replied:

> His [the Commissioner's] terms of reference have specific relation to the Northern Territory. His findings, however, will be the basis upon which the Commonwealth will act not only in the Northern Territory ... but also in the States where Aborigines are still exercising traditional land rights.[2]

This interpretation of the constitutional rights given to the federal government by the 1967 referendum is not in accord with what was actually said in the statement provided to voters at the time of the referendum, which spoke of federal and state governments working hand in hand for the welfare of Aboriginal people. Likewise, Whitlam took Blackburn's comments in the Yirrkala case as sufficient evidence that a connection between the people and the land existed, and that it existed not only in the case of the Yirrkala Aborigines but for all Aborigines— another very sweeping assumption.

At the beginning of 1973 Prime Minister Whitlam appointed A. E. Woodward, QC, as a single Commissioner to handle an inquiry into Aboriginal land rights. Woodward had represented the Yirrkala Aborigines in their action against the Nabalco mining company and the federal government, and had been made a judge of the Supreme Court of Australia shortly after the case concluded. His new brief was to recommend the most appropriate ways of recognising and establishing land rights. Tackling his task with great energy, Woodward visited many remote communities, often sitting out in the open air under a tree listening to statements from a group of Aborigines with only a stenographer to assist him. Despite being a one-man commission, or perhaps because of it, he was able to submit an interim report six months after his appointment.

In tabling the report in parliament, Minister for Aboriginal Affairs Gordon Bryant said that the government was prepared to act immediately on two of its key recommendations. First, it would establish land councils that would act as custodians of the land granted to Aboriginal people; second, it would incorporate Aboriginal communities and groups so they could become the beneficial owners of the land. The idea of incorporating communities and electing town councils was Whitlam's way of providing a legal solution to the question of Aboriginal ownership, but it created some serious cultural problems. The power structures of Aboriginal communities are not always amenable to Western legal systems, the democratically elected town councils, for example, posing a real threat to non-elected traditional clan leaders. In some communities, therefore, the elected town councils simply became 'shop windows' to satisfy the legal requirements of the government. The real control of the communities remained with the traditional clan leaders.

Having set in motion its plans for the Northern Territory, the Whitlam government moved to involve itself in the affairs of the six states. But since key areas such as health and education could only be tackled through existing state departments, the role of the newly formed Commonwealth Department of Aboriginal Affairs became that of a coordinator, aimed at developing national policies for Aboriginal people. The implementation of these policies provided the Coalition parties now in Opposition with their first opportunity to engage in a full-scale debate on the decisions to dump assimilation and to intervene in the states. Ralph Hunt, Minister for the Interior in the previous government, attacked the government on its land policy:

> We [the McMahon government] were determined to apply to Aborigines generally, the law that applied to other Australians. This was leasehold title in the Northern Territory. The Aborigines themselves were happy with this arrangement to the extent that 180 applications were made to a Land Board to which I appointed two Aboriginal members. What the present Government has succeeded in doing has frozen all mining leases.[3]

While Labor stuck to its guns with respect to the granting of land rights, Bryant admitted that it had modified its original determination to give Aborigines absolute control over mineral rights. The initial land rights policy of the ALP (1971 Conference) had included the statement: 'Aboriginal land rights shall carry with them full rights to minerals in those lands'. This was amended in 1973 to: 'All Aborigines jointly to share the benefit from the development of natural resources, including minerals, on Aboriginal land'.

The government's intention to reform Aboriginal Affairs and vastly increase the amounts of money allocated to it was not easily translatable into immediate and effective action. It has been said that it takes a newly created government department five or six years to settle down to the point where it can run efficiently. The new Department of Aboriginal Affairs had the additional burden of entering into previously uncharted and predictably stormy waters. Other federal departments such as

Health and Education were unwilling to accept the authority it had been given to formulate policies for Aborigines. Barrie Dexter, a former diplomat and member of the Council of Aboriginal Affairs, became the first Secretary of the new Department of Aboriginal Affairs. He soon found that he needed all his diplomatic skills to prevent his bureaucratic baby from being stillborn.

A particular headache for Dexter was Charles Perkins, the man appointed to be his assistant. Perkins was not averse to speaking his mind publicly, even when it meant breaching the protocol of the Public Service. His comments about the racist attitudes of the Liberal and Country parties so infuriated them that Dexter was forced to charge him with breaching the *Public Service Act*. Another source of conflict for the new department was that many of the senior staff of the Northern Territory public service administration remained firmly wedded to the policy of assimilation. They were already at odds with the new government, which had created a Department of the Northern Territory and swept out many of the old guard. The result was that the new department was staffed with people who had little experience in the field.

Perhaps the greatest difficulty facing the government was the need to create procedures by which the policy of self-determination could be introduced. The appointment of town councils to run their communities was one way, as was the establishment of Aboriginal Land Councils. But none of the Aborigines involved in these bodies had any real experience in administration. The government also decided to set up a National Aboriginal Consultative Committee of 41 members elected from various regions around the country. Its task was to advise the government on Aboriginal needs. The resulting bureaucracy was complex, untried, often unwieldy and frequently confusing.

Another difficult change involved removing control of Aboriginal reserves from the hands of missionaries and government administrators. At best these administrations had been paternalistic and benevolent, at worst dictatorial and destructive. But the abrupt and sometimes traumatic transfer of power to the Aboriginal people themselves often led to vital community services and projects falling into disuse and disrepair. This was particularly true of services that required technical or professional expertise from such people as electricians and motor mechanics. Missions had been able to provide these services through committed people who were prepared to accept low salaries, but many of the advisers brought in by the Aboriginal town councils and paid big salaries failed to perform and did not last long in the remote communities.

Providing services to the Aborigines was further complicated by what came to be known as the 'homeland movement'. The reserves and mission stations into which the Aborigines had been herded hadn't always been located on their traditional lands. When they were no longer duty bound to remain on the reserves, some Aborigines began to move back to their traditional places. In this homeland (or outstation) movement, new communities, some comprising no more than 15 or 20 people, attempted to re-establish their traditional lifestyles. White people were not allowed to live in the new communities so that services such as medical care and mechanical assistance had to be flown in. Airstrips were mostly simple clearings carved out of the bush, which made landing and takeoff at times hazardous.

The Labor government quickly realised that if the self-determination policy were to work, it would require a heavy emphasis on education, and therefore introduced a five-year programme designed to upgrade educational buildings and facilities in Aboriginal communities. To assist in the learning process they encouraged bilingual education, in which children learned their tribal language and culture alongside the language and culture of mainstream Australia. Secondary education residential colleges were established in Darwin and Alice Springs where bilingual education was also encouraged. But as there are about 130 languages and dialects in use in the Northern Territory alone, bilingual education was always going to be a formidable challenge.

Prime Minister Whitlam continued to assert his belief that the 1967 referendum had given the Commonwealth power to override the states in matters relating to the Aboriginal people. In a speech to parliament he said, 'We will establish once and for all, Aborigines' rights to land and insist that whatever the law of George III says, a tribe and a race with an identity of centuries millennia [sic], is as much entitled to own land as even a proprietary company.'

In May 1974 the second and final land rights report from Commissioner Woodward was tabled in parliament.[4] His brief had been to recommend appropriate ways of establishing the traditional rights and interests of the Aborigines in the land and then to recommend procedures for examining land claims and arrangements for vesting the reserves in Aboriginal bodies. Woodward held the view that traditional Aboriginal life was 'land based' and that a weakening of the traditional relationship with the land had tended to break down social organisation. In retrospect the validity of parts of his report has been seriously questioned. For example, the report begins with a number of 'main principles'. This was not part of the original brief but something Woodward took upon himself to undertake. The first of his principles stated: 'At the beginning of the year 1788 the whole of Australia was occupied by the Aboriginal people of this country. It was divided between groups in a way which was understood and respected by all.' Further on, he said that this principle was based on 'simple historical facts which provide the background for the Government's expressed intention to recognise Aboriginal land rights'.

However, 'the simple historical facts' of Woodward's first principle were an oversimplification of a much more complex situation. There was no proof that in 1788 the Aborigines occupied the whole of Australia, nor that the degree of mutual understanding and respect between tribes was as complete as he suggested. To his credit Woodward acknowledged the dangers inherent in his assumptions. In a section concerning the comparable situation of the indigenous peoples of North America, he wrote: 'I find it hard to believe that claims based solely on historical circumstances and depending on the availability of historical evidence, are likely to produce as satisfactory and fair results as claims based mainly on present needs.'

Another contentious part of the report had to do with how the finalising of any decisions about Aboriginal land rights would be reached. Woodward's view on this was expressed in another of his principles:

> Any scheme for recognition of Aboriginal rights to land must be sufficiently flexible to allow for changing ideas and changing needs among Aboriginal people over a period of years. This is so for a number of reasons. Surrounding circumstances may change. Certain widely held expectations about, for example, the ease of reaching a consensus on certain matters, may prove false. For all these reasons future generations should not be committed by this generation's ideas any more than is necessary.[5]

These predictions have subsequently proved to be correct.

Woodward's second report also dealt with what was probably the most sensitive issue of all, the question of Aboriginal identity. When the matter of land rights is under consideration the questions must ultimately be asked, 'Who is an Aborigine?' and 'Which Aborigines are entitled to what land?' The assimilation policy was based on the assumption that Aborigines were divided broadly into two groups, those who continued to live a near traditional lifestyle in traditional areas and those who in varying degrees had moved away and were living in or on the fringes of urban society. A further assumption was that eventually all Aborigines would become part of the total Australian community, albeit at various speeds. In the past the method used to assess Aboriginality had been determined by a person's proportion of Aboriginal blood—one-half, one-quarter, one-eighth and so on. This process reached the point of absurdity where public servants had to decide whether or not a person was eligible for welfare benefits on the basis of their 'blood level'. Woodward felt compelled to say something on the subject of Aboriginal identity because it obviously impinged on the matter of who was entitled to land:

> Differences between Aborigines should be allowed for, but any artificial barriers, in particular those based on degrees of Aboriginal blood, must be avoided. In saying that differences should be allowed for, I have in mind that

the Aborigines of mixed descent in New South Wales share only some of the beliefs and aims of the tribal Aborigines of Arnhem Land. People from one background should not readily be accepted as spokesmen for people of the other. On the other hand, I believe it is vital that no artificial wedge should be driven between people whose Aboriginal ancestry is the [same] dominant factor in their upbringing and their thinking. Their similarities should be built upon and their cooperation encouraged.[6]

Wisely, Woodward didn't try to answer the question, 'Who is an Aborigine?', but in some ways his comments raise more questions than they provide answers. He tried to balance the need to recognise the differences between groups with the need to foster a sense of common identity. As future events would reveal, developing such a sense among different groups of Aborigines became almost as difficult a task as reconciliation with the rest of the community. Despite the many minefields through which he dared to tread, Woodward's report has been described as 'a sensible account of past failures and a sensible approach to remedy the ills, real or imaginary, which these failures have caused'.[7]

Woodward recognised that land claims would inevitably become sources of conflict with other vested interests such as tourism, conservation, road-making and similar enterprises. But one matter concerned him most: 'Of all the questions I have had to consider, that of mineral rights has caused me the most difficulty and concern ... The claims that land rights include minerals under the ground [conflict with] the national interest'. After giving the matter considerable thought he finally recommended that: 'There should be no new mining on Aboriginal land for over two years and then only if the owners of the land and other Aboriginal people want it, or if the Government says it is very important for the national interest'.[8]

Woodward's concern was soon to be realised. While the government was announcing its intention to legislate for land rights in the Northern Territory, another storm was brewing in that region, as serious as any of the cyclones which smite it from time to time. This storm was centred on proposals to mine uranium in the Alligator River region of Arnhem Land. It would put the government's land rights policy to the test faster and more fiercely than anyone had anticipated.

4

Legislating for Land Rights

Today Kakadu is widely known, in Australia and overseas, as a national park of great beauty. But in 1974 few Australians, let alone the rest of the world, had ever heard of it. Kakadu is about 200 kilometres east of Darwin in the region we call Arnhem Land, an area inhabited by Aboriginal people for thousands of years. Their first contact with white people came only in 1906, when a pastoral lease was granted to one Paddy Cahill. Twenty years later, the Missionary Society of the Anglican Church began working with the Aborigines in the Kakadu region and established the settlement of Oenpelli. Like other missions in remote parts of Australia, Oenpelli attracted many Aborigines because the missionaries provided handouts. Some came only for brief and irregular visits, but the settled population grew steadily. By 1974, there were about 600 Aborigines in more or less permanent residence at Oenpelli.

The discovery and mining of bauxite at Yirrkala was the first major crack in the wall of isolation that protected the Arnhem Land Aborigines from the outside world. Then, hot on the heels of the bauxite discovery, came another important mineral find. The mineral was uranium and it was found in the Kakadu region. Uranium is used to produce atomic energy, one of the most controversial and threatening legacies of World War II. The threat did not go away when the war ended, for the subsequent escalation of the Cold War spurred the superpowers to build arsenals of nuclear weapons at the same time as a worldwide shortage of fossil fuels and oil led to the building of nuclear power stations. Uranium became greatly sought after.

Australia had known for some time that significant uranium deposits existed in the outback and had been determined to cash in on the global demand. Uranium was first discovered at Radium Hill in South Australia in the 1920s, but the deposit was too small to be developed. The first really big discovery was made at Rum Jungle in the Northern Territory in 1949; another big discovery at Mary Kathleen in 1954 made Australia a major player in uranium production. Almost at the same time, however, concerns about uranium mining began to mount, triggered by the threat of radiation fall-out from the atomic explosions which took place at the Woomera rocket range in South Australia. There was also concern about the possible effect on people living in the surrounding region, nearly all of whom were Aborigines. Concern about fall-out escalated in 1956, when two large atomic bombs were exploded in the Monte Bello Islands off the coast of Western Australia, despite world-famous scientists like Professor Ernest Titterton saying there was little cause for concern. In the following decade, Radium Hill, Rum Jungle and Mary Kathleen were all phased out of production, and concern about the effects of radiation began to diminish.

In 1972, alarm bells rang again when Australia learned that big deposits of uranium had been discovered in Arnhem Land. These discoveries coincided with the election of the Whitlam government, whose policies on uranium mining were strongly opposed to those of its predecessors. The Labor Party had been agitating for nuclear disarmament, the protection of the environment and the advancement of Aboriginal land rights, and the discovery of uranium at Ranger in Kakadu impinged on all three policies. An existing piece of legislation, the *Atomic Energy Act* of 1953, gave the Atomic Energy Commission authority to explore for uranium in that part of Arnhem Land, and it was anxious for mining to commence, but opposition from sections of the community began to mount, chiefly through the activities of two groups. One group fiercely opposed any mining or export of the ore on the grounds that it only enhanced the possibility of nuclear warfare, the other was equally opposed on the grounds of environmental pollution. Aborigines joined in the fray when Narbalec, the mining company involved, offered $3.3 million to compensate for any adverse effect the mining of uranium might have on the Aborigines. They rejected the offer out of hand.

Environmental objections were based on the fear that mining would result in radioactive material being drained into the East, South and West Alligator river systems, which interlace the Kakadu region. The Whitlam government dealt with this issue by passing the *Environment Protection (Impact of Proposals) Act* of 1974, and in September 1975 set up a Ranger Uranium Environment Inquiry, chaired by Mr Justice Fox. In its first report, issued a year later, the Fox Inquiry examined the argument that the risks and problems associated with the use of uranium in the nuclear power industry were such that it should recommend against the proposals to mine and export it, and reached the provisional conclusion that the only real danger was the global proliferation of nuclear weapons. Regarding the environment, the Inquiry concluded that uranium mining didn't appear to constitute any real threat.

At the same time as Mr Justice Fox and his fellow commissioners were about their uranium business, Mr Justice Woodward was about his land rights business. His report was received and accepted by the Whitlam government before the second stage of the Fox Inquiry was completed, and Woodward's recommendations about land rights legislation substantially influenced what Fox subsequently recommended. It has to be emphasised that the purpose of the Woodward Commission was not to prove the relationship between Aborigines and the land, but to recommend ways of implementing their traditional rights and interests. The key to this relationship was to be found in the recognition of traditional landowners. Woodward explained it this way:

> [Traditional landowners are] a local descent group of Aboriginals, who have a common spiritual affiliation to a site of land, [which] places the group

under a primary spiritual responsibility for that site and for the land, and are entitled by Aboriginal traditions to forage as of right over that land.[1]

But traditional owners were in many cases either one person or a small group of people whose capacities to manage large landholdings and deal with Western economic and legal systems were extremely limited. Woodward therefore recommended the appointment of land trusts, whose functions were to hold the titles of land vested in them and exercise the legal powers of ownership for the benefit of the traditional owners.

Secondly, Woodward proposed the appointment of land councils whose role, as distinct from that of the land trusts, was not ownership but management. The 1979 *Aboriginal Land Rights (N.T.) Act*, s.23, described their functions as follows:

> [The function of a land council is] to ascertain and express the wishes of the Aborigines living in the area, as to the management of the land; to protect the interests of the traditional owners and other interested Aborigines and to consult with the traditional owners, etc, regarding proposals; to negotiate on behalf of the traditional owners with persons desiring to use, occupy or obtain an interest; to assist Aboriginals in making claims and to supervise and provide administrative assistance to the Land Trusts.

The land councils were also given responsibility for the protection of sacred sites and the issue of permits for entry onto Aboriginal land. Membership of both the land trusts and the land councils was restricted to Aborigines living in the defined area.

A third tier of involvement was created by Woodward's recommendation for the institution of an Aboriginal Lands Commission, to deal with land rights claims and make appropriate recommendations to the federal minister for Aboriginal Affairs. In this respect the minister became the fourth tier and had the final decision in the granting of land rights claims. The minister also had the power to appoint members to the land trusts and the land councils. In retrospect it became obvious that, apart from the minister, the real power in matters of land rights lay with the land councils who were the managers of the land. R. J. Ellicott, QC, the Solicitor-General involved in the Yirrkala land rights case, later became the Opposition's shadow minister for Aboriginal Affairs. He wasn't happy about Woodward's proposals for land councils, saying that they could become political bodies and not always representative of the Aboriginal people whom they were supposed to serve. He felt that a different structure, in which the clan leaders would be involved, should be set up to hold land. Despite Ellicott's concerns, land councils in the form recommended by Woodward were included in Liberal Party policy.

Woodward himself was concerned that conflicts would arise over proposals for mining and made recommendations as to how exploration and mining leases should be granted. Briefly, there were two alternatives. If the appropriate land council, after due consultation with the traditional owners, approved an application from a mining company, then, with the consent of the Minister for Aboriginal Affairs, it could be granted. Alternatively, if the land council did not approve an application from a mining company, it was within the power of the Governor-General to declare that the national interest required that it be granted. Thus the government retained the final decision as to whether mining would or would not be allowed on Aboriginal land. While this reservation of power aroused considerable opposition from Aboriginal groups, the Aboriginal Land Rights (N.T.) Bill was introduced into Parliament by the Whitlam government in 1975. In presenting the Bill, Minister for Aboriginal Affairs Les Johnson said:

> It will provide freehold title over all reserves and certain other lands to be vested in Aboriginal ownership and gives the Aborigines control over mining developments. It will establish in our law those aspects of Aboriginal traditional law relating to the land, which Mr Justice Blackburn could not uphold in the Gove [Yirrkala] land rights case. It creates for Aborigines, property interests in, and community title to land and makes that title inalienable.[2]

When he came to the section of the Bill which said that any Aboriginal veto on mining could be overruled 'in the national interest', the minister acknowledged that there would be many interpretations of what constituted 'the national interest'. He expressed the hope that it would not be necessary to invoke the provision, and that sensible agreement could be reached between the parties concerned. He went on to make specific reference to the proposal to mine uranium at Kakadu in Arnhem Land:

> International assurances had been given by Australia that it would meet the uranium requirements of its major trading partners until 1990. Moreover the very substantial increase in the national welfare which could be derived from development of the Ranger project could not lightly be overlooked. Should the Government feel obliged to invoke the national interest provisions in the Bill in view of these factors, discussions would be held with those affected. Any decision to proceed ... will depend on the Government's consideration of the findings of the Ranger uranium environmental inquiry, which is now taking place.[3]

Although the Bill was debated at length, there appeared no question that it would be passed with Opposition approval. The second reading was passed on 5 November 1975 without any real difficulty. Had that been the only matter of concern to parliament at the time, the final stages of the Bill would have had a clear passage. Parliament, however, did have other things on its mind. During the time that the Bill was being debated in the House of Representatives, another debate, far more ferocious in its intensity, was taking place in the Senate. This debate had to do with a threat from the Coalition to withhold Supply from the Whitlam government, which it subsequently did. On 11 November 1975, a week after the second reading of the Bill, Opposition Leader Malcolm Fraser moved a motion of no confidence in the government. In scenes of tension unequalled in Australian political history, Governor-General Sir John Kerr dismissed Gough Whitlam as prime minister. All legislation before parliament, including the Aboriginal Land Rights (N.T.) Bill, was put on hold until such time as an election could be held and the new government determined its policies. The dismissal of the Whitlam government did not, however, affect the Ranger Uranium Environment Inquiry. Mr Justice Fox and his colleagues continued their work, not presenting their final report until 17 May 1977. By that time the newly elected Fraser government had resubmitted the Aboriginal Land Rights (N.T.) Bill substantially unchanged, and it had been passed in the latter part of 1976.

In due course the final recommendations of the Fox Inquiry were presented to parliament. One of the matters of interest that emerged was how much these recommendations had been influenced by the contents of the *Aboriginal Land Rights (N.T.) Act*. The focal point of this interest was the way in which the report interpreted the term 'the environment'. This can best be understood by reference to the report itself:

> The matters which have been debated before us are seen by some in the light of a contest between environmentalists and despoilers of the environment— between conservationists and developers. These contrasts are false. The question is a single one—what is best for the environment—that term being unlimited in relation to its physical and its social aspects ... In terms of human welfare, it is a question of accepting responsibility towards future generations, as well as for those now living.[4]
>
> [And later] The greatest threat to the environment and particularly to the welfare, well-being and culture of the Aboriginal people, may prove to be the large white populations which the mining ventures will bring ... There is also the related matter of tourists.

The interpretation given to the meaning of 'environment' was a radical departure from the simple traditional understanding of 'concern for the physical environment', as was acknowledged in the report's conclusion:

> We acknowledge that we adopt a sensitive approach to the position of the Aboriginal people ... the *[Aboriginal] Land Rights Act* based on the Woodward report, is an acknowledgment of a turning point ... The changed attitude is not as we understand it, a matter of conscience but of justice, based on a fuller, better understanding. It is no longer expected of them that they adopt the customs and lifestyle of the white man if they do not wish to do so. Land is central to the attainment of the necessary confidence and purpose and self-esteem.[5]

The most significant aspect of the Fox report was that it enlarged the focus of attention to include human aspects of the environment as well as the physical. It insisted that strict safety controls should be placed on uranium mining projects, that construction of mines should be sequential and with appropriate time intervals, and that the construction of further mines should be deferred. The recommendations also included strict control on the number of tourists allowed into the area, minimisation of the population of the proposed mining town of Jabiru, and the involvement of Aborigines in planning, management and jobs such as rangers and health workers. One highly significant recommendation was for the development of a large national park from which future mining developments would be excluded. The adoption of that proposal resulted in the establishment of Kakadu National Park, which has become one of Australia's major tourist attractions.

The Fox report contains a very clear description of what the commissioners came to understand as the relationship between the Aborigines and the land:

> The spiritual relationship between the Aborigines and the land is given emphasis in the belief that for a child to be born, a spirit must first enter the mother's womb to give the child life. The spirit derives from one of the various sites associated with the Dreamtime heroes. Consequently there is a direct personal link between the spirit being, the child, and the place from which the spirit came. That place is the source of the person's life force and he or she is inseparably connected with it. The spirit is part of the land and therefore the land is very much part of the Aborigines. The relationship is not broken even on death, as the Aborigine's spirit returns to the site from which it came.[6]

As had Blackburn and Woodward before him, Fox and his fellow commissioners developed a profound compassion for the Aboriginal people they encountered, and a deep respect for the traditions which were at the foundation of their lives. They saw them as 'faced with progress involving rapid social change ... a depressed group whose standards of living are far below that acceptable to the wider Australian community'.[7]

However, while the Woodward report, the Fox inquiry and all the legislative and judicial procedures which were set up during those years were well intentioned, they happened all too fast for the Aboriginal people. Up to this time, Aboriginal communities in the Northern Territory, and the buildings and equipment and considerable funds which had been poured into them, had been controlled and administered either by government departments or by mission organisations. The new policies of self-determination and self-management now required these communities to be responsible for the ownership of their properties and the conduct of their financial affairs. To achieve this, the government deemed it necessary for Aborigines to set up incorporated bodies to receive money, spend it, and be accountable for the way it was spent. Therefore, at the same time as the *Aboriginal Land Rights (N.T.) Act* was before parliament, a parallel piece of legislation, the *Aboriginal Councils and Associations Act*, was being processed.

Its purpose was twofold. The first was to enable Aborigines to have the equivalent of the incorporated municipal bodies of mainstream Australia. The Act allowed that where ten or more Aborigines lived in a particular area, they could apply for incorporation and form a town council. This would enable the small homeland communities with only 20 or 30 members to manage their own affairs. The number of councillors appointed would depend largely on the wishes of the Aborigines themselves. The second purpose of the Act was to enable Aboriginal groups wishing to engage in commercial activities such as fishing, running a cattle station or a store, to be incorporated. They could then assume ownership of buildings and other property previously owned by the government or the missions. The *Aboriginal Land Rights (N.T.) Act* and the *Aboriginal Councils and Associations Act* provided the legal and administrative frameworks through which Aborigines in the Northern Territory could acquire title to land and organise their lives in ways that maximised their freedom and responsibility.

Thus, within the space of four decades, the Aboriginal people of Arnhem Land had come from being almost totally isolated from whitefellas and their ways to having close and continuous contact, first through the missionaries, then through World War II, and finally through mining. All these encounters drew them deeper and deeper into a conflict of cultures. But Aboriginal communities in Arnhem Land, and indeed in all of the Northern Territory, differed from those in the rest of Australia because from 1911 they had been directly under the jurisdiction of the Commonwealth Government. It could be said that Commonwealth policies on Aboriginal affairs were more enlightened than those of the states, especially after

World War II, when international human rights movements began to influence political decision making. Protagonists for the states would argue that it was one thing to make high-sounding decisions in Canberra, but quite another to translate them into the delivery of services to remote communities of Aboriginal people. Be that as it may, the Whitlam government, impatient to right the wrongs of past generations, produced a rapid succession of Royal Commissions, judicial inquiries and Acts of parliament which left many Aboriginal people bemused, to say the least.

The Whitlam government tried to ensure that Aboriginal people were consulted in these determinations as far as was practical, given its driving desire to have reform legislation passed. It's doubtful whether any other matter in Australian political history has received such concentrated attention and resulted in such radical reform in such a short time as did Aboriginal affairs in the early 1970s. But many of the people to whom the reforms were directed were still, by and large, living in 'another country'. The formal recognition of their rights as Australian citizens had been achieved in 1967, through the referendum, but in many cases their contact with the rest of Australia and its ways of life remained minimal. To present Aborigines in remote areas with economic, social and political freedom and responsibility within the space of a few short years and in unparalleled measure, and to expect them to absorb and cope with these things was, to use a contemporary expression, a 'big ask'.

5

Queensland Stirs the Pot

Power struggles between the Commonwealth and the states have always been a feature of Australia's federated system of government. Some have been titanic, but none has been greater than that of the 1970s between the Commonwealth and the State of Queensland. It was made all the more so because the two chief characters in the battle were dominant, forceful and colourful men. Prime Minister Gough Whitlam was an imposing figure with a commanding grasp of the English language. By contrast, Joh Bjelke-Petersen, Premier of Queensland, was often mocked for the ineptness of his utterances—but a wilier and more determined politician would be hard to find.

The battle lines were drawn when Whitlam threatened to 'bring the states into line' in matters relating to Aboriginal affairs. Some states were amenable to his proposals but the Queensland Government, led by Bjelke-Petersen, refused to amend its policies to conform with those of the Commonwealth. Bjelke-Petersen was not going to have Whitlam riding roughshod over Queensland. Equally determined to have his way, Whitlam introduced into federal parliament the Aboriginal and Torres Strait Islanders (Queensland Discriminatory Laws) Bill, 1975. In presenting the Bill, Gordon Bryant, Minister for Aboriginal Affairs, said: 'The purpose of the Bill is to supersede certain provisions of the laws of Queensland that discriminate against Aboriginal and Torres Strait Islanders and deny them basic human rights.'[1]

The particular target of the Bill was Queensland's restrictive practices regarding Aboriginal reserves. Movement in and out of the reserves was controlled by a permit system, and the Whitlam government took the view that this practice was a violation of human rights and a form of racial discrimination. Pointing this out in his speech, Bryant cited a clause from the Universal Declaration of Human Rights which referred to 'the right to freedom of movement and residence and no one shall be subject to arbitrary interference with his privacy, family, or house'. The restrictions placed on Aborigines living on reserves in Queensland, said Bryant, were a violation of this right.

The Queensland Discriminatory Laws Bill was hotly debated in the House of Representatives, both on the matter of the rights of Queensland Aborigines and on the broader issue of racial discrimination. Ralph Hunt from the Opposition claimed that the Aborigines in Queensland hadn't been consulted about the Bill, and supported his claim with a telegram from Les Stewart, Chairman of the Queensland Aboriginal Advisory Council, which said that his people didn't want the legislation.[2] W. C. Wentworth, also of the Opposition, said that the Queensland Government should retain the right to refuse entry to the reserves, quoting the sale of alcohol as one example of the dangers of freedom of access. Said Clarrie Millar, also of the Opposition:

> The Bill is another example of those advanced by contemporary society, which at first blush immediately attracts the attention and sympathy of the ordinary man in the street. It evidences a torment of conscience in contemporary society for the way in which it has been derelict in its duties and responsibilities over the years, to some of its unfortunate minorities. But our torment of guilt should not prompt us to act indiscreetly in a futile effort to remedy the problem.[3]

Bryant stuck to his guns: 'The principle before us tonight is the claim by the Australian Government that it has the right, the duty, to deal directly with the Australian people no matter whether they are Aboriginal people or non-Aboriginal people.'[4]

The debate about the Queensland Bill was mild, however, compared with the furore which arose when the Whitlam government introduced the Racial Discrimination Bill (1975). First introduced into the Senate in October 1973 by the Attorney-General, Senator Lionel Murphy, it came to the House of Representatives in 1975. Introducing the Bill, Kep Enderby said: 'The introduction of [this] legislation will furnish legal background on which to rest charges reflecting basic community attitudes. The fact that racial discrimination is unlawful will make it easier for people to resist social pressures that result in discrimination.'[5]

The Opposition thought otherwise. Rather than enhancing human rights, it saw the Bill as a serious threat to an individual's privacy and freedom. Queenslander Jim Killen was particularly outspoken, asserting that the Commonwealth had no intrinsic power to legislate on the matter of racial discrimination. The government, he claimed, had introduced the Bill as a derivative of its external affairs powers based on the signing by Australia of the International Convention on Racial Discrimination. (The use of external affairs powers to justify domestic legislation by the Commonwealth was first affirmed by the High Court of Australia in a decision handed down by Justices Evatt and McTiernan in 1930. The validity of this decision has been hotly debated ever since.)

'Racial discrimination' was defined in Section 9 of the Bill in these words:

> It is unlawful for a person to do any act involving a distinction, exclusion, restriction, or preference, based on race, colour, descent, or national or ethnic origin, which has the purpose or effect of nullifying or impairing the recognition, enjoyment or exercise on an equal footing, of any human right or fundamental freedom, in the political, economic, social, cultural, or any other field of public life.[6]

Examples of 'exclusions', 'restrictions' and 'preferences' were provided in an attempt to clarify this complex definition. They included exclusion from public places or facilities, the right of access to land, housing or accommodation, the provision of goods and services, and employment. Referring to Clause 13 of the proposed Bill, which stated that it was unlawful to refuse to supply goods or services to people on the grounds of race, colour or ethnic origin, Wentworth again raised the problem of access to alcohol. The application of this clause, according to him, would mean that any attempt to regulate or prohibit the sale of alcohol to Aboriginal communities would be illegal— and, he protested:

> This provision, well-meaning though it is, will make it more difficult for us or for any Parliament, to give adequate protection to the Aboriginal people, against the destruction which they themselves see and which they themselves have asked us to do something about.[7]

John Howard from the Opposition benches submitted a proposal to establish a conciliatory process for the resolution of claims of racial prejudice, which was adopted.[8] However, there was one proviso in the Racial Discrimination Bill (Paragraph 4 of Article 1 of the Schedule), which has subsequently been ignored or overlooked, that has important long-term ramifications. Referring to the enforcement of the Act, it says: 'provided however, that such measures do not as a consequence, lead to the maintenance of separate rights for different racial groups and that they shall not be continued after the objective for which they were taken, has been achieved'.

Generally known as a 'sunset clause', this statement assumes that the time will come when enforcement of the Act will no longer be reasonable or necessary. It is remarkable that more frequent reference to this proviso has not been made in subsequent commentary, because in essence it foresees the ultimate dismantling of the Act. Having introduced the two Bills, it seemed that their passing would be no more than a formality and the Commonwealth would be suitably armed to take action against Queensland. However, on 11 November 1975, the Labor-appointed Governor-General dismissed the Whitlam government and appointed Malcolm Fraser to head a caretaker government. At the election which followed, the Coalition parties were swept into power and Fraser became Prime Minister.

With the change of government it seemed that Whitlam's visionary plans to radically reshape the face of Aboriginal Affairs would come to nothing, as it was assumed the new government would consign the two Bills to the political scrap-heap. But Prime Minister Fraser had barely had time to settle into office when a crisis blew up in Queensland, reminiscent of what had happened in Arnhem Land five years earlier. This time the controversial mining project in question was located at the Aboriginal reserve at Aurukun on Cape York Peninsula. Patrick Weller, in his biography of Fraser, described what happened:

> During the distraction of the 1975 [Commonwealth] election, the Queensland Government had pushed through the *Aurukun Association Agreement Act,* which would allow mining to take place without Aboriginal approval. Fifteen years earlier, the neighbouring Aboriginal community of Weipa had been moved to make way for bauxite mining operations. Although there was some unhappiness at the time, the Presbyterian Church mission involved had not raised strong objection. However since that time there had been the Yirrkala protest, the Blackburn judgment, the Woodward Commission and the introduction of the Land Rights Bill. So when Queensland Premier Joh Bjelke-Petersen pushed through the *Aurukun Association Agreement Act,* the Presbyterian Church was much better prepared to support the Aborigines.[9]

Fraser had two concerns about the actions of the Queensland Government. First, it was highly questionable whether there had been adequate consultation with the Aborigines before the legislation was introduced. Second, the proposals involved a mining company which was 100 per cent foreign owned, and that contravened federal policy. Any action Fraser might have contemplated was pre-empted by the Aurukun Aborigines themselves, however, when they took out an injunction against the Queensland Government to prevent mining on the reserve. The Queensland Supreme Court upheld the injunction but Bjelke-Petersen, determined to prevail, appealed to the Privy Council in Great Britain. For the next two years all parties to the dispute had to bide their time as they waited for the Privy Council to reach a decision.

In the meantime, the Labor Opposition kept the issue alive in federal parliament, and the government was not unsympathetic to its point of view. When Kim Beazley senior moved that the government take action to protect the interests of the Aborigines at Aurukun, Ian Viner, Minister for Aboriginal Affairs, said:

When mining companies and others go in to confer with Aboriginal communities, they must first take time to do their homework and learn the basis of Aboriginal social structure, the nature of Aboriginal tradition, the lines of authority, who can speak with authority, who ought to speak when they are conferring; because only if this is done can any adequate consultation be carried out. That is the lesson that has been learned at Aurukun.[10]

However, during the long wait for the Privy Council to make a decision on the Aurukun situation, the focus of interest in Aboriginal affairs shifted to other parts of Australia.

6

Malcolm Fraser's Many Headaches

Gough Whitlam bequeathed Malcolm Fraser more than one headache in the realm of Aboriginal affairs. In addition to the belligerence of Joh Bjelke-Petersen were several other matters that required sensitive handling. The first was Whitlam's somewhat reckless approach to funding for Aboriginal purposes. During his government's halcyon days, unheard-of amounts of money were allocated to a wide range of projects. Housing, health and education were three areas where money was freely available to almost anyone who could present a convincing submission, and the rise in Commonwealth expenditure was spectacular. Contributions to the states and direct Commonwealth funding of Aboriginal projects in the financial year 1972/73, prior to Labor's coming to office, had amounted to $83 million. Two years later the same allocations had risen to a staggering $233 million, a 300 per cent increase in two years. As one public servant later reflected:

> It was the time of the 'money' scandals. You threw money at a problem but there wasn't the machinery to absorb it. The motivation and the rhetoric were of the highest level, but the tyranny of the 'Annual Budget process' meant that money was spent [within the financial year], irrespective of whether the programs were in place.[1]

In Opposition, Fraser and the Coalition parties had constantly attacked what they called the extravagant and wasteful expenditure of the Labor government. Now that Fraser was prime minister there was much speculation and apprehension as to where, and how hard, his axe would fall. One of the chief targets of the former Opposition had been unemployment benefits to Aborigines, derisively referred to as 'sit-down pay'. It was claimed that unemployment benefits and similar 'hand-outs' were largely being spent on alcohol, which in turn was destroying what little was left of Aboriginal culture and self-esteem. To attack this problem, the Fraser government decided that employment would be its number one spending priority. Early in 1977, the new Minister for Aboriginal Affairs, Ian Viner, said that 50 per cent of Aborigines were unemployed compared with a figure of 4.4 per cent for the nation as a whole.[2] One of the main reasons for this huge unemployment rate, he said, was the exodus of many Aborigines from their traditional places and lifestyles to become fringe dwellers on the edges of remote and rural towns. This meant that they had no access to traditional bush tucker and so became heavily dependent on the foods of mainstream society. This in turn led to a greater need for money to purchase food and in turn, in the absence of employment opportunities, a growing dependence on welfare benefits. The loss of an active lifestyle and an increasing level of dependency on welfare payments, said Viner, had created many social problems for Aborigines, the most serious of which was alcoholism.

The Fraser government, Viner went on, proposed to tackle the unemployment problem on two levels. One was the Community Development Employment Projects (CDEP) scheme, aimed at encouraging Aboriginal town councils in remote regions to develop new projects which would employ people. Roads, rubbish collection and water supply were some examples. A second scheme would be introduced to increase the employment of Aborigines who had moved to rural communities and towns. Called the National Employment and Training System (NEAT), this programme was designed to encourage employers to admit more Aborigines into their workplaces. By providing substantial sums of money to the CDEP and NEAT programmes, the government believed it would help create more employment in remote and rural regions.

The next big challenge that Fraser inherited was that of making positive inroads into the problems of Aboriginal health and, in particular, alcoholism. Despite massive expenditure and elaborate programmes, Whitlam's strategies had been largely unsuccessful. In 1976 the House of Representatives Standing Committee on Aboriginal Affairs was asked to investigate this problem and its report was presented to the October-November sitting. Introducing the committee's report, chairman Philip Ruddock said:

> Alcohol is the greatest present threat to the Aborigines of the Northern Territory and unless strong immediate action is taken, they could be destroyed ... It has led to a breakdown in traditional authority and the discipline of the clan elders ... Communities should decide whether alcohol should be permitted on settlements ... There is a need to recruit and train police especially for this purpose.[3]

Les Johnson of the Labor Party, another member of the committee, said that drinking reflected a despondency which had arisen from the loss of traditional land and lifestyle and added that the effect of alcohol on Aborigines was 'very public and very visible':

> All this clearly reveals a great human tragedy. We were told of a community, and I quote, 'collapsing in a great bloody brawling sprawling drunken heap'; white men selling flagons of wine to Aborigines at $20 a flagon. One Aboriginal 'drunk pick up' service picks up 50 to 60 per night. One Northern Territory town has 52 liquor outlets ... a community rationing beer to 12 cans per adult a day and 24 cans on Saturday.[4]

The problem of alcoholism in Aboriginal communities aroused a great deal of emotional debate in parliament during 1976, with much discussion about its causes and possible cures. Despite this emotional catharsis, there was still more bad news to come before parliament adjourned for the Christmas break. Reports surfaced of an alarming increase in clashes between Aborigines and police, in almost all cases alcohol related. (Unfortunately most of the police stationed in or near Aboriginal communities at that time had little or no training in Aboriginal culture.) One example given was that of Laverton, a small mining community north of Kalgoorlie in Western Australia. Aborigines from distant desert communities where alcohol was banned frequently visited Laverton and engaged in excessive drinking that led to disturbances. The police stationed in the town were responsible for maintaining law and order over one of the biggest, most sparsely populated regions on the continent. Responding to calls for assistance when disturbances occurred in remote communities took a day or two, the police almost inevitably arriving to find the culprits had vanished into the desert.

The poor state of Aboriginal health was often believed to be linked to the appalling conditions under which they lived, and most efforts at improving health were directed towards changing living habits. One aim of the policy of assimilation was to introduce Aborigines to better living conditions and consequently to improved health, but the extent to which this succeeded or failed is difficult to determine. Certainly many Aborigines who left their traditional settings and ended up as urban fringe dwellers lived in conditions as bad as, if not worse than, those they left. The change from the policy of assimilation to that of land rights and self-determination was based partly on the belief that Aboriginal health and wellbeing could be improved by turning the clock back to their traditional ways of living, which would include a closer relationship with the land. It could be expected, therefore, that for those Aborigines who had their land rights restored and were able to determine their destiny, there would be a consequent improvement in health.

Some diseases which had become endemic in Aboriginal communities were not likely to disappear overnight simply by reverting to more culturally satisfying surroundings. The problem was how to eliminate such diseases without intruding too much into Aboriginal culture. Speaking in a parliamentary debate on Aboriginal health, Kim Beazley senior stressed the need to eliminate diseases and disabilities such as yaws, leprosy, hookworm, trachoma, pulmonary infections, deafness and malnutrition. Referring to the work of Professor Fred Hollows in the elimination of eye diseases and the work of Doctor Randy Spargo, Director of Community Health in the Kimberley region, Beazley said that similar concentrated programmes were needed to attack each of these problems. Ralph Hunt, Minister for Health, commended the strong bipartisan spirit of the debate and congratulated Beazley on his speech, but added to his list of Aboriginal health problems those of infant mortality and alcoholism. Reference was also made in the debate to the difficulty of recruiting appropriately skilled medical staff prepared to work in isolated communities and to the fact that the growth of the homeland movement had complicated the problem of service delivery.

The other big Aboriginal Affairs headache that Fraser inherited when he became prime minister was the continuing battle over land rights. Contrary to public expectation, Fraser took up the Land Rights and Racial Discrimination Bills introduced by Whitlam and submitted them to parliament. The Acts passed peacefully through both Houses and were cemented into the legislative framework of Australia. The passing of the *Aboriginal Land Rights (N.T.) Act* and the *Aboriginal Councils and Associations Act* in 1976 marked the beginning of a new era for Aboriginal people and represented a complete policy turnaround, from assimilation to self-determination and self-management. But there yet were other issues involved. The most important of these was whether the Aborigines' claim to land rights simply affirmed their traditional relationship with the land, or whether land ownership could and should provide them with an economic power base. The passing of the *Aboriginal Land Rights (N.T.) Act* achieved both. It ensured that Aborigines could retain a traditional relationship with the land, and it provided economic power by giving them the right to negotiate with mining companies and receive royalties. For some more militant Aboriginal activists, the Act didn't go far enough, in that it reserved to the Commonwealth the final decision to permit mining if the project was considered to be in 'the national interest'. Likewise, while the *Aboriginal Councils and Associations Act* gave Aborigines the means of controlling their communities through elected town councils, and the capacity to engage in projects of social and economic development, much of the Act was so complex in its regulatory language it was beyond the understanding of many of those it was intended to help.

Finally, and perhaps most critically for Fraser, the policies of anti-discrimination, though now given legislative status and authority through the *Racial Discrimination Act*, had yet to be tested in the field. Queensland, the major target of this legislation, was not about to lie down in front of the Commonwealth legislative steamroller without a fight. At the end of 1976, the position regarding the rights of the Aurukun and Mornington Island Aborigines was still in limbo, with the Queensland Government's appeal to the Privy Council yet to be resolved. What Fraser had to decide was whether to force a head-on confrontation with Queensland, or to strive for a negotiated settlement. He chose negotiation, but it was to be a long and difficult process. In the face of Queensland's continuing opposition to its policies, the Commonwealth, under pressure to uphold the rights of the communities of Aurukun and Mornington Island, introduced the Aboriginal and Torres Strait Islanders (Queensland Reserves and Communities Self-Management) Bill. Introducing the Bill, Minister for Aboriginal Affairs Ian Viner was careful to point out that this was not an attempt by the Commonwealth to take over the powers of the State of Queensland. He quoted from a speech which Fraser had given at the inaugural meeting of the National Aboriginal Congress:

> It was never good enough for politicians or bureaucrats, whether at the federal or state level, to impose on the Aboriginal peoples their concept of what was good for the Aboriginal people. Aboriginal people have the same right as other Australian citizens; to determine what is best for them ... These communities have turned to us. We will not fail them.[5]

Both sides of the House were in agreement that action against Queensland was necessary, and the Queensland Reserves and Communities Self-Management Bill was passed with reasonable speed. Before the Act could be promulgated, however, the politico-legal time bomb which had been ticking away for three years suddenly exploded. In March 1978, the Privy Council announced that the Queensland Government's appeal against the decision of the High Court of Australia in the Aurukun case had been upheld. Queensland immediately announced it would take over the management of the Aboriginal communities at Aurukun and Mornington Island. This meant that the Uniting Church in Australia, which had managed the communities and had vigorously supported them, was sacked.

The Aurukun and Mornington Island affair aroused tremendous interest throughout Australia as the two communities, together with the Uniting Church, appealed to the Commonwealth for help. The appeal came before parliament in a 'matter of public importance' debate, initiated by Dr Everingham, Labor member for Capricorn. Everingham said that the Queensland Government had sacked the Uniting Church because, it claimed, the church was unable to provide health and education services; since it was the government's responsibility to provide these services, this gave Queensland the excuse to take over. But the real agenda, said Everingham, was the Queensland Government's desire to commence a billion-dollar bauxite-mining project on the Aurukun land, for which approval had been given to an overseas consortium. Everingham made a strong personal attack on Premier Bjelke-Petersen, saying he was 'dangerous and sick'.

Viner also voiced grave concern. He said that the Uniting Church had been promoting the Commonwealth's policy of self-management in the two communities and he had received a letter from the church President, strongly urging the Commonwealth to take over direct responsibility for them. Worse was to come. It was learned that Queensland intended to enact a Local Government (Aboriginal Lands) Bill, which would give the government power to amend the boundaries of the shires of Aurukun and Mornington Island, dissolve their councils, and reserve areas for mining. By switching the status of the land from 'Reserve' to 'Crown', the Queensland Government was virtually taking it out of the reach of the Commonwealth.

The situation appeared to be heading for a massive confrontation. Bjelke-Petersen was fiercely opposed to anything which savoured of an attempt by the Commonwealth to usurp states' rights. He was also convinced that Aboriginal communities in Queensland were being stirred up by communists and left-wing agitators, which included, in his view, officials of the Uniting Church. Bjelke-Petersen was a shrewd and seasoned political campaigner, capable of keeping his opponents off balance. He was aware that the Commonwealth's *Aboriginal Land Rights (N.T.) Act* only applied to the Northern Territory; although some states had cooperated by enacting parallel legislation, Queensland had steadfastly stood out against such moves, and Prime Minister Fraser was now faced with an extremely sensitive and potentially dangerous situation.

Fraser took the line that the issue at stake was the right of Queensland Aboriginal people to self-management and that to widen the dispute at this stage to include land rights, or to threaten a cutback of funds, would only exacerbate the situation. Rather than enter into a personal confrontation with Bjelke-Petersen, Fraser employed Ian Viner, Peter Nixon and a few highly skilled public servants to maintain a steady flow of communication with him and ensure that his personal agreement was obtained for every decision. One top federal public servant was jokingly referred to at the time as 'the Ambassador to Queensland'. The Aurukun and Mornington Island saga took another dramatic turn when the two Aboriginal communities sought and obtained an injunction restraining the Queensland Government from dissolving their councils. Viner expressed the hope that the injunction would provide a 'cooling off' period and enable the various parties to get together and work out a way of achieving self-management for the communities.

Rather than cooling off, however, Queensland responded by cutting off funding to the two communities. Viner, as the federal Minister for Aboriginal Affairs, countered by providing the Uniting Church with $240 000 to continue its work with the communities on the understanding that when Queensland reimbursed the church, it would repay the money. In sticking to his guns and saying that the proper approach was for Queensland to provide funds to enable the communities to be self-managing, Viner was avoiding any semblance of usurping states' rights. But Queensland further exacerbated the situation by serving notice of eviction to three Uniting Church advisers at Aurukun, plus the local representative of the federal Department of Aboriginal Affairs. Viner insisted that the DAA representative should stay. In the midst of all the argument and political manoeuvring, one old Aborigine was heard to say, 'Why can't you leave us in peace and simply agree between your governments about the man who will advise us?'[6]

Negotiations dragged along through 1978. At times it would seem that Bjelke-Petersen was beginning to soften his resistance to the Commonwealth's proposals, but in the next breath he would sheer right away again. Despite his assurances that Queensland's Local Government (Aboriginal Lands) Bill would accommodate all Commonwealth concerns, when the first draft was presented it contained nothing that satisfied the Commonwealth. Viner and the other Commonwealth representatives persevered with their negotiations. They found to their relief that Russ Hinze, a larger than life cabinet minister and trusted adviser to Bjelke-Petersen, was prepared to accommodate Commonwealth demands in matters such as the terms of the leases, the role of advisory committees and rights of entry. So successful was this new round of negotiation that when the Bill was finally introduced in the Queensland Parliament it was substantially as the Commonwealth wanted.

Despite the apparent success of negotiations over the Bill, it became obvious that the Queensland Department of Aboriginal and Islander Affairs had not relinquished the purse-strings of the two communities, nor had any real control had been handed over. The normally calm Viner was furious, threatening to fund the communities directly. The communities themselves were still very hostile towards the Queensland Government, and at times poured fuel on the fire by refusing to receive or speak to the premier. Further protracted negotiations took place, with the Commonwealth appointing negotiators and intermediaries whom they believed would get on best with the Queensland people concerned. By November 1978, Viner was able to

announce that the Aurukun and Mornington Island communities
had interviewed applicants for the positions of town clerk and
appointments had been made. Viner also announced that, for
the first time in the history of Queensland, leases were being
negotiated which would grant to the Aboriginal communities
security of tenure over their traditional lands, and that new
elections would shortly be held for town councils. Thus the
Commonwealth's twin goals of achieving self-management
and security of tenure for the Aurukun and Mornington Island
Aborigines were close to achievement.

During 1977 and 1978, federal parliament spent an
extraordinary amount of time debating the Aurukun and
Mornington Island issue, with the Opposition constantly
attacking the government with a series of 'matters of public
importance' or 'urgency' motions. Sometimes they were
directed towards the threats which mining on Aboriginal land
presented, sometimes towards the question of security of tenure
of land, and sometimes to the question of human rights. The
Aboriginal communities became extremely unhappy at times,
impatient with the slowness of proceedings and feeling that
the Commonwealth had let them down. Likewise, the Uniting
Church strongly criticised the government for its failure to take
strong and decisive action. But in January 1979, Viner was able
to announce in the House of Representatives that new councils
had been elected in each community and that practically all the
previous councillors had been re-elected. 'As from this time,'
he said, 'the former administration ceases to function and the
councils will be self-governing bodies.'[7]

The eventual outcome was that the Aurukun and Mornington
Island communities received the right of self-management and
long-term leases over their lands. While the Commonwealth
always had a fallback position in the form of compulsory
acquisition of the lands in question, it preferred the approach
of gradually steering the 'recalcitrant' Queensland Government
in the right direction. As Fraser put it:

> We could have asserted our power and secured their future, but there
> would then be two warring administrations and it would have made

sensible resolutions almost impossible. They [the Aboriginal communities] are dependent on the State for education, health and all sorts of services, which they are equipped for and we're not. That's one path and I would be really fearful of the consequences. The other path was for us to be resolute and to extract everything we can possibly extract from the Queensland Government. It would be extremely difficult but it would enable us to preserve a relationship with the Queensland Government.[8]

By the end of 1979, the Fraser government couldn't claim that it had solved all the problems of Aboriginal Affairs, but it had begun to tackle what it perceived to be the major issues. By passing the *Aboriginal Land Rights (N.T.) Act* and the *Aboriginal Councils and Associations Act*, it had established a process in the Northern Territory which gave Aboriginal people considerable control over their traditional land and their communities. The Northern Territory pattern provided a model for other states to emulate. The Fraser government also initiated programmes to tackle the serious problems of housing, health and employment, restructured organisational processes so that Aborigines could play a bigger part in influencing the policies and programmes which affected them, and overhauled expenditure processes to eliminate waste and extravagance. Even so, budget allocations to Aboriginal Affairs continued to increase.

Despite these achievements, turbulence in Aboriginal Affairs continued. Even as the Queensland situation was being resolved, another storm was brewing in the west. The eye of this storm was Noonkanbah, a cattle station in the remote northwest Kimberley, and the protagonists were the local Aboriginal community and the Western Australian Government. Fraser was about to face another challenge in Aboriginal Affairs, and he would have to contend with another tough state premier in the person of Sir Charles Court.

7

High Noon at Noonkanbah

Mining is an explosive business. Using explosives to blast ore into manageable pieces is conventional practice in the mining industry, whether in tunnels deep under the ground or in an open-cut operation. The 'mining explosion' was also the term used to refer to the rapid and dramatic sequence of new mining projects that occurred across the Australian outback in the 1960s and 1970s. Bauxite, coal, iron, copper and uranium were just some of the rich ore deposits discovered during those two decades. The economic benefit to Australia that resulted from the mining explosion was as great as in any period of its history, and the share prices of some of the mining companies involved rocketed to unheard-of (and unsustainable) levels.

The social impact of some of these new mining projects had two equally explosive but less productive results. One was their impact on the environment, the other their impact on the lives of Aboriginal people. We have already seen how the mining of bauxite in Arnhem Land and on Cape York Peninsula led to protracted and painful disputes, and how the discovery of uranium in Kakadu also aroused highly emotional reactions. The next mining explosion occurred in the remote Kimberley region of Western Australia. The Kimberley had always been a kind of ill-fated Shangri La where mining was concerned. Great hopes of rich discoveries had driven many prospectors there in the days of the Gold Rush. Most were doomed to disappointment, and in the case of the ill-equipped, to their death. One hundred years later, in the middle of the twentieth century, a new generation of prospectors hoped that large deposits of copper would be found there, but again success proved elusive. Hope dies hard, however, and people still dreamed that one day the region would 'strike it rich.'

Relationships between Aboriginal and white people had a tragic history in the Kimberley. Early contact between Aborigines and cattlemen was marred by conflict and violence. Nor was the situation helped when desert Aborigines moved into the coastal regions, displacing others from their traditional lands. A clear picture of the situation between 1880 and 1930 is not easy to obtain, but by the beginning of World War II most of the Aborigines in the Kimberley were living subdued lives in primitive camps either on cattle stations or the fringes of towns and settlements, those who had jobs being paid paltry under-award wages, those who did not subsisting on hand-outs. Observers at the time were shocked by the appalling conditions in which the Aborigines lived. But little if anything was done to alleviate the situation.

This passive pattern of poverty was turned upside down in 1969 when the government awarded Aborigines the basic wage and full unemployment benefits. Pastoralists found themselves unable, or were unwilling, to pay the higher rates, forcing the Aborigines to move away from their station camps and apply for the dole. One of the centres to which they drifted was Fitzroy Crossing, the site of a causeway that crosses the Fitzroy River on the long road from the coastal town of Derby inland to Halls Creek and thence to Darwin. In 1969, Fitzroy Crossing was no more than a pub, a post office, a police station and an Australian Inland Mission nursing outpost hospital established by Flynn of the Inland. This was a place certainly not equipped to cope with the hundreds of people who moved in from the cattle stations. The situation was exacerbated by the fact that as part of their new citizen rights Aborigines now had the right to drink alcohol, a right they embraced with enthusiasm. Drinking excesses led to outbreaks of violence that dramatically increased the workload of the two nurses who staffed the little hospital.

I had first visited Fitzroy Crossing in 1965, four years earlier, when I had become acutely aware that Aboriginal health problems were reaching crisis levels. The Western Australian Government shared this opinion and after Whitlam came to power financed our organisation to employ more nurses in an attempt to improve health services. Many of the professional staff who came to live and work in the Kimberley with us were appalled by the conditions in which the Aborigines lived and became ardent supporters of land rights.

Success in achieving land rights in the Northern Territory led militant white advocates to encourage Kimberley Aborigines to pursue similar claims. When their first land rights claim was lodged in 1972, the cattle industry was in a depressed state and several station owners were contemplating selling and moving out. In January 1975, the cattle station Noonkanbah was put up for sale, and in August that year the Aboriginal Land Trusts negotiated its purchase on behalf of the local Yungngora Aboriginal community. Aboriginal ownership was not without its problems, however, the most serious being a dispute over the way in which the station should be managed. One option was to adopt the traditional Aboriginal style, where control lay in the hands of the old men. The other was to follow a 'community development' model which had been created by a group of Aborigines and their white advisers on Strelley, a pastoral station in the Pilbara. The community development model involved greater participation in decision making by the community as a whole, especially the younger men. The victory of the proponents of the community development model at Noonkanbah led to a decline in the power of the older men and the emergence of some of the younger men into leadership roles.

Spurred on by this success, many younger men in the Kimberley became aggressive in their pursuit of land rights. As was the case in Queensland, the chief obstacle to their claims was the attitude of the state government. Premier Sir Charles Court, whose political success was founded on the development of the iron ore industry in the Pilbara, was keen to achieve similar results in the Kimberley. The first development venture, a massive irrigation scheme based on damming the Ord River, failed to achieve the results he had anticipated, and Court's main hope now lay with the mining industry.

Mining exploration had been going on in the Kimberley for some time, and a number of claims, mainly related to searches for diamonds and oil, had been pegged on Noonkanbah before the Aborigines took control. While exploration for diamonds soon shifted to the East Kimberley and to the discovery of the rich Argyle diamond mine, Australia's heavy dependence on the importation of oil led to intensified oil exploration in the area. In March 1978 a letter from Amax, one of the companies engaged in this exploration, was delivered to the Noonkanbah community, stating that the company intended to drill a well on their property. It was delivered by a representative of the Western Australian Community Welfare Department, who departed with the impression that there would be no opposition. But after the representative left the old men in the community changed their minds, concerned that drilling would constitute a threat to their sacred sites.

Wishing to avoid unnecessary trouble, the Western Australian Government and Amax agreed to defer drilling until a survey could determine the location of the sacred sites. The anthropologist appointed to carry out the survey, Peter Bindon, duly reported that there was 'a conflict between the proposed drilling location and the need for protection of the [sacred] site complex'.[1] Bindon suggested some alternative sites for drilling, but by this time the situation had become complicated by other factors. Steve Hawke, a young white activist (and son of future Labor prime minister Bob Hawke), was acting as an adviser to the Noonkanbah people, and with his encouragement the focal point of their objection changed from the protection of sacred sites to the wider agenda of land rights. Premier Court came to the conclusion that Hawke and other activists were manipulating the situation in order to embarrass his government. Once again isolation was a key factor in the dispute. The government representatives nearest to Noonkanbah were 200 kilometres away in Derby, and were not really equipped to handle a potentially explosive situation. Hawke, on the other hand, was living in the community and as a journalist could use his experience to exploit the media to the full. Further complications arose when other parties entered the fray, the Aboriginal Cultural Materials Committee, for example, seeking temporary protected status for the proposed drilling site.

Both Amax and the state government were keen to get on with the drilling and in June 1979 Amax again informed the Noonkanbah community that it intended entering the station to commence work. The community sought and obtained an injunction to restrain drilling, but it was soon lifted, and the Aboriginal Legal Service in Western Australia advised the Noonkanbah people that there was no chance of winning a permanent injunction. As the situation entered the second half of 1979, Noonkanbah began to experience a rising tension. The Kimberley is a vast area with a small and scattered population, but incidents of any size are widely broadcast, and when the heat and oppressive humidity of the wet season arrives, tempers begin to snap, especially when combined with excessive drinking. The pressure began to take its toll.

On the federal front, the new Minister for Aboriginal Affairs, Senator Fred Chaney, himself a West Australian, began to take an active interest in the Noonkanbah situation, urging both sides to engage in consultation and moderation. The community asked for a three-year moratorium while the issue of sacred sites was properly investigated, a proposal which Amax rejected. In March 1980, Amax again announced that it proposed to commence drilling. Dicky Skinner, the leader of the Noonkanbah community, immediately called the Aborigines of the Kimberley to 'battle stations'. Premier Court sent some of his cabinet ministers to Noonkanbah to negotiate. One asked Skinner whether the community was saying 'no' to mining anywhere on Noonkanbah, to which Skinner replied 'Yes, that's what the people think.'[2] Despite Skinner's assertion, and the added pressure from the presence of television crews filming the drama, the Noonkanbah community eventually agreed to allow drilling at another site. On 21 March it reversed this decision, and sought and obtained an injunction against any drilling within 5 kilometres of Pea Hill, the sacred site at the heart of the controversy. This effectively prevented drilling on the new agreed site, which was within the 5-kilometre radius.

The drilling contractors withdrew until the injunction was lifted a few days later, on 27 March. However, when they came on site again, the Aborigines ordered them off and locked the gate. This led to a heated confrontation between Amax representatives and the Noonkanbah people, but the Aborigines stood firm. On 1 April, while the drillers cooled their heels outside the locked gates, the Noonkanbah lawmen danced and performed at the Amax camp all night, in what Steve Hawke described as 'a masterly piece of psychological warfare'.[3] The Aborigines continued to exert this kind of pressure, repeatedly telling Amax and the drilling contractors to go. The contractors, together with a squad of police who had been sent to prevent violence, pulled out from the site and the Aborigines celebrated their victory. Premier Court issued a statement expressing his strong condemnation of the Aborigines' actions and gave Amax an extension of time to complete the drilling.

Heartened by the success of their tactics, the Aborigines held a big rally at Noonkanbah attended by many outside supporters. The media began to talk of Premier Court losing the initiative and being forced to back down. Amax threatened to pull out entirely unless a breakthrough was achieved. Court flew to Noonkanbah and the stage was set for a showdown at a meeting which took place there on 30 May 1980. Court made a conciliatory offer to the community, which he later committed to writing, although the community seems to have suggested to him that they didn't want mining to take place under any circumstances. Later they wrote to reject his proposal, although the letter was somewhat ambiguous. In the meantime, however, the drilling equipment had been moved down the coast to Eneabba near Geraldton, where other commitments needed to be completed. Drilling at Noonkanbah was thus deferred yet again.

The next move in the drama was the announcement that Amax was sending water-drilling equipment to Noonkanbah. The Aborigines set up a road blockade to prevent its entry, but eventually they dispersed and the drill got through. Events began to move towards a dramatic climax. With the accompaniment of huge media contingent, a convoy of trucks headed north from Perth to pick up the oil-drilling equipment at Eneabba and transport it to Noonkanbah. Thanks to television coverage, the progress of the convoy was seen all over Australia. Trade unions in the iron ore industry threatened to take disruptive action as the convoy passed through the Pilbara, but when it arrived there was only a token protest. Nonetheless, inflamed by media attention the drama was building, and it was generally agreed that the real confrontation would occur when the convoy reached Noonkanbah.

As the convoy drew closer the Aborigines decided to bar the access road to Noonkanbah where it crossed a creek called Mickey's Pool. Sixty people, including five ministers of religion, and seven vehicles formed a blockade to prevent the convoy getting through. Police delivered a warning to the protesters and when they refused to budge, removed the vehicles. Following a further warning, the police proceeded to move the protesters. Despite the emotionally charged situation, there is no evidence that any violence occurred, although some of the protesters, including ministers of religion, spent the night in the Fitzroy Crossing gaol.

With the blockade removed, the convoy was able to move on to the drilling site, but this was not the end of Amax's troubles—the drillers who had contracted to operate the equipment suddenly refused to proceed with the job. They changed their minds a few days later and drilling commenced. The Noonkanbah drama ended with a totally unexpected anticlimax. After all the time, money, energy and emotion spent on getting the project off the ground, drilling results proved disappointing and Amax decided not to proceed with their search for oil.

Remarkably, the events at Noonkanbah did not become the subject of debate in the House of Representatives until the drama was reaching its height early in 1980. Labor's Clive Holding, who was to become Minister for Aboriginal Affairs in the Hawke government, suggested that the Noonkanbah community should 'fly a different flag, declare themselves a republic and ask for overseas aid'.[4] Mick Cotter, Coalition member for the electorate of Kalgoorlie, which in the extraordinary political geography of Australia includes the Kimberley region, reminded the House that the Aborigines held Noonkanbah under a pastoral lease and that the property was thus subject to the same conditions regarding mining as any other pastoral lease in Australia.[5] John Dawkins, of the Labor Opposition, took the line that the Noonkanbah issue related to human rights and referred particularly to the right of religious freedom: 'There is no way that the Aboriginal people of Australia can pursue their religious beliefs without the control and ownership of the land which holds the symbols of their religious beliefs'.[6]

In the weeks that followed, the Opposition continued to attack the government for its failure to take action on the Noonkanbah situation. Sir Charles Court was accused of running a 'police state', and Labor compared the 'courteous' relationship which had been developed between the Aborigines and mining company CRA over the mining of diamonds in the Kimberley with the confrontational situation at Noonkanbah. In a lengthy statement in reply, Minister for Aboriginal Affairs Ian Viner outlined the government's position:

> Let me state clearly the Commonwealth's position. The Commonwealth has consistently expressed its view to all parties that conflict should be settled by negotiation not by confrontation ... If there is one lesson that has been learned over many years of Aboriginal affairs, it is that confrontation does not succeed. It is easy to advocate development projects regardless of all other consequences ... It is also easy to argue for the protection of Aboriginal interests at all costs ... But the real challenge is to allow development of Australia's natural resources—so essential for the benefits of all Australians—to proceed and at the same time, to provide properly for accommodation of Aboriginal interests.[7]

By the end of August 1980, with Amax's failure to achieve encouraging results from its drilling, Noonkanbah was no longer a front-page issue in the papers and no longer an issue in parliament. Despite all the drama that surrounded it at the time, and the great anticlimax, Noonkanbah was not a one-off incident, but part of an historical and political process in the arena of Aboriginal affairs that continued to unfold for another decade or more. While some of the key characters in the affair disappeared from centre stage, the ideology that was the real catalyst for what occurred remained very much alive. The confrontation which this ideology produced eventually moved from the heat and dust of remote Aboriginal communities such as Yirrkala, Aurukun and Noonkanbah to the more sedate, air-conditioned ambience of the High Court of Australia. It was here that the drama of *Mabo and Others v. State of Queensland* was played out and the legal status of land rights eventually decided.

8

A Proliferation of Policies: Bob Hawke

The Australian political pendulum often swings in response to the economic conditions of the time. Such was the case in 1983 when a stagnant economy and high unemployment were the key issues in a federal election in which, under the charismatic leadership of Bob Hawke, the Labor Party swept into power. Initially Aboriginal affairs didn't rate highly on Hawke's list of policy priorities, and it wasn't until the end of 1983 that Labor policies on Aboriginal affairs were presented to parliament. It's interesting to note that Clyde Holding, who became the first Minister for Aboriginal Affairs in the Hawke government, was the eighth person to be appointed to that office in the ten years since 1972. His predecessors were Gordon Bryant, George Cavanaugh and Les Johnson in Whitlam's government, and Ian Viner, Fred Chaney, Peter Baume and Ian Wilson in Fraser's government. Obviously the burn-out rate in the portfolio was extremely high.

Holding began his ministry by launching an avalanche of inquiries—into the *Aboriginal Land Rights (N.T.) Act*, Aboriginal Legal Aid, the Department of Aboriginal Affairs, the National Aboriginal Conference, the Aboriginal Development Commission, Aboriginal Hostels Ltd, Commonwealth/States uniform land rights and Aboriginal training and employment. The results of these inquiries were never revealed to parliament, but in the last session for 1983, Holding produced a wide-reaching statement of the government's Aboriginal Affairs policies. Most controversial of these was the land rights policy which, said Holding, was based on five principles:

- Aborigines to have inalienable freehold title to land.
- Protection of sacred sites.
- Aboriginal control of decision making in relation to mining.
- Compulsory payment of royalties by mining companies.
- Compensation for lost land.

Included in the policy statement were promises to achieve equality for Aboriginal people with other Australians in matters of health, education, housing, employment and welfare services. There would be protection of Aboriginal cultural identity, language, oral history, rites and artefacts, and encouragement for both traditional and contemporary forms of arts such as painting and dancing. Holding waxed eloquent about Aboriginal culture: 'Aboriginal culture is the oldest culture known to mankind. In Australia, at a time when our European forebears still lived in caves, art and dance, song and ceremony, language and religion had been a recognised part of this great ancient culture.'[1]

Underlying these grandiose aspirations was another agenda. It concerned the fast-approaching year of 1988, which would mark the bicentennial celebration of the first white settlement in Australia. Hawke's fear was that Aborigines would use the occasion to embarrass the government by expressing their feelings about what had happened to them over the previous 200 years. In an attempt to forestall the possibility of an Aboriginal protest, Holding said:

> The Bicentennial year of 1988 provides an immediate focal point towards which all Australians can work together to achieve the objective set out in this resolution ... I have made it quite clear to Aboriginal people that neither the grant of land nor the recognition of Aboriginal prior occupation and ownership, in any way puts Australian sovereignty in question. Sovereignty is vested in the Crown and the Parliaments, for a single people united in the Commonwealth. The people who are so united are all Australians.[2]

Holding inherited the Aboriginal Affairs portfolio at a difficult time. Seven years had passed since the *Aboriginal Land Rights (N.T.) Act* had been passed, and a review was urgently needed. In fact it was overdue, especially since the Act was, to say the least, uniquely innovative in Australian political history. The government commissioned Mr Justice Toohey to carry out a review and in due course he presented his report, which bore the title 'Seven Years On'. It included a number of suggested amendments to the original Act, about which Toohey said:

> The number of amendments to the *Land Rights Act* may be thought to suggest substantial defects. Given the legislative novelty of the subject matter of the Act and the need to marry complex notions of traditional Aboriginal law and culture with European institutions and administrative procedures, the Act has worked surprisingly well. But it is inevitable that after seven years, cracks in the edifice have started to show.[3]

Landowners who had felt threatened by the *Land Rights Act* became even more anxious when in 1984 the Labor government introduced the Aboriginal and Torres Strait Islander (ATSI) Heritage Bill, the purpose of which was to give the government power to 'protect' land that had been declared part of Aboriginal heritage. Once again Aboriginal affairs entered hitherto uncharted waters. For the first time parliament was forced to look critically at the definition of some of the words being used. For example, the word 'heritage' as used in the Bill carried a different meaning from that used in international conventions. Internationally, the term 'heritage protection' applied to buildings or other specific objects. In the ATSI Heritage Bill, 'heritage' also applied to land. Other definitions which gave landowners cause for concern related to the Bill's application to land which might be declared as being of 'particular significance to Aboriginals in accordance with Aboriginal tradition'. Like 'heritage', the word 'tradition' was given a convoluted meaning. The Bill described Aboriginal tradition as including: 'the body of traditions, observances, customs and beliefs of Aborigines generally or of a particular community or group of Aborigines and includes any such tradition, observance customs or beliefs relating to particular persons, areas, objects or relationships'.[4] As one parliamentarian was driven to comment, 'The big question is, what doesn't it include?' But the most controversial aspect of the Bill was the vague definition given to the term 'Aboriginal': '"Aboriginal" means a member of the Aboriginal race of Australia and includes a descendant of the indigenous inhabitants of the Torres Strait Islands'.

In retrospect it's extraordinary that despite the inherent threats to existing landholders and the potential for lengthy and expensive legal disputes created by the language of the Bill, it was passed with little resistance from the Opposition.

The *Aboriginal Land Rights (N.T.) Act* was not the only Aboriginal matter up for review. Seven years after its creation, the Aboriginal Development Commission (ADC) had been subjected to uncomfortable scrutiny even before the review was announced. Under pressure from the media, the chairman of the House of Representative's Expenditure Committee, Steven Lusher, launched an investigation into the purchase by the ADC of a hotel at Walgett in outback New South Wales and a licensed club in Sydney. Lusher, a member of the Coalition Opposition, was accused by government members of political and racial motivation in initiating this investigation, but defended himself by saying there was a need for financial scrutiny of all expenditure of taxpayers' money, including that by Aborigines.

However, just as the Expenditure Committee began looking into the financial affairs of the ADC, Minister Holding suddenly announced a reorganisation of the Department of Aboriginal Affairs. The major item of interest in his announcement was the appointment of Charles Perkins as Secretary of the Department. This was an historic step as Perkins was the first Aborigine to be appointed to a senior federal public service position. Much was made of Perkins' new appointment, and people of every political persuasion congratulated him. But it fell to Charles Porter, shadow minister for Aboriginal Affairs, to raise the question as to whether the credibility of Perkins' new appointment was jeopardised by his leaving the post of Chairman of the ADC just at the time its financial affairs were being investigated.

In October 1984 the House of Representatives Standing Committee on Expenditure presented an interim report on the ADC. In presenting it, Leo McLeay, a government member, said:

> The Committee has found in the course of its investigation that the ADC has had some significant weaknesses during its brief history. Some of the weaknesses described by the Committee stem from the normal establishment difficulties of a new organisation. Others are more serious and need to be corrected if the Aboriginal Development Commission is to fulfil its potential to promote Aboriginal self-development and self-management.[5]

In another important area of Labor's Aboriginal Affairs policy, attempts to persuade the states to accept uniform national land rights legislation ran into trouble at the end of 1984. The Labor premier of Western Australia, Brian Burke, refused to agree to the proposals. Obviously the federal government was worried about where its Aboriginal Affairs policy was going, because no more than a year after its launch it was suddenly replaced with a new policy aimed at achieving a 'stronger, fairer and more equitable Australia'.[6] Self-determination, national land rights legislation and a review of the anti-discrimination laws were the major issues to be tackled, together with the hardy perennials of health, education, housing and employment. In the course of the debate on this new policy, Michael Cobb, Opposition member for Parkes, referred to the situation in the far west New South Wales town of Bourke which was rife with Aboriginal vandalism and robbery. He said that Bourke had 27 policemen, more per capita than any other town of similar size in Australia, that shopkeepers had to board up their windows and that all public telephones had been vandalised:

> We are destroying them [the Aborigines] as a race. By patronising them, by treating them differently from whites and by lavishing them with money and hand-outs, we are creating a bitter division between the white and black communities ... For goodness sake stop thinking we can solve the so-called Aboriginal problem by writing more cheques in ever increasing amounts.[7]

The next body to come under investigation by Holding was the National Aboriginal Council (NAC). Dr H. C. Coombs was commissioned to conduct an inquiry into its affairs; in his report he recommended that the government had to accept the fact that 'in its present form, the NAC is unsuitable for and ineffective as a national Aboriginal representative body'; that the changes needed were 'fundamental and comprehensive', and that 'the existing members, especially the Executive, are too identified with the existing practices to accept fully the need for change'.

Coombs also said that the fundamental problem with the NAC was that it was based on a 'white model'; he recommended that it be abolished. Holding rejected this recommendation, but in 1985, when an audit of NAC accounts became public, he had to acknowledge that there was a serious problem. Holding admitted that he had become aware of 'serious deficiencies in the NAC financial situation but [he] didn't interfere because of his allegiance to the principles of self-determination and self-management'.[8]

Attacking Holding, Roger Shipton of the Opposition said the Hawke government in its first Budget had nearly doubled the funds available to the NAC: 'Any organisation would have difficulty in absorbing such an increase'.[9]

In April 1985, parliament was informed of another crisis in the administration of the NAC. It happened at a time when Holding was overseas. Acting Minister Senator Susan Ryan ordered NAC funds to be frozen, but its executive continued to spend money in defiance of the order and when Department of Aboriginal Affairs officers tried to enter its premises they were locked out. Subsequently the minister announced that the NAC would be wound up. Later in 1985, it was revealed that the NAC's overdraft had increased from $100 000 to $500 000, despite the ordered freeze on spending. 'It is a matter of record,' said Holding on his return, 'that the NAC overspent the notional budget quite considerably and it did so in spite of repeated warnings from me and directions not to do so'.[10]

Meanwhile debate over the proposed uniform national land rights legislation continued, with cracks appearing on the Labor side. Holding took issue with Prime Minister Hawke's assurances to the Western Australian premier, and continued a dispute with Burke. Seizing the opportunity presented by the division in Labor's ranks, the Opposition launched an attack through a 'matter of public importance' procedure. The subject, the failure of government policies in Aboriginal affairs, was particularly directed to Holding's lack of competence.

In the August-September 1985 session of parliament, the Standing Committee on Expenditure presented its final report on the inquiry into the ADC. It recommended that the commission's role be 'maintained and strengthened' with an increasing emphasis on programmes associated with commercial enterprises and land acquisition. It further said that the ADC should take over some of the responsibilities previously associated with the Department of Aboriginal Affairs, such as housing, water supply, sewerage and power. The report also stressed the need for better administration, pointing especially to the questionable lending of money for property, saying there was a need to clarify the purposes of the properties purchased. Speaking to the report, David Connolly of the Opposition said that the background to this part of the report was the allegations of serious misspending, including those against the previous chairman of the ADC, Charles Perkins. He quoted Perkins as saying to a meeting of Aborigines regarding the financial plight of the ADC: 'We have got what they call a moratorium on business enterprises for individuals. Why we have done this is because we've got 460 business enterprises out at the moment and they're all going bad, or most of them are anyhow.'[11]

Connolly continued his attack on Aboriginal expenditure when the Appropriations Bill came before the House of Representatives: 'Since 1967 [to 1985] we have spent absolutely enormous amounts of money on Aboriginal assistance, in fact some $4.5 billion. And we are talking about a population which is somewhere between 160 000 and 300 000.'[12]

Endeavouring to regain some grip on his portfolio, Holding made a ministerial statement to parliament at the beginning of 1986 on the subject of Aboriginal land rights, noting that in February 1985 the government had released for public discussion a draft set of proposals for a national land rights model and in

August of that year had endorsed the principles of this proposal. Holding insisted that the referendum of 1967 had given the Commonwealth 'a special and overriding responsibility for the welfare of the Aboriginal people'. Connolly again went on the attack, saying that Holding was stepping back from his policy of achieving uniform national land rights legislation mainly because of pressure from the Premier of Western Australia. He also quoted from a letter which Liberal Senator Fred Chaney had written to Prime Minister Hawke:

> I urge you to rethink your position as soon as possible. The last thing Aborigines and other Australians need is another year of doubt and another year of strident argument. You are very remote from the Australian community if you do not understand what harm that is doing to the Aboriginal people and to race relations in Australia. It is my own assessment that your Government will eventually do little or nothing in this area.[13]

Hawke later acknowledged that the land rights policy had been changed because the Australian people were no longer as sympathetic toward the problems faced by the Aboriginal community as they might have been in the past. In the five years since its election the Hawke government had learned some hard lessons about the complexities of Aboriginal Affairs. Beginning with a plethora of investigations and inquiries into almost every aspect of policy and administration, and with a determination to achieve uniform land rights, it had been forced to amend its objectives and accept the fact that in many respects no real progress had been made in improving the conditions in which many Aborigines lived. At the beginning of 1987 the Bicentennial celebration of 1988 was looming uncomfortably close and the government was acutely aware that Aboriginal protest on a large scale was an increasing possibility. The government desperately needed to mount a new approach to Aboriginal Affairs and this, inevitably, would require a new minister to tackle it. Holding was moved out of the portfolio and Gerry Hand installed as the new minister.

Nothing puts more pressure on a government than the threat of severe embarrassment, so in an attempt to forestall Aboriginal resistance to the Bicentennial celebrations the

Labor government announced that it was formulating another 'new' policy for Aboriginal Affairs, the third in three years. In his speech to open parliament in 1987, the Governor-General said that the government's policy had three objectives:

- How best to reflect recognition of over 40 000 years of Aboriginal history.
- The appointment of a Royal Commission to inquire into Aboriginal deaths in custody.
- The formation of a new commission to replace both the Department of Aboriginal Affairs and the Aboriginal Development Commission.

Titled 'Foundations for the Future', the new policy was officially launched as the nation's response to Aboriginal needs. It had eight major components:

- The formation of an Aboriginal and Torres Strait Islander Commission (ATSIC).
- A Compact of Agreement, which would be called Makarrata.
- The formation of an Aboriginal Economic Development Commission.
- The development of an Aboriginal land base.
- A Royal Commission into Aboriginal Deaths in Custody.
- Better employment opportunities.
- Improvement of Aboriginal health.
- Improvement in Commonwealth–State relationships.[14]

On these foundations the Labor government planned to build a better future for the Aboriginal people. It was a comprehensive and ambitious policy, described by its advocates as 'bold' and 'visionary', while its detractors questioned how long it would survive after lift-off from the Bicentennial celebration launching pad. Responsibility for implementation of the new policy lay with Hand who, in his first speech as Minister for Aboriginal Affairs, said: 'The Government is determined to increase and improve Aboriginal economic independence and to ensure that essential services are delivered to Aboriginal communities'.[15]

Like his predecessors, Hand took up the portfolio determined to get it right. He set himself the daunting task of consulting as widely as possible with Aboriginal communities and organisations. In February 1988, six months after he took office, he announced to parliament that consultation had taken place with 1000 Aboriginal communities and organisations and that he himself had been involved in 46 meetings with 6000 people, representing 1200 community groups. Two months later, in another ministerial statement, he claimed that the widespread consultations had produced strong support among Aboriginal people for the proposed Aboriginal and Torres Strait Islander Commission (ATSIC). The statute which created ATSIC, he said, would have a preamble that recognised the prior occupation and prior ownership of Australia by the Aboriginal people.

The proposal to include such a preamble aroused heated debate. On 24 March 1988, the Opposition launched an attack on the government's Aboriginal Affairs policies by raising 'a matter of public importance'. The subject of the debate was: 'The damage done by the Government to prospects for continuing reconciliation between Aboriginal and other Australians by its insensitivity and unrealistic raising of expectations'. In speaking to the motion, Chris Miles, shadow minister for Aboriginal Affairs, said:

> The simple staggering and tragic fact is that not one of the recognised social indicators has shown an improvement. In fact two or three of the key social indicators have got dramatically worse even though $2.5 billion has been allocated to Aboriginal advancement in the past five years under the Government.[16]

Miles cited some of the promises made in the early days of the Hawke government, such as providing 1000 Aboriginal teachers by 1990, commenting that the target had no hope of attainment. He added that the greatest impact of government policies on the Aboriginal people had been their introduction to a cash economy, which had eroded virtually every aspect of their culture. 'Many of us would have preferred some of the things that happened not to have occurred, but we cannot turn back the clock'.[17]

On 24 August 1988, Hand introduced the Aboriginal and Torres Strait Islander Commission Bill, again emphasising the amount of consultation with Aboriginal people which had taken place before the Bill was drafted. It is interesting to note just how much faith he placed in the effectiveness of the consultative process, which included the use of videos and similar methods of mass communication. Hand also emphasised that the constitutional authority on which the Bill was based was 'a concurrent one shared between the Commonwealth and the States', in which the states would still need to be responsible for meeting the needs and requirements of Aborigines and Torres Strait Islanders for such basic services as water, sewerage and education.[18] Emphasis was again placed on the preamble to the Bill, with Hand saying that it was fitting in the Bicentennial year to make recognition that Aboriginal and Torres Strait Islanders were prior occupiers and original owners of this land. But he tempered this by adding: 'It is the Government's intention that the language applicable would be neutral and have no legal consequences for present or future litigation in regard to land claims.'[19]

The debate on the ATSIC Bill continued right through 1988 into 1989. Unfortunately for Hand, it became enmeshed with several critical investigations into the conduct of the ADC and the Department of Aboriginal Affairs. In so far as ATSIC would inherit their functions it was important that any flaws in the existing system be first removed, but in the process of this administrative surgery there was plenty of political embarrassment for the government. When the debate on the second reading of the ATSIC Bill was resumed on 1 September 1988, Miles pointed out that with 60 regional councils, each with 20 members, there would be a total of 1200 councillors spread across Australia. He also noted that the Makarrata Treaty (Compact of Agreement) which featured prominently in the Foundations for the Future policy, had disappeared from sight.[20] And in a somewhat prophetic statement, Michael Cobb of the Opposition said:

> I believe that we must let Aborigines accept the consequences of their actions more than we have, whether the consequences are successful or whether

they be failures, because people need to both succeed and fail ... It always intrigues me that a person who is, say, 49 per cent Aboriginal blood and 51 per cent Chinese blood, which is not an unusual mix in my electorate, always calls himself an Aboriginal. Why does he not sometimes call himself a Chinese ethnic or whatever? So many people see this as becoming farcical ... I think that one year, five years, even ten years down the track, the position of Aboriginal people regrettably may not be much changed.[21]

Undaunted by these criticisms, Hand expressed his confidence in the ATSIC Bill, saying: 'The legislation will work. The programs will work better.'[22] On 8 November 1988 the Opposition launched another attack on the government in the form of yet another 'matter of public importance' debate, titled, 'The Government's failure in priorities and policies to address the needs of the Aboriginal and Torres Strait Islanders.'[23] Shadow minister Miles spoke of a 'chaotic period' in the administration of the Department of Aboriginal Affairs, noting that nine leading Aboriginal administrators had been sacked, including the Secretary of the Department, Charles Perkins, so recently lauded by Hand. Miles quoted Michelle Grattan, the Canberra correspondent for the Melbourne *Age*, writing about the administration of Aboriginal Affairs in November 1988:

But the dreadful verdict at the fag end of party time is hard to avoid. The opportunity has been wasted, indeed squandered. The year is ending in futility and farce. Why, having gone through ten months of this Bicentennial Year have we ended up with a farce and chaos in this administrative area?[24]

The debate highlighted the failure of a number of Aboriginal commercial enterprises, including the Oasis Hotel at Walgett, the Woden Club in Canberra and various pastoral stations. The government's intention to make the bicentennial year a landmark in Aboriginal Affairs had certainly been achieved, but not in the way it had hoped. The ATSIC Bill was still being debated and the administration of Aboriginal Affairs had been exposed as something of a shambles. In 1989 the Opposition renewed its attack on the government for 'the failure of its policies and the collapse of effective administration in Aboriginal Affairs', Miles referring to a special audit into the Department which found that it was unable to confirm that funds provided for over 1700 projects had been expended on the purposes for which they had been provided.[25] Hand finally admitted that all was not well:

> From our travels around the communities as members of the House of
> Representatives Standing Committee on Aboriginal Affairs, it was obvious
> to everybody that the system was not working ... Aboriginal Affairs is an
> incredibly difficult area to work ... It is an incredibly difficult area to administer
> in terms of government and programmes. The history of Aboriginal Affairs
> is littered with mistakes but I have to say that the mistakes were not made
> by Aboriginal people.[26]

Towards the end of the debate on the matter of public importance, Prime Minister Hawke felt constrained to make a contribution. He began by saying that the Auditor-General's report into the administration of Aboriginal Affairs would not be published generally.[27] He acknowledged that there had been administrative shortcomings, some serious, in the administration of the Department, but said that the major criticisms of the report were directed towards the way in which the ADC administered its enterprise funds, where there had been a number of failed programmes and 'less than rigorous oversight'. Nonetheless, Hawke reaffirmed his faith in the policy of self-management and said that Aborigines and Torres Strait Islanders were the best judges of their needs and priorities. There was a need, said Hawke, for a balance between self-management and ministerial responsibility, and he promised that the ATSIC legislation would be amended accordingly.

John Howard, Treasurer in the former Fraser government, attacked the present government for its maladministration of the Department of Aboriginal Affairs and quoted the Auditor-General's report, which described its policy guidelines as 'out of date, unrealistic, not relevant, not measurable, ambiguous and too narrow'. Said Howard: 'The audit found that $500 000 provided for consultation in relation to the "treaty" [Makarrata], was contrary to the purposes of the ADC Act and consequently illegal.'[28]

Embarrassed by these revelations and the lengthy delay since the ATSIC Bill was first presented to parliament (on 11 April 1989), Hand made a lengthy ministerial statement titled 'ATSI. The Way Ahead', which began: 'It is now 16 months since I first made a statement in this House outlining the Government's proposals to significantly restructure the Aboriginal Affairs portfolio'. Hand announced further changes to the proposed legislation which mainly dealt with issues of accountability: 'During consultations, ATSI people stressed to me that they did not want to be set up to fail and would only accept responsibility if properly trained'.[29] The basics of the proposed Bill had not changed, he said, but there would be more accountability from ATSIC to the minister. There would also be a better distinction between commercial and non-commercial activities for funding purposes. Some zones would be split up and the number of ATSIC commissioners would be increased to seventeen. The preamble to the Bill, which was a statement about Aboriginal prior occupancy and ownership, would be maintained despite advice from the Senate to treat it as a separate document. Hand concluded that the target now was to have ATSIC operational as from 1 October 1989: 'Now for the first time, Aboriginal and Torres Strait Islander Australians will have a real say in matters affecting them. We are putting an end at last to paternalism'.[30]

In the consultations leading up to the presentation of the ATSIC Bill, Dr H. C. Coombs argued against the formation of ATSIC as a separate statutory commission and expressed support for the retention of a federal Department of Aboriginal Affairs. But anthropologist C. D. Rowley argued that the 'client/department relationship' model was inappropriate in Aboriginal Affairs and should be replaced by a 'bargaining' relationship between the government and an independent institution representing Aboriginal pressure groups. Shadow minister Miles commented that the government's action in setting up ATSIC was 'based on an ideology of the seventies rather than the administrative reality of the eighties and it would lead to separation ... Aboriginal Australians should be assisted on the basis of needs and not on the basis of race'.[31] He predicted that ATSIC would be confronted with conflicting interests and pressure groups and that the commissioners would ultimately choose to support the interests of their separate constituencies. While the ATSIC Bill had its third reading on 23 May 1989 and was eventually passed in the early hours of the following morning, the Opposition continued its attack on the underlying philosophies of the government's Aboriginal Affairs policies. On 11 May 1989, Neil Cowper moved that 'this House rejects the principle of separate development for Aboriginal or any other Australians'.[32] Separate development, he claimed, was producing conditions such as those he had seen in his electorate at Burnt Ridge, an Aboriginal community of 57 people:

> There are two decent houses but the great bulk of people are living in wood and tin humpies with dirt floors and no running water. They have to fill buckets to get water from the decent houses. There is no sewerage and the electricity is supplied in a very dangerous fashion by power leads from the two decent houses.

Graeme Campbell, Labor member for Kalgoorlie, also voiced his concerns about the direction of the government's policy:

> ATSIC is just another mishmash, another rehash. It is not solving the problems because Aboriginal people are sick to death of consultation. The concept of self-management was bright as a noble view but the reality is that self-management is a recipe for doing nothing.[33]

The inquiry into the administration of the Department of Aboriginal Affairs and the ADC continued through the first half of 1989, and on 15 August David Hawker presented its final report:

> This final report brings out some further shortcomings in administration in the area of Aboriginal Affairs, in some cases, shortcomings for which Mr Perkins as the Department Secretary over much of the period had to bear ultimate responsibility ... but most of the deficiencies identified were in the Aboriginal Development Commission.[34]

Immediately after the report had been tabled Prime Minister Hawke rose to defend Perkins, speaking warmly about him and his work before announcing that he would be retiring from the Public Service. Referring to the new body, ATSIC, Hawke said that all the necessary reforms would be implemented in it: 'This new Commission is the logical and appropriate next step for the advancement of both the great principles of self-management and ministerial responsibility'.[35]

The Leader of the Opposition, Andrew Peacock, confirmed that the report clearly exonerated Perkins from any wrongdoing even though Hand, the Minister for Aboriginal Affairs, had condemned him. Having supported Perkins, Peacock then went on to give reasons why the ATSIC proposals were flawed. The Senate Select Committee which examined them, said Peacock, had found they were 'unjustified, unnecessary, culturally inappropriate and would operate to the detriment of the Aborigines'.[36]

The creation of ATSIC was the cornerstone of the Foundations for the Future policy of the Hawke government. The policy was designed to demonstrate that the Aborigines and their welfare were seen as integral to the nation's future; this would be achieved by recognising past wrongs and assisting Aborigines to determine and manage their future directions. But the fact that, despite Hand's exhaustive consultative process with Aboriginal people, it took nearly eighteen months of parliamentary surgery before the Bill was finally passed was evidence that the place of Aboriginal people in Australian society was far from settled. The fact that the parliamentary debate took place against the background of continuing inquiries into the administration of Aboriginal Affairs was evidence that legislative empowerment does not necessarily lead to administrative efficiency and effectiveness. The fact that the gloomy prophecies about the future of ATSIC were subsequently realised is cause for reflection about the philosophy on which Aboriginal Affairs has been based ever since the 1967 referendum.

9

From Rage to Reconciliation

It's been said that short of death, the greatest punishment that can be inflicted on Aboriginal people is to lock them up. This especially applies to those who are incarcerated in a prison cell, but to a lesser degree also applies to those confined in a hospital ward. It was not uncommon for Aboriginal women taken from their remote communities to the hospital in Alice Springs for delivery of their babies to abscond and return home even before the baby was born, some infants being delivered in the back of a truck as their mothers were being taken back to the hospital. Incarceration in a prison cell had far more serious consequences. In the period leading up to the launch of Labor's Foundations for the Future policy in 1987, evidence was coming to light that the rate of incarceration of Aboriginal people was many times higher than in the rest of the community. Even more serious were claims that Aborigines were dying in prison cells at a rate far exceeding that for the rest of the community, and that police brutality was a key contributor to many of these deaths. The emotionally charged atmosphere surrounding the issue finally forced the government to take action. Included in its Foundations for the Future policy was a commitment to investigate Aboriginal deaths in custody and in due course a Royal Commission was appointed to do so. The Commission commenced work on 16 October 1987 with the confident prediction that its task would be completed within fourteen months, with a cost estimate of $2.2 million.

The estimates of both time and cost proved wildly inaccurate. In August 1989, almost a year after it was scheduled to complete its work, the Royal Commission into Aboriginal Deaths in Custody disclosed it had already cost $12 million for the eight months to 30 June 1989 and that the final cost was estimated at $29 million, nearly fifteen times the original amount. It was also revealed that the Commission had commenced with a staff of twelve, which by June 1989 had increased to 110, or tenfold. The staff blow-out was attributed in part to the creation of an Aboriginal Issues Unit, which employed a large number of Aborigines on salary levels in excess of $40 000 a year. Another factor contributing to the staggering cost increase was the provision of financial assistance to 129 Aboriginal families to enable them to be legally represented at the commission, an amount of $1.5 million.[1]

The 'Deaths in Custody' Commission was one example of the escalating amount of money being spent on Aboriginal Affairs. In September 1989, a document tabled in the House of Representatives listed federal government expenditure on Aboriginal Affairs from 1971 to 1990.[2] The summary figures were:

Year	$m
1971	24.5
1973	58.5
1975	158.9
1980	184
1983	300
1985	467
1988	671
1990	917

In real money terms, these figures represented a sixfold increase in expenditure in nineteen years. As would be expected, their tabling raised many questions. Warren Smith of the Opposition described Aboriginal Affairs as a 'billion dollar a year industry'.

Posing the question 'What is it doing?', he quoted the Labor premier of Western Australia, Peter Dowding, as saying: 'The arrangements between the State and Commonwealth for the delivery of Aboriginal services were doing nothing to improve the outcome. There was great confusion and all they were doing was hampering the benefits that were supposed to flow to Aboriginal people.'[3]

Criticism of 'wasteful' and 'extravagant' expenditure on Aboriginal Affairs came at a bad time politically and economically. Christopher Skase and Alan Bond, two of the more colourful high-flyers of the 1980s, had put their corporations into receivership with debts running into billions of dollars, but far worse, the OECD had declared Australia to be fourth on the world's debtors' list, with foreign debt running close to $100 billion. It was against this background of economic gloom and doom that federal parliament adjourned for the Christmas break on 22 December 1989. Soon after its return in 1990, parliament was dissolved for an election and, in a closely fought contest, the Labor Party was returned to government. Prime Minister Bob Hawke now appointed Robert Tickner as Minister for Aboriginal Affairs, partly because Tickner at one stage of his career had worked with Aboriginal people in the Northern Territory.

On 9 May 1991, three and a half years after it began its work, the Royal Commission into Aboriginal Deaths in Custody brought its final report to parliament. In that time the commission had inquired into the deaths of 99 Aboriginal people who had been 'in custody of police, in prison and in youth detention institutions'. The original commissioner, Justice Muirhead, had been requested to report by 31 December 1988, but as the work expanded and staff expanded, the number of commissioners also increased, from one to five. The final report filled eleven volumes, contained 5000 pages and 399 recommendations. In presenting the report to parliament, Minister Tickner said:

> The final Report does not accord with initial expectations of foul play. The Commissioners have not found that any deaths were the result of deliberate

unlawful violence or brutality by police or prison officers ... Families and friends in their continuing grief have found this difficult to accept ... [but] there is a failure to live up to the standards of care for those in custody.[4]

The report said that 30 of the 99 deaths resulted from hanging, and other forms of suicide accounted for many more. The average age of those who died was 32 years. Forty-three of the people whose deaths were investigated had experienced childhood separation from their families. Eighty-three were unemployed at the time of detention and 43 had been charged with offences before the age of fifteen. Tickner commented on some other aspects of the report:

The report documents in a way never before achieved the impact of European settlement upon Australia's indigenous people, their dispossession and subordination with a dominant and often hostile society frequently motivated by self-interest ... Aboriginal Australians themselves must have the will and the capacity to put an end to their disadvantaged situation and take charge of their own lives.[5]

Aboriginal Affairs seemed destined to lurch from one crisis to the next. No sooner had the Aboriginal Deaths in Custody inquiry been brought to a conclusion than another vexatious issue erupted. Once again the triumvirate of Aboriginal sacred sites, environmental issues and mining came into conflict in one of Australia's remote and sparsely populated regions. A decade after the dramas of Aurukun, Mornington Island and Noonkanbah, the focus of attention turned to Arnhem Land, specifically to the Kakadu region. Giant mining company BHP had discovered gold at a site called Coronation Hill and, naturally, wished to exploit their find. The company couldn't have chosen a more sensitive location or a greater source of embarrassment for the Hawke government. Faced as it was with a national financial crisis, the government couldn't ignore any project which might assist Australia's economic recovery—and the income which gold mining at Coronation Hill was expected to generate was considerable—but it also had to contend with the pressure being exerted by the environmental lobby. The Greens claimed that Coronation Hill was a conservation zone lying within a national park. The government also had to take into account the position of the Aborigines themselves, which was uncertain, because they appeared to be split in their views about whether mining could or should proceed. Those against mining argued that Coronation Hill was a sacred site because of its association with a mythical beast called Bula.

In seeking to resolve the issue, the government resorted to a tactic which had been employed in the past, namely, appointing a prominent judge to head a commission of inquiry. In this case the appointee was Mr Justice Stewart, who had achieved considerable fame as the head of a corruption inquiry in New South Wales. The new body was called the Resources Assessment Commission and its task was to examine the Coronation Hill mining proposal, taking into account its impact on environmental and Aboriginal issues. The Coronation Hill issue was raised for the first time in the House of Representatives on 13 May 1991. Referring to the division of opinion among the Aboriginal people, Opposition member Garry Johns said:

> Among some Jawoyn people the controversy over mining in the Conservation Zone also appears to have become an overtly political issue. According to the Stewart Inquiry's consultants, the debate about mining at Coronation Hill is not just a matter of traditional religion but a move clearly political.[6]

Stewart admitted that while three elders of the Jawoyn community were passionately anti-mining, they were not always so, and younger people in the community were more open-minded. The women were also more open to the possibility of mining. Debate also raged as to the authenticity of the beast Bula. It was alleged that before the Coronation Hill issue arose, Bula had never been identified with the site. Stewart more or less recognised this but tactfully expressed his view in the following terms: 'There seems little doubt that these opportunities and pressures have helped to restore specific form and content to a religious field of power known from preceding generations.'[7]

Stewart concluded that the beast Bula didn't exist at Coronation Hill, but had 'attachments to it'. However, taking into account environmental as well as Aboriginal issues, he came to the conclusion that mining shouldn't proceed. Faced with the Stewart inquiry's recommendation, Prime Minister

Hawke also had to contend with the fact that a substantial number of his cabinet ministers held the opposing view. When debate on Coronation Hill was resumed in parliament on 30 June 1991, John Hewson, Leader of the Opposition, asked Hawke why he chose to ban mining at Coronation Hill when the majority of his cabinet was in favour of it. Hawke defended his decision with the assertion that Coronation Hill was an authentic sacred site which needed to be protected. The Opposition was not convinced about the authenticity of this claim, and counter-attacked with a quote from Labor Senator Bob Collins, who represented the Northern Territory, concerning Coronation Hill:

> It is with some resignation that I note the debate on this matter is proceeding along familiar lines. The new key players who are now running this debate are all well known to me. A small number of them are consummate ratbags. All of them are running on an agenda that has nothing whatever to do with the long-term interests of the Jawoyn community. The Jawoyn are simply convenient cannon fodder.[8]

The division which occurred in the ranks of the Labor government over the Coronation Hill issue was symptomatic of the wider concerns affecting it. In particular, Hawke's leadership was under question and although 'the pretender to the throne', Paul Keating, had been banished to the backbenches in June, it was only a matter of time before he made another attempt. In December 1991, after nine years as Prime Minister of Australia, Bob Hawke was defeated in a Caucus vote and Paul Keating assumed the mantle of leadership.

While the Coronation Hill debate was occupying the spotlight during 1991, other Aboriginal issues were also being debated in parliament. For example, the report of the Standing Committee on Aboriginal Affairs emphasised the difficulties and frustrations experienced in implementing government policies:

> You cannot marry a system which has not changed for at least 200 years with a system which is constantly evolving. The intervention of the Commonwealth since 1967 has only served to multiply the bureaucratic processes and inhibit the progress of the Aborigines.[9]

Despite the criticism, the government persevered with attempts to achieve more of the objectives it had set in the Foundations for the Future programme of 1987. One of these was to create a process by which reconciliation between Aborigines and the rest of Australia might become a reality. On 30 June 1991, Minister for Aboriginal Affairs Robert Tickner introduced the Council for Reconciliation Bill, which would, he said, 'signal the beginning of a decade of reform and social justice for the Aborigines and Torres Strait Islanders'.[10] Tickner said that the objectives of the Bill were to promote reconciliation; deepen understanding of the Aborigines; provide a forum for discussion, and lead to the issue of some kind of formal document. The Opposition supported the Bill but warned about not raising the expectations of the Aborigines beyond reality. The Coalition's Dr Michael Wooldridge quoted Anglican Bishop Malcolm of Northern Australia, himself an Aborigine, as saying: 'All that Aboriginal people want is for someone to say "Sorry". We cannot undo the past. We have to look at the future. The first essential step in that is just simply saying "Sorry".'[11]

By and large, that particular debate on the Reconciliation Bill was carried out in a bipartisan spirit. The same bipartisan spirit wasn't present later in the year when questions were raised about the effectiveness of government programmes. Indeed, the government faced some awkward questions from members of its own side. On 13 November 1991, Labor's Graeme Campbell asked questions about grants to the Kalgoorlie Aboriginal Medical Service in his electorate. It was revealed that the service had sixteen staff and eight vehicles and had received $750 000 in capital grants and $491 937 in recurrent funding for the nine-month period from January to September 1991 with little to show for it. On 14 November 1991 another Labor member, John Anderson, who represented Gwydir in New South Wales, spoke about the Barwon Aboriginal Community, a registered company operating out of Walgett and engaged in several enterprises including Aboriginal housing, a bus service for elderly Aborigines, self-drive rental cars, social work and the leasing of the now infamous Oasis Hotel. Anderson alleged that the first manager of the Barwon Aboriginal Community had been dismissed for stealing and had a MasterCard debt of

$36 000. The second manager also had a dubious record. When he took over the company, its debt was $120 000. When he left, it was $340 000. He was replaced by a third manager, to whom ATSIC said it would not provide funds while he held that position. By now, the Barwon Aboriginal Community had suffered a total loss of $2 million and many assets had been sold off at grossly less than value. According to the member for Gwydir, ATSIC had said it was under no obligation to investigate the company, even though it had cancelled its $2 million annual funding:

> When repeated instances of mismanagement, fraud, theft, blatant incompetence ... are continually shoved into the too hard basket by politicians and bureaucrats afraid to bite the bullet for fear of being branded 'racist', then you have an acceptance of second, third, or even tenth best as being the norm for Aboriginal organisations.[12]

As 1991 drew to a close it was apparent that Paul Keating, now Prime Minister, was seeking to overcome any electoral disadvantage the government might be suffering by attacking the Opposition on every available front. One of these fronts was the 'republican issue', which included the 'colonial' treatment of Aboriginal people by the British. It was increasingly obvious that Aboriginal issues were becoming a political football and part of a much wider ideological battle. Five years earlier the political point of reference for Aboriginal Affairs had been the impending Bicentennial celebrations and the need to appease Aboriginal feelings about the event. The new point of reference was the centenary celebration of the founding of the Commonwealth of Australia, scheduled for 2001, and with it the goal of achieving reconciliation between Aborigines and the rest of the Australian community. On the same political agenda was the move to make Australia a republic by that date. The Labor government had taken the initiative on both issues and Aboriginal Affairs were set to achieve a higher public profile than ever before. The tragedy was that while Aboriginal Affairs might have achieved this status in Canberra, the health, education and employment status of Aboriginal people in remote communities were as low as ever.

10

The Mabo
High Court Case

Ticking time-bombs are not unusual in Australian political and legal history but few have exploded with such ferocity as did the now famous High Court case popularly known as Mabo. It is the name of a man on whose behalf were fought legal battles that changed the whole basis of land ownership in Australia and achieved for the Aboriginal people recognition of their right to hold land under a doctrine called 'native title'.

Remarkably, Eddie Mabo, the man in question, was not himself an Aborigine. He was born on one of the three tiny islands in the Torres Strait called the Murray Islands. The people who lived there were generally referred to as the Meriam people and their ancestors were of Melanesian origin, probably from New Guinea. Because of the size of the islands the number of residents had never been more than 1000 and on one occasion fell as low as 400. Christian missionaries were the first to establish a permanent relationship with the Meriam people. Government involvement came later, as a result of concern for their welfare at a time when 'blackbirding' (abducting native people into virtual slavery) was rampant. The Murray Islands were not originally part of Queensland, but government concern about outsiders using the islands and their inhabitants for questionable purposes led to a proclamation on 21 July 1879 under which the Murray Islands were annexed to Queensland and subject to its law. Under a further proclamation in 1882 the islands were reserved for the native population, with the exception of a small parcel of land that was leased to the London Missionary Society. The other significant fact about the Murray Islands was that the Meriam people had a social system distinct from that of the mainland Aborigines. The islands had a clearly defined geographical area, a well-recognised system of land ownership and inheritance, and a land use (market gardening), which was more use-specific than the nomadic mainland Aboriginal practices of hunting and gathering.

This was the background and community life from which Eddie Mabo came. As a young man he had gone across to the mainland to find work in Cairns but in the late 1970s he sought to return to the Murray Islands. At that time the Protector of Aborigines in Queensland still held the power to prevent people from entering a reserve, which the Murray Islands were, and he refused Mabo's request. Mabo went to the Aboriginal Legal Service for help. The thought of mounting a High Court challenge to the Queensland government would have been the last thing on his mind at the time. But it happened that in other parts of Australia there were people concerned about Aboriginal rights in relationship to the land and looking for an avenue through which to take action. Eddie Mabo's situation provided them with that opportunity.

How the refusal to allow a Torres Strait Islander to return to his homeland led to the granting of land rights for Aboriginal people on the Australian mainland requires an explanation of the background to the land rights movement. Some authorities trace it back to the activities of the international communist movement after World War II. With the disintegration of colonialism, former colonies in Africa and Asia became independent nations and their predominantly indigenous populations assumed control. International communism became a powerful influence in their affairs. But there were other countries in which the indigenous population was a very small minority, the United States and Australia, for example, where indigenous people constituted somewhere between 1 and 2 per cent of the population. It was part of the international communist philosophy that even in these countries the indigenous population should strive to achieve separate sovereignty. In the United States, however, the race issue was focused on the former African Negroes rather than on the indigenous Americans, and because the African Americans had no 'traditional land rights' the idea of separate sovereignty was eventually discarded there. But the notion was never totally discarded in Australia, and became strongly linked to the land rights movement.

The evolution of the land rights movement has already been documented in this book, but it's worth reviewing some of the landmark decisions along the way. The first was the decision of the Australian people in the 1967 referendum to give the Commonwealth Government power to make special laws for the Aboriginal people. Whatever interpretation was later given to that decision, a comment by Sir Paul Hasluck is worth noting:

> I would doubt, myself, whether this was a well-considered judgment of the Australian people on the constitutional question alone. Rather it was an expression of opinion that we should do more to help the Aborigines and to redress the wrongs they had suffered ... The amendment to the Constitution certainly does not appear to me to mean that there shall be two different systems of law in Australia or two different classes of Australians.[1]

The next landmark in the history of Aboriginal land rights was the decision of Mr Justice Blackburn in the case of *Milirrpum and Others v. Nabalco Pty Ltd and the Commonwealth of Australia* (Supreme Court of the Northern Territory, 1971). In this case counsel representing the Aboriginal plaintiffs argued that communal native title to the land under dispute had never been extinguished and that therefore the granting of mining leases by the government was unlawful. However, the claim of the plaintiffs that they had been deprived of the use and enjoyment of their land was dismissed. The principal reasons for this decision were that it had not been proved that communal native title was an accepted fact in common law, and that it had not been proved that the clans had a recognisable and proprietary interest in the land in question. Despite these decisions, the judge and the two counsel involved came to the conclusion that something should be done to recognise the special nature of the relationship between the Aborigines and the land.

The next landmark was the appointment by the Whitlam government of a commission to inquire into how that relationship could be recognised. A. E. Woodward was appointed a sole commissioner to conduct the inquiry and as a result of his recommendations the Aboriginal Land Rights (N.T.) Bill was introduced to parliament and subsequently passed by the Fraser government.

The next significant event in the history of the land rights movement was the decision of the Queensland Government to oppose any attempt to impose the principles of the Commonwealth land rights legislation onto its state laws. The climax of this battle was the Aurukun case, which was fought over the unwillingness of the Queensland Government to give ownership of reserves and the right of self-government to remote Aboriginal communities. To counter this, federal parliament passed the *ATSI (Queensland Discriminatory Laws) Act*, although as it transpired the Commonwealth didn't have to exercise its powers, for the matter was settled by negotiation. The most vexatious issue for Aboriginal people in Queensland was the law that prevented them from moving in and out of the reserves without permission. The government argued that this was a protective measure designed to prevent social dangers such as the introduction of alcohol to the reserves, but many Aborigines regarded it as a denial of a fundamental freedom. It was this restriction which led Eddie Mabo to seek redress against what he alleged to be an infringement of his freedom.

In 1981 a conference titled 'Race Relations and Land Rights' was held at James Cook University in Townsville. It was organised by people from around Australia who were dissatisfied with the Blackburn judgment in the *Milirrpum v. Nabalco* case and were looking for another way to achieve recognition of Aboriginal land rights. Eddie Mabo and Father Dave Passi, who also became one of the plaintiffs in the Mabo case, were both present. One of the presenters at the conference was Barbara Hocking, whose paper was the only one to tackle the validity of the doctrine of *terra nullius* and argue for taking a challenge to the High Court. She received little support from other lawyers present, although the Aboriginal Legal Aid solicitor from Cairns, Greg McIntyre, took careful note of what she said. Afterwards McIntyre, who was advising Mabo, said to Hocking, 'You'll be hearing from us.' Subsequently Hocking was briefed to advise in the preparation of the case to the High Court and spent the next ten years researching the relevant law in the United States, Canada, New Zealand and New Guinea, as well as other former colonies of Great Britain.

Another speaker at the conference was Nonie Sharp, who had been carrying out anthropological studies on the Murray Islands and was aware of Eddie Mabo's grievance.[2] Sharp's subsequent role in the Mabo case can be appreciated by this extract from an article she wrote some years later for the magazine *Arena*:

> Some nine years ago a critical step towards this case was made at a small meeting of Islanders and others interested in challenging the principle of *terra nullius* upon which the white Australian nation is founded. It seemed likely to those present that as a sedentary people who cultivated garden land clearly demarcated by boundaries, the Murray Islanders would be able to present to a Western court more clear cut and comprehensible evidence than was possible for the Yirrkala witnesses in the Supreme Court of the Northern Territory.[3]

In the meantime the movement to make Mabo the test case for Aboriginal land rights was gathering momentum. Professor Henry Reynolds of James Cook University (who was also present at the conference but didn't present a paper) had published two books, *The Other Side of the Frontier* and *The Law of the Land*, in which he included some of Hocking's arguments. Reynolds' influential role in the Mabo case is recognised by both supporters and detractors of the High Court decision. In *The Australian History of Henry Reynolds*, Geoffrey Partington quotes a number of opinions about Reynolds' role, including that of Gordon Briscoe, a research scholar of Aboriginal descent, who observed: 'The weakness of the Mabo decision lies in the way that one historical idea raised by one historian

[Reynolds], and one ethnographic document, made up the sole proof relied on by the Court.'[4]

On the other side of the argument, Noel Pearson, an Aboriginal leader in north Queensland, holds that it was Reynolds who demonstrated 'that native title was recognised by the Imperial government ... and respect for this title was supposed to govern colonial settlement in Australia. Reynolds shows how the colonists contrived to deny those rights.'[5]

Partington also quotes from the introduction to the second edition of another book by Reynolds, *Race Relations in North Queensland*: 'There can be little doubt that the History Department [of James Cook University] played a major role in the fundamental reinterpretation of Australia's past which found expression in the Mabo decision.'[6]

Mabo was employed as a groundsman at James Cook University during the 1980s and later as a research assistant to Henry Reynolds, so there can be no dispute about Reynolds' role in the litigation that followed. There may be others, known and unknown, who would claim to have contributed to the success of the Mabo case, but the work of Hocking has probably received the least recognition. Of course, the role of H. C. Coombs as the *eminence grise* of Aboriginal affairs should never be underestimated, and the influence of Henry Reynolds and his writings is unquestioned.

In 1982 Mabo, David Passi and James Rice, all from the Murray Islands, launched a High Court action against the Queensland and Commonwealth governments claiming that Crown sovereignty over the islands was subject to the land rights of the Meriam people which were based on local custom and traditional native title. The three plaintiffs sought a three-part declaration from the High Court: first, that they were owners and holders of traditional title; second, that this had not been impaired, and third, that as owners they were entitled to protection in terms of the fiduciary duty of the Queensland Government. They further sought a declaration from the High Court that Queensland was not entitled to impair their traditional ownership. The State of Queensland announced that it would rebut the claim that such land rights existed in law.

The case did not come before the High Court for another three years (1985) and in the interim the Queensland parliament passed the *Coastal Islands Declaration Act (1985)* which declared that the annexation of the Murray Islands in 1879 vested them in the Crown. The matter was further delayed when in 1986 the Chief Justice of the High Court, Sir Harry Gibbs, remitted the whole issue to the Supreme Court of Queensland for hearing and determination of all issues of fact raised by the pleading. This task was carried out by Mr Justice Moynihan, who visited the Murray Islands to acquaint himself with the life of the people. Moynihan duly reported his investigations to the High Court in 1988 and on the basis of his findings the High Court held that 'on the assumption the plaintiffs could establish the land rights claimed, the State *Coastal Islands Act* was inconsistent with the [Commonwealth] *Racial Discrimination Act* of 1975'.[7]

This decision, generally referred to as *Mabo v. Queensland 1*, cleared the way for Mabo and his co-plaintiffs to have the case re-opened in the High Court. While these legal battles were proceeding, other things were happening that would profoundly affect the outcome of the Mabo case. The most significant was the proclamation of the *Australia Act* of 2 March 1986. In this Act Queen Elizabeth II signed away the last vestiges of British legal powers over the Commonwealth of Australia, which among other things put an end to the right of appeal from the courts of Australia to the Privy Council in England. Where on previous occasions the Queensland Government had appealed to the Privy Council and won, this would not now be possible in Mabo or any subsequent cases. The second significant factor was that the Chief Justice of the High Court, Sir Harry Gibbs, had retired from the Bench and the federal Labor government had appointed two new judges, swinging the balance of the Court away from its previous conservative character. Thirdly, changes from Coalition to Labor governments at both federal level and in Queensland meant that the two governments which were the defendants in the case were not now as enthusiastic about winning as had been their predecessors. Indeed, the Commonwealth dropped out in 1991 before the hearing began.

While the second and final High Court case, known as *Mabo v. Queensland 2*, had to deal with a large number of complex issues, in essence it amounted to this—three Murray Islanders brought an action in the High Court against the Government of Queensland and asked the Court to declare that:

- The Meriam people were entitled to the Murray Islands as owners, possessors, occupiers and as persons entitled to use and enjoy the Islands.

- The State of Queensland had no power to extinguish the Meriam people's title.[8]

The hearing took place in the first half of 1992 before a Bench of six. After considerable deliberation the High Court, with one judge dissenting, delivered its finding as follows:

1. The Meriam people are entitled to possession, occupation, use and enjoyment of the Murray Islands.

2. The Queensland Parliament and the Queensland Governor have the power to extinguish the Meriam people's title, as long as they exercise that power validly and in a manner consistent with Commonwealth laws.[9]

The far-reaching significance of the first part of this judgment can be understood in this extract from the judgment of Mr Justice Toohey:

Although this case concerns the Meriam people, the legal issues must be determined according to fundamental principles of law that apply throughout Australia. The Meriam people differ in culturally significant ways from the Aboriginal peoples of Australia, who in turn differ from each other. But when it comes to determining what interests exist in ancestral lands of Australia's indigenous peoples, no basic distinction need be made between the Meriam people and those who occupy the mainland. The principles are the same.[10]

Thus the position of the Aboriginal people on the continent of Australia was determined on the basis of a case involving a small group of people on three tiny islands in the Torres Strait.

The 'fundamental principles of law that apply throughout Australia', to which Mr Justice Toohey referred, are generally known as the common law. This is the body of decisions and precedents which had been built up in England over the centuries and which, when Australia was first settled, became the law of this land. In earlier centuries, when the great European powers were expanding their empires and setting up colonies in the newly discovered parts of the world, there developed a form of international law by which these colonies could be acquired. There were three ways: by conquest, by cession, and by occupation of land which was *terra nullius*. It was this last method which England applied to its occupation of Australia. *Terra nullius* literally means 'land of no one.' In the case of Australia it was reckoned that because the native population appeared to have no form of social organisation or system of law, then technically the land was *terra nullius* and therefore its occupation by the British was the first real settlement of the country.

The plaintiffs in the Mabo case claimed that the indigenous people did have fully developed social organisations and systems of law, therefore Australia was not *terra nullius* when the British settlers arrived. While the High Court judges who gave the majority decision were reluctant to overturn the body of law which Australia had inherited from England, they did feel that they could 'modify our legal system to make it conform to contemporary notions of justice and human rights' and that the concept of *terra nullius* 'seriously offends the values of justice and human rights, especially equality before the law which are the aspirations of the contemporary Australian legal system' (Justice Brennan).[11] Justices Deane and Gaudron further elaborated on how the existing law had

> seriously offended the values of justice and human rights ... The dispossession of the Aboriginal people from their traditional land constitutes the darkest aspect of the history of this nation. In these circumstances the court is under a clear duty to re-examine past practices.[12]

The judges rejected the doctrine of *terra nullius* and declared that a form of native title existed which was recognisable in the 'contemporary' common law of Australia. Brennan spoke of:

> The use of the term 'native title' to describe indigenous inhabitants' interests and rights in land, whether communal, group or individual, under their traditional laws and customs ... To discover the nature of native title we must look to those laws and customs.[13]

The second part of the judgment had to do with the power to extinguish native title. The court held that the Queensland Government and the State Governor had the power to extinguish native title as long as they exercised that power validly and in a manner consistent with Commonwealth laws. Under British law in 1788, the Crown had the power to extend its sovereignty to territory over which it had not previously exercised sovereignty: 'Sovereignty carries the power to create and extinguish private rights and interests in land within the sovereign's territory' (Justice Brennan).[14] Having acknowledged this, however, the judges went on to say that nothing had been done to extinguish native title in the Murray Islands, apart from some small parcels of land.

Justices Deane and Gaudron held that where the right of the Crown to extinguish native title had been applied, 'it would involve a wrongful infringement by the Crown of the rights of the Aboriginal title holders', but the majority of the Bench thought otherwise. Brennan then made a statement which was probably the most far reaching of all: 'There may be other areas of Australia where native title has not been extinguished and where Aboriginal people, maintaining their identity and their culture, are entitled to enjoy their native title.'[15]

This comment has been interpreted as a clear invitation to Aboriginal people to institute land claims on the mainland just as the three Torres Strait Islanders had done with the Murray Islands. While the judges varied in their attitude to some aspects of the Mabo case, only Justice Dawson dissented from the final ruling, in a minority judgment saying:

> Upon annexation of the Murray islands, the Crown acquired the 'ultimate' title (sometimes called the 'absolute' or 'radical' title) to the lands comprising the Islands. As a result, any rights others might have in it must be derived from the Crown and amount to something less than absolute ownership.[16]

Dawson didn't oppose Aboriginal people holding title to land but insisted that such title must be by direct grant of the Crown or by its acquiescence to existing occupancy: 'The Crown's acquisition of the radical title to the land upon assuming sovereignty is incompatible with the continued existence of any pre-existing rights in precisely the same form." After outlining his understanding of the history of the treatment of the Aborigines, Dawson said:

> There may not be a great deal to be proud of in this history of events. But a dispassionate appraisal of what occurred is essential to determine the legal consequences, despite the degree of condemnation which is nowadays apt to accompany any account. The policy which lay behind the legal regime was determined politically, and however insensitive the politics may now seem to have been, a change in view does not of itself mean a change in law. To do that requires a new policy, a matter for government rather than the courts. It would be wrong to attempt to revise history or to fail to recognise its legal impact, however unpalatable it may now see. To do so would undermine the foundations of the very legal system under which this case must be decided.[17]

These last comments reflect what came to be the major criticism of the decision of the High Court in the case of *Mabo v. Queensland 2*—that the court had engaged in making legislation rather than making a judicial decision. In fact the High Court virtually rewrote the common law of Australia with respect to land title. In his summary, Brennan said:

> I summarise what I hold to be the common law of Australia regarding land titles:
>
> 1. The Crown's acquisition of sovereignty over the various parts of Australia cannot be challenged in an Australian court.
>
> 2. When it acquired sovereignty over a particular part of Australia, the Crown acquired a 'radical' title to the land in that part.
>
> 3. Native title to land survived the Crown's acquisition of sovereignty and 'radical' title. However the acquisition of sovereignty exposed native title to extinguishment, by a valid exercise of sovereign power inconsistent with the continued right to enjoy native title.
>
> 4. Where the Crown has validly granted an interest in land that is wholly inconsistent with a continuing right to enjoy native title, native title is extinguished to the extent of the inconsistency. Thus native title has been extinguished by grants of freehold or of leases, but not necessarily by grants of lesser interests such as authorities to prospect for minerals.
>
> 5. [This clause deals with land acquired by the Crown for purposes such as roads, railways, etc., and says that native title is extinguished in such cases, but not in cases of land set aside for such purposes as a national park.]
>
> 6. Native title ... is ascertained according to the laws and customs of the

indigenous people who by those laws and customs have a connection with the land ... Membership of the indigenous people depends on biological descent from the indigenous people and on mutual recognition of a particular person's membership by that person and by the elders or other persons enjoying traditional authority among those people.[18]

The year of the Mabo decision, 1992, was a landmark year in the history of Aboriginal affairs, among other things being the twenty-fifth anniversary of the referendum of 1967. The loudness of the rhetoric in parliament marking that occasion was quickly drowned out by an event which would become the most momentous and controversial in the history of Aboriginal affairs. On 4 June 1992, Labor member Les Scott asked in the House of Representatives if 'the Prime Minister can inform the House about the implications of the High Court decision in the Mabo case handed down yesterday'.[19]

The significance of the question can be assessed by Prime Minister Keating's reply. The High Court's decision to uphold Mabo's claim for land rights, he said:

> ... does finally quash the outrageous notion of *terra nullius* which, as Professor Henry Reynolds has said, was surely the distinctive and unconscionable contribution of the Australian jurisprudence to the history of relations between European and the indigenous people of the non-European world, to deny the right and even the fact of possession to people who had lived on the land for 40 000 years. With this decision one more barrier, historically perhaps the greatest barrier, has been effectively removed and the foundations of discrimination and prejudice have been kicked away. At least that is what I am sure all the Members of this House hope and want to see pursued in the next decade.[20]

In view of the immense public prominence which the Mabo decision achieved, it is remarkable that the case was not given greater attention in the House of Representatives before the legal proceedings were completed. The first mention of Mabo came in September 1988, during the debate on the ATSIC Bill, by which time the High Court case had been in process for nearly seven years. From then until 1992, not a murmur about Mabo was heard in the House until Les Scott asked his question the day after the decision was handed down.

The Mabo decision exploded like a bombshell in the Australian community and led to great celebrations on the part of the Aborigines and their supporters. In so far as the High Court had made a judgment for the whole of Australia based on the claims of representatives of a small Torres Strait Islander community living on three minuscule islands, it aroused a furore of controversy, of not only legal, but also social and economic dimensions. Mabo was both the end product of a long battle to achieve full recognition of Aboriginal land rights and the foundation on which was built one of the most complex and controversial pieces of legislation ever to confront the Commonwealth of Australia—the *Native Title Act.*

11

The Native Title Act

Inevitably the legal shock waves created by the High Court's Mabo decision came surging into the political arena. If federal parliament had little to say about Mabo before the decision was handed down, it certainly made up for lost time afterwards. Parliamentary debates during 1993 focused on Aboriginal affairs with a degree of intensity never previously experienced. Some people have gone so far as to say that no subject of any kind has so absorbed the attention of parliament as did the Mabo case and the Native Title Bill which stemmed from it. The Mabo decision also aroused sustained and heated debate in the community. Aboriginal and civil libertarian groups hailed it as a triumph, but others, including some distinguished jurists, criticised not only the decision but also the High Court's handling of the case. They were particularly critical of the way that evidence used to support the claims of the Torres Strait Islanders was extrapolated to become the basis for pronouncements about mainland Aborigines. As leading barrister S. E. K. Hulme, QC, said:

> With no mainland issue, with no evidence as to the mainland, with no parties concerned with any mainland issue, without argument as to any mainland issue, the High Court proceeded to destroy what Deane and Gaudron JJ described (175 CLR at p. 120) as 'a basis of the real property law for this country for more than a hundred and fifty years.'[1]

Hulme criticised the decision, saying that a wise judge interpreting the Constitution in matters of political disputation, where passions run high and his decision might decide what governments can or cannot do, should exercise judicial restraint and limit any statement accordingly, for otherwise the decision might exacerbate the political situation and inflame community reaction. Hulme cited several contemporary cases where judges had extrapolated from a statement about one particular woman to a statement about women in general, with predictable reactions from the community.

The question raised by Hulme as to where the High Court obtained the facts to substantiate its comments about Aborigines on the mainland was also raised by historian Professor Geoffrey Blainey, in a speech he gave in Adelaide:

> As an historian I am puzzled especially by the judgment of Justice Deane and Justice Gaudron. It is an emotive judgment as they themselves concede: 'We have used language and expressed conclusions which some may think to be unusually emotive for a judgment of this court.' ...
>
> The case for more land or compensation for Aborigines has become a crusade among many intellectuals and journalists and now the High Court. While it is a crusade among intellectuals it is not an intellectual crusade. The High Court's judgments have been coloured by this crusade ... The Aboriginal history did not come from evidence given to the Court but presumably from the justices' own reading, their research assistants and the atmosphere they breathe and the circles they move in.
>
> When a judgment of profound importance to Australia seems to rest partly on prejudice and misguided research, it is time for the High Court for the sake of its own reputation to defend itself in detail ... It is in his [the Chief Justice's] interests to reveal the evidence that led him and most of his colleagues to such an unusual view of Australian history especially from 1788 to 1900.[2]

The mining industry's reaction to the Mabo judgment, as expressed by one of its leaders, Hugh Morgan of Western Mining Corporation, was one of equal concern about its implications:

> Although the High Court decision per se will not yet have any immediate implications for property rights in Australia, the judgments recorded by the Justices and the reasons underlying the decision, are a very different thing. I see these judgments on the Mabo case raising great concerns for the future political and legal stability of Australia ... My concern was increased when the Jesuit priest, Father Frank Brennan, when launching his book, *Sharing the Country*, on June 11 last, told us that: 'The Mabo decision changes the law of the land ... Aboriginals and Torres Strait Islanders may claim more than half of Western Australia and demand payment for the land taken by

governments ... The decision gave indigenous Australians a bargaining chip for a treaty with white Australians.'[3]

The widespread public furore over the Mabo decision triggered off a political war in parliament and spread to embrace the whole arena of Aboriginal affairs. Continued criticisms of the operations of the Aboriginal and Torres Strait Islander Commission forced the Labor government to introduce the ATSIC Amendment Bill, designed to give greater powers of decision making to regional councils and also to require of them greater accountability. The Opposition supported the general thrust of the Bill, but was still critical of the lack of progress in implementing the government's policies in Aboriginal Affairs. Seeking to deflect the debate away from ATSIC, Minister for Aboriginal Affairs Robert Tickner announced that the government was in the process of preparing legislation (the Native Title Bill) which would constitute its response to the Mabo decision. Knowing that the debate surrounding it would be vehement and protracted, he urged that it should be as constructive as possible. On 13 August Prime Minister Keating, in reply to a question from a hostile Opposition about a referendum on Mabo, said:

> The Government's position in respect to the High Court's historic decision is that it will do what is necessary to protect native title in this country. We are in the process now of bringing together a piece of generic legislation which will introduce a system of national principles whereby native title can be ascertained, protected and awarded.[4]

Uncertainty about the validity of existing titles and leases began to dominate Question Time during the latter months of 1993. On 30 September, Peter Reith of the Opposition asked whether responsibility for dealing with native title claims would lie with the states, and whether the states could extinguish native title provided they adhered to laws regarding compensation. Minister for State Frank Walker replied: 'The States can extinguish native title ... the High Court decided that ... But not in a way that is discriminatory against Aboriginal people ... The High Court also decided that.'[5]

On 16 November 1993, seventeen months after the Mabo

decision was handed down, the government brought the Native Title Bill to the House of Representatives. Introducing the Bill, Prime Minister Keating said, 'Today is a milestone, a response to another milestone, the High Court decision in the Mabo case.' Quoting from Justice Brennan's judgment, Keating declared: 'Australian law should not be frozen in an era of racial discrimination.'[6]

The Native Title Bill which Keating proceeded to outline had four key points:

- The recognition and protection of native title.
- Provision for clear and certain validation of past acts of Governments, including titles and leases.
- A just and practical regime governing future grants and acts affecting native title.
- Tribunal and court processes for determining claims to native title and for negotiations and decisions on proposed grants over native title to land.

Keating said the Bill recognised that the bulk of dealings in land were done by the states. The Bill didn't seek to change that, but would be a way of establishing a national framework for dealing with native title. Each land claim, he said, would be determined on its own merits. There would be provision for validating existing grants, and access to tribunal and court procedures. With regard to compensation, the Commonwealth would provide monetary compensation or, alternatively, land, and there would be a land fund set up for achieving this. Keating quoted Lois O'Donohue, then Chairwoman of ATSIC, who described the Bill as 'a remarkable settlement and historic agreement ... indigenous affairs will never be the same again.'[7]

As the government was anxious to have the Bill passed before the end of the year, the second reading was resumed on 23 November. On that occasion, John Hewson presented the Opposition's response:

> We on this side of the House, accept the existence of native title as decided by the High Court ... but we totally reject the Native Title Bill because we believe it is neither a just nor a workable response to the High Court Mabo

decision ... The Opposition opposes it because it is bad for Australia and goes beyond what the High Court decided in the Mabo case ... It [the Bill] creates enormous complexity, delay, uncertainty and division in Australian society ... It assumes a mistaken view of the root causes of Aboriginal and Islander disadvantage, constrains future opportunities for national development and creates future financial liabilities the scale of which no one can predict.[8]

States' rights had become one of the most contentious issues in the debate on the Native Title Bill; Richard Court, Premier of Western Australia, was threatening to take legal action to overturn it. The Western Australians saw the Mabo decision as an example of 'judicial activism', a term which would later become widely used in criticism of a number of High Court decisions. The debate on the Native Title Bill began on 16 November and continued through to 25 November, when the second reading was passed. It was then debated extensively in the Senate, with hundreds of amendments being proposed. Eventually the Greens and the Democrats, who had been opposing the Bill, agreed to pass it. On 22 December 1993, the Native Title Bill was returned from the Senate, with amendments, to the House of Representatives. A parliamentary joint committee was then appointed to deal with the amendments. When the committee's report was brought to the House of Representatives, Prime Minister Keating moved that the amendments be approved. The Native Title Bill was finally passed on the last sitting day of parliament for 1993.[9] It was a remarkably swift passage for such an important piece of legislation—which later would be subject to much parliamentary surgery.

The *Native Title Act* took effect on 1 January 1994. Despite the euphoria which surrounded its proclamation, few Australians really understood the radical nature of the legislation, let alone the Mabo case on which it was based. In essence, the High Court had turned the clock back 200 years and revised the whole basis on which title to land in Australia was held. The key to understanding Mabo and the subsequent *Native Title Act* can be found in the Preamble to the Act, which says that the High Court in the Mabo case 'held that the common law of Australia recognises a form of native title that reflects the entitlement of the indigenous inhabitants of Australia, in accordance with their laws and customs, to their traditional lands.'[10]

The relationship of the Aborigines to the land as described by the High Court was 'a form of native title' and in the Act's List of Definitions, native title is defined thus:

> The expression 'native title' or 'native title rights and interests' means the communal, group or individual rights and interests of Aboriginal peoples or Torres Strait Islanders in relation to land where:
>
> a. the rights and interests are possessed under the traditional laws acknowledged and the traditional customs observed by the Aboriginal peoples or Torres Strait Islanders; and
>
> b. the Aboriginal peoples or Torres Strait Islanders by those laws and customs have a connection with the land or waters; and
>
> c. the rights and interests are recognised by the common law of Australia.[11]

Thus native title to land is not recognised by a title deed or entry in a register or even by a form of physical demarcation such as a fence, but rather by the extent to which the traditional laws and customs of the Aborigines reflect the connection they have with the land. The High Court stated that this connection existed over the whole continent of Australia and its surrounding waters prior to the coming of the white man. But because the Aboriginal peoples were not unified as the one nation with one set of laws, it would be necessary for each community, group or individual to demonstrate that laws and customs had existed and still existed, by which they were connected with particular tracts of land. In principle, therefore, the recognition of 'a form of native title' in the common law of Australia exposed the whole of the continent and its surrounding waters to native title claims. The High Court, however, recognising the injustices this would create to those who now held valid title to land, held that native title was extinguished if the government had by 'valid acts' granted freehold or leasehold titles to land. But even in this eventuality the *Native Title Act* stated that: 'Justice requires that if acts that extinguish native title are to be validated or to be allowed, compensation on just terms and with a special right to negotiate its form must be provided to the holders of the native title.'[12]

In essence the *Native Title Act* was concerned with how native title was recognised, how it was extinguished, and how compensation was to be determined in cases where native title had been extinguished. The Act was extremely complex. For example, it spoke of 'acts affecting native title' which are essentially acts of government in passing legislation or granting interests in land such as freehold title or lease. Under the Act, freehold titles and leases are largely validated and therefore extinguish native title, but in cases where leases are granted, say, for mining or pastoral activities, the renewal of such leases may be invalid if there are any variations in the terms of the lease. Such would be the case if a pastoral lease were to be turned into a mining lease. This is one of the aspects of the Act which caused concern because many mining operations were carried out on land held under a pastoral lease.

The *Native Title Act* stated that applications for the determination of native title could be made to the Native Title Registrar and were then to be heard by the National Native Title Tribunal. Once the tribunal heard an application and made a determination, it lodged the application with the Federal Court for decision. (The Federal Court has jurisdiction to hear and determine applications lodged with it and its jurisdiction is exclusive of all other courts except the High Court.) Although the Federal Court made the final determinations regarding native title matters, it was the National Native Title Tribunal which in effect performed the major tasks of examining claims, arranging negotiations between parties, determining appropriate compensation and making recommendations to the Federal Court. It is interesting to note that with all the complexity of procedure and interpretation which the *Native Title Act* contains, the all-important question as to who can make claim to native title is defined with deceptive simplicity: "Aboriginal peoples" means peoples of the Aboriginal race of Australia ... "Torres Strait Islander" means a descendant of an indigenous inhabitant of the Torres Strait Islands.'[13]

While the passing of the *Native Title Act* almost immediately aroused a number of strong and often emotional responses, such was the complexity of the legislation that detailed analyses and criticisms were not so quickly forthcoming. As is often the case, the real problems associated with parliamentary legislation did not emerge until the legislation was put into practice. Although the Commonwealth had claimed that Aborigines had no right of veto over mining proposals under native title, Geoffrey Ewing of the Australian Mining Council, in a speech to a Law Council of Australia conference, pointed out that the tribunal was obliged to take into consideration the 'wishes' and 'opinions' of Aboriginal people. He said that this was parallel language to that used in the *Aboriginal Land Rights (N.T.) Act* of 1976, which had considerably inhibited mining development in the Northern Territory. Citing again the situation in the Northern Territory, Ewing said that there was an enormous difference between the granting of mining leases on non-Aboriginal land compared with those granted on Aboriginal land. In the 22 years to 1993, of 3102 applications made on non-Aboriginal land, 2096 were granted, whereas on Aboriginal land only 43 of 587 applications were granted. Ewing concluded his address by saying:

> Unimpeachable title is a fundamental basis for any investment and particularly for mining, where the committed sums involved may run into many hundreds of millions of dollars. The *Native Title Act* provides little comfort for mining companies [wishing] to invest in areas where native title may be claimed.[14]

With the right of appeal to the Privy Council now ended, the High Court judgment in Mabo had to be accepted by all parties, however much they might disagree with its legal soundness or wisdom. But the *Native Title Act* was another matter. In so far as it impinged on relationships between the Commonwealth and the states, the question of its constitutional competence could be raised. In February 1994, several petitions to the federal parliament were received from Western Australia, saying that the majority of people in that state were opposed to any form of title based on a High Court decision. The petitions also stated that while the majority of Australians acknowledged the specific rights granted to the Murray Islands people, they also believed that the question of claims for native title on the mainland should be decided by a referendum.[15] The Western Australian Government had already announced its intention of appealing to the High Court. But as the High Court had, in a sense, 'parented' the *Native Title Act*, the odds on the appeal being upheld were not favourable. The more likely attack on the Act would come from within parliament itself, if and when the political pendulum swung again and the Coalition came back into power.

12

Social Justice versus Fiscal Responsibility

Land rights for Aboriginal people had been one of the major elements of the Labor Party's Foundations for the Future policy of 1987. The Mabo decision of 1992 made possible the achievement of land rights beyond the Labor Party's wildest dreams. Other objectives of the Foundations for the Future policy had not been quite as successful, however. One of them, the Aboriginal and Torres Strait Islander Commission (ATSIC), had endured some very rocky passages but was still afloat. Another, the Royal Commission into Aboriginal Deaths in Custody, had taken four years to complete its work despite a projected time span of twelve months. In that time it had not been able to produce evidence that the death rate of Aborigines in custody was any different from the rest of the population. A fourth objective, the proposal to achieve a Compact of Agreement (Makarrata), had gradually dropped out of sight and been replaced by a Council for Aboriginal Reconciliation, while other critical policy objectives such as improvements in Aboriginal health and employment seemed just as far away as ever. Nor could it be said that there was any marked improvement in Commonwealth/State relationships, another policy objective, especially with Queensland, Western Australia and the Northern Territory, where most Aborigines lived.

The lengthy Inquiry into Aboriginal Deaths in Custody finally ended with the presentation of its report to parliament in the opening session for 1994. Introducing the report, Minister for

Aboriginal Affairs Robert Tickner outlined several of its major findings. After the severity of the allegations which had sparked the inquiry, the findings constituted something of an anticlimax. First, 99 Aboriginal deaths in custody within the given time span of the inquiry was not a disproportionate rate of death compared with that in the wider custodial population. Second, the inquiry found that matters of criminal justice, police, prison and coronial reform were the business of the states and the territories, not of the federal government. The third finding was that the root cause of the disproportionate rate of Aboriginal imprisonment was their extremely disadvantaged position on every socio-economic measure in Australian society. Fourthly, said Tickner, this disadvantage could be effectively addressed only if the Commonwealth, state and territory governments allocated their resources equitably: 'Mainstream programmes in all jurisdictions must aim to deliver social justice to Aboriginal and Islander people. ATSIC's specialist programs must be seen as supplementary. On their own they can never redress the extreme disadvantages experienced by ATSI people.'[1]

This statement was a clear confession that the federal government was limited in its capacity to implement the policies it had initiated under Foundations for the Future. The problems which needed to be addressed, said Tickner, were fundamentally the 'exclusive jurisdiction' of the states. This inability of the federal government to implement its policies was also demonstrated in the Auditor-General's report for that year which, among other things, raised the question of the Commonwealth's funding of infrastructure such as water supply and sewerage in remote Aboriginal communities. The Audit Office found: 'The respective responsibilities of Commonwealth, State and local Government, in the provision of community infrastructure to indigenous communities, are unclear and ATSIC may be funding projects properly the responsibility of other levels of government.'[2]

In other words, introducing ATSIC as a fourth level of administration had led to untold confusion and complexity, to the detriment of Aboriginal communities. ATSIC hotly disputed the findings. Where the federal government believed that responsibility for such services as water supply and sewerage in remote communities should belong to state or local government authorities, ATSIC disagreed, saying that ATSIC regional councils were responsible for proposing the allocation of funds.

Heated debate on Aboriginal affairs continued in parliament during 1994, due mainly to the government's announcement that it intended to introduce a Land Fund Bill which would be used to purchase land for Aborigines who were unable to achieve it through native title claims. But even more serious, according to the Opposition, was the United Nations' intention to draw up a Universal Declaration of the Rights of Indigenous Peoples which, if it came to fruition, would grant rights of self-determination and self-government to indigenous people. Protested Warren Truss of the Opposition:

> Article 32 [of the proposed Declaration] talks about establishing their [indigenous people's] own citizenship. Article 33 gives indigenous people the right to have their own distinctive customs and traditions, their own judicial systems. Other Articles talk about power sharing in various different levels of government. This treaty gives in practice the right to set up a country within a country.[3]

Debates on land rights issues were revived when the Standing Committee on Aboriginal and Torres Strait Islander Affairs presented an efficiency audit of the Northern Land Council, conducted by the Auditor-General. The report identified 52 examples of financial mismanagement and made recommendations as to how they might be rectified. One practice which the Audit Committee criticised was the making of advances to the chairman and members of the Northern Land Council, sometimes for non-council purposes such as the payment of personal credit cards, a procedure which the committee said was inappropriate and in contravention of the Land Council's own ruling.[4] However, debate about existing legislation and practices in Aboriginal Affairs was soon to be overtaken by the long-awaited announcement of the government's intention to establish a land fund. On 12 May, in answer to a 'Dorothy Dix' question from one of his colleagues about the proposed land fund, Prime Minister Keating said:

I am very pleased to say that the Budget delivers that land fund. The Government will allocate $200 million in 1994/95 and $121 million thereafter for each of nine years, to a fund which will be established by legislation later this year. The money will be invested so as to accumulate a self-sustaining fund for the acquisition and management of both existing and newly acquired indigenous land.[5]

On 30 August 1994, the Prime Minister finally introduced the ATSIC Amendment (Indigenous Land Corporation and Land Fund) Bill, 1994, which became known as the Land Fund Bill. Keating said in part:

> The facility of the Bill and the high order of funding provided under it, will give indigenous Australians a significant and recurring opportunity to re establish their relationship with the land. The land fund will be the centrepiece of the social justice measures to be undertaken by the government and represents the major financial element of these proposals.
>
> Our colleagues on the other side have expressed their opposition to the concept of the land fund, saying there are higher priorities in Aboriginal affairs ... but we maintain that land ownership is fundamental to the wellbeing of the indigenous community and should be addressed as a matter of priority.[6]

The debate which followed the introduction of the Bill exceeded even the debate on the *Native Title Act* in terms of bitterness and acrimony, and gave the new Leader of the Opposition, Alexander Downer, an opportunity to demonstrate his capacity to confront the Prime Minister on a major issue. Downer had already publicly stated in Perth that the Opposition opposed the establishment of a Land Fund.

In parliament, he said: 'It is the firm belief of the Coalition that this Bill does not address in an adequate way the unacceptable deprivation of the Aboriginal people in Australia.'[7] He challenged the government to accept the amendments the Opposition was proposing, which he claimed went to the heart of Aboriginal economic and social disadvantage:

> Land is important but to focus on land to the exclusion of other pressing issues is to ignore the facts and simply rerun previously failed policies. Land is no panacea for Aboriginal health, education, and social problems ... Does the government seriously believe that by simply purchasing more land the health, education and economic independence of indigenous Australians will be significantly improved? Is it not the case that where significant areas

of land are in Aboriginal hands the ill health and economic dependency of those people still remain unsatisfactory?[8]

The debate in the House of Representatives began to focus on whether the acquisition of land by Aboriginal people was a prerequisite to all else that might be done for them, or whether it had to be linked from the beginning with the critical issues of health, education and employment. As 1994 entered its concluding months, and with the threat of a protracted debate in the Senate, it became apparent that the government's objective of having the new Indigenous Land Corporation operational as from 1 January 1995 was a rapidly diminishing possibility.

With the Land Fund Bill now in the Senate, the government signalled its intention to implement the next stage of its Foundations for the Future package. This was destined to become a source of emotional outbursts even exceeding those provoked by the Deaths in Custody debates.

On 17 November, the Minister for Aboriginal Affairs was asked by a member of his party: 'What action is being taken to address the continuing problems arising from the past practices of removing Aboriginal children from their families?' Tickner replied that the government proposed to institute a study into the practice.[9] This practice, begun in the early part of the twentieth century, had continued to operate in some parts of Australia at least until the 1930s and there were many Aboriginal people still alive who had experienced the trauma of separation. The government believed that one benefit of the Land Fund Bill would be to give such people a chance of being reunited with their families through the purchase of land on which they could relocate.

While this emotional debate was beginning to take shape another debate was drawing to a close. On 5 December 1994, Marjorie Henzell presented a report from the Standing Committee on Aboriginal and Torres Strait Islander Affairs titled 'Justice under Scrutiny'. It was a review of the Aboriginal Deaths in Custody recommendations and the extent to which they had been implemented. Speaking to the report, Henzell said:

> Much of the Royal Commission's report and its recommendations, were directed towards reducing the over-representation of Aboriginal people in

custody. Despite considerable outlays, in excess of $100 million from the Commonwealth to date, the incarceration of Aboriginal and Torres Strait Islander people has increased substantially when it should be decreasing. This is a prime performance indicator on which the Royal Commission implementation can be readily assessed. The performance on this measure has been appalling ...[10]

The major thrust of the speeches of those who spoke to the report reflected frustration that there had been so little progress in the implementation of the recommendations of the Royal Commission. Peter Nugent, a member of the Standing Committee, highlighted part of the frustration by quoting from the report: 'The committee found gross failures to implement the Royal Commission's recommendations, with crucial funding being used for internal bureaucratic conferences and meetings rather than community consultations and program delivery.'[11] The committee, Nugent said, was keen to ensure that the report of the Royal Commission was not left to 'gather dust on the shelf', as had so many other reports. But with seven years having elapsed since the commission began its work, it seemed a sad but real possibility.

Meanwhile the Land Fund Bill was receiving major surgery in the Senate, which made 67 amendments and one request for an amendment. The Bill was referred back to the House of Representatives, where the government rejected the amendments and returned the Bill to the Senate, which then appointed a committee to investigate the matter. By the beginning of March 1995 the Land Fund Bill had been subjected to a five-month impasse in the Senate, with the Coalition and the Greens proposing more than 120 amendments. While accepting 30 minor amendments, the government continued to reject the key amendments, especially those that would link land acquisition with the provision of health and education services, especially for the most severely dispossessed Aborigines. On 1 March 1995, the Prime Minister threatened the Opposition with the prospect of a double dissolution of parliament if the Land Fund Bill was not passed. To add to the drama, when the Bill in its amended form was finally passed by the Senate, it had been necessary to vote twice. The first vote was tied because a

Liberal senator was absent and the two Green senators, after supporting the amendments, had surprisingly abstained from voting. On the second count, with the absent Liberal senator now present, the amended Bill was carried.

Then, after all the fuss and bother, the government almost immediately announced that it intended to drop the Land Fund Bill and introduce a new Bill into the House of Representatives. *The Age* in Melbourne commented on the move in an editorial with the heading, 'An unlikely crisis'. The gist of the editorial was that the possibility of the Land Fund Bill sparking a constitutional crisis was causing little interest outside Canberra.[12] In another surprising turn of events, the new Leader of the Opposition, John Howard, announced that the Coalition would allow the new version of the Land Fund Bill to be passed in both Houses. 'Far from becoming a model for reconciliation,' said Howard, 'the [previous] legislation was on the verge of becoming dangerously divisive.'[13]

In an article on 4 March headed 'Black dreaming is the haunting of Howard', *The Age* attacked Howard for being opportunistic. Referring to the attempts of his predecessor Alexander Downer to cope with Aboriginal affairs, *The Age* said that the Opposition's disastrous management of Aboriginal issues had returned to haunt Howard, and attacked the Opposition for changing its attitude on the Land Fund Bill.[14] Howard's response to this criticism was that he would no longer oppose the Bill because if the deadlock continued, the people who suffered most would be the people the Bill was intended to benefit.[15] The ATSIC Amendment (Indigenous Land Corporation and Land Fund) Bill was eventually passed in March 1995.

The Land Fund saga was only one of a number of issues in Aboriginal affairs claiming public attention at the beginning of 1995 and before long it was forgotten in a morass of other issues which kept the media fully occupied.

13

The Swings and Roundabouts of Public Opinion

Political pragmatism is always finely tuned to public opinion; hence the results of opinion polls are always of interest to politicians despite protestations that they ignore them. The 1967 referendum was in a sense a public opinion poll on the Aboriginal people, with the overwhelming 'yes' vote indicating strong public support and sympathy for their cause. Thereafter expressions of public support were generally associated with highly emotional issues such as the Deaths in Custody and 'Stolen Generation' inquiries. It was inevitable, however, that support based on highly emotionally charged issues would reach a plateau and begin to decline. Just when that happened is a matter of conjecture. In the first half of 1995 hardly a day went by without prominent media coverage being given to one or more aspects of Aboriginal issues—and not all the coverage was sympathetic. Certainly there continued to be revelations of past and present Aboriginal sufferings and demands for their redress. But there was a growing crop of revelations of scandals in the management of Aboriginal affairs.

Allegations of mismanagement in Aboriginal organisations were not new, but from early 1994 they began to escalate. For example, on 21 April 1994 *The Age* in Melbourne published a full-page article titled, 'Koori Inc. A patriarchy not a party, dominates Aboriginal politics', analysing the power held by Alfred (Alf) Bamblett in the peak Aboriginal organisations of

Victoria. It alleged that Bamblett had a strong personal control over these organisations and that members of his family were entrenched in positions of power. Added to this were allegations that he had used his power and influence to his own advantage and to the advantage of commercial enterprises he owned in partnership with others. According to the article, an Aboriginal Justice and Reform Group, dissatisfied with the way Bamblett was running things, opposed him and his candidates in the December 1993 election for the ATSIC regional council. The Reform Group had a convincing win, claiming that the ever-expanding management structures in Aboriginal organisations had grown fat on increasing government funding: 'The Aboriginal community had become a mega-buck business but we weren't getting value for money.'[1]

A few days after the ATSIC regional council elections, Bamblett and his supporters staged a counter-coup by winning control of the Aboriginal Advancement League, the oldest and most prestigious Aboriginal organisation in Victoria. *The Age* made the following comment on that situation:

> On claims of nepotism, Mr Bamblett argues that the family lies at the heart of Aboriginal culture … Critics say the involvement of such a small group in so many influential organisations … raises a serious problem of potential conflict of interest.[2]

The list of positions held by Bamblett was impressive, but according to *The Age* the heart of his 'empire' was an organisation called the Victorian Aboriginal Community Services Association Inc. (VACSAI). This organisation had been deregistered by Victorian Corporate Affairs for several months during 1991. At the same time there was a fraud investigation into the loss of more than $100000 by the Victorian Legal Service, of which Bamblett was a director. When the article appeared, Bamblett vehemently denied having greatly benefited from his involvement in Koori politics. In response to the investigations by *The Age*, he 'warned "whitefellas" not to apply non-Aboriginal assumptions and values when looking at the Koori community and to understand the importance of "family constellations" within it'.[3]

But such was the pressure aroused by the media stoush that

the Victorian Government appointed Ian Viner, QC, a former minister for Aboriginal Affairs in the Fraser government, to conduct an inquiry into the allegations. Viner completed his investigations at the end of 1994 and for some reason his report was handed not to the Victorian Government but to the federal Minister for Aboriginal Affairs, Robert Tickner. On 15 February 1995 *The Age* published an article headed, 'Battles on two fronts over controversial ATSIC reports', which revealed that in parallel to Viner's investigation, the Commonwealth Ombudsman had been conducting an inquiry into allegations of a similar financial scandal in New South Wales. Neither report had been released and the Aboriginal Justice and Reform Group in Victoria was taking legal steps to have access to Viner's report.

'Aboriginal leader breached act: report' was the front-page headline in *The Age* on 10 March 1995. In his report, tabled in the federal parliament, Viner stated that Bamblett had failed to observe 'the highest standards of honesty and integrity' and might have broken Commonwealth and state laws. Also, according to Viner, Bamblett's interest in a firm called Koori Fleet Management was inherently in conflict with his public duty as a commissioner of ATSIC. The following day, *The Age* published another article, titled 'Rise and fall of Koori Inc.', which said that Viner's investigation would reveal improprieties in Bamblett's conduct of his various roles and his business affairs, and that 'the previously unchallenged reign of Koori Inc. was finally drawing to a close.'[4] Viner's report, released two days later, suggested that there had been a misuse of funds, and also contained an allegation that a $10 000 payment to an organisation run by Bamblett's brother and sister had 'every appearance of being an improper use of VAEIA funds'.[5] Bamblett attacked the report as a sham and a 'shortsighted witch hunt', but Viner stood by his findings and said that a balance had to be struck between Aboriginal self-determination and accountability. The three Victorian ATSIC councillors who first raised the allegations were reported as calling for Tickner to sack Bamblett. In an editorial titled 'Questions for ATSIC', *The Age* on 13 March 1995 criticised Tickner for not acting until three months after he received Viner's report.

On 14 April, five months after the completion of Viner's inquiry, Bamblett resigned from ATSIC, still denying any wrongdoing. Tickner described his resignation as 'appropriate'. In its report next day on the resignation, *The Age* said that Bamblett had boasted that he was the 'tallest Koori poppy in the State'. Those who had pushed for reform in Aboriginal Affairs claimed that more than a decade of indifference on the part of both state and federal governments had allowed a culture of corruption, dishonesty and lack of accountability to spread like a 'cancer' through Aboriginal organisations. *The Age* editorial of the following day was titled 'One rule for all'. It said that Koori bodies which received government funding must observe proper business standards and be publicly accountable for their actions like the rest of the community. ATSIC came under considerable criticism during the course of several investigations into mismanagement and fraud involving various Aboriginal organisations. Much of this criticism came from Aborigines themselves, especially when efforts were made to hush up damaging reports. For example, some ATSIC leaders claimed they hadn't been consulted on a court action to prevent the release of an Ombudsman's report, that the action had been taken by Lois O'Donohue, Chairwoman of ATSIC, without the knowledge of the other commissioners.[6] Tickner quickly sprang to the defence of ATSIC, saying that it was 'in good shape', and on the same day *The Age* reported: 'The commission's deputy chairman Mr Charles Perkins said ATSIC had made a "number of mistakes" but had nothing to hide. "We are the most researched, scrutinised and accountable people in Australia for the amount of money we get."'[7]

But the trade union which represented the majority of ATSIC staff wrote to its chief executive claiming that the legal bid to suppress a damaging Commonwealth Ombudsman's report could backfire. Tickner also admitted that he was 'uneasy' about ATSIC's decision to take legal action. Then *The Age* published another half-page article headed 'Self-destruction? The crisis of confidence inside and outside ATSIC now seen by many as a somewhat tarnished experiment in Aboriginal self-determination through bureaucracy'. The article said there was a fear that ATSIC lacked independence from the federal government and repeated the claim that attempts to suppress the Ombudsman's report were more damaging than its release. Added to these problems were reports of a growing tension between ATSIC's chairwoman Lois O'Donohue and deputy chairman Charles Perkins, in a leadership struggle. The article concluded: 'There is little doubt the ATSIC experiment in self-determination is coming rapidly to a crossroads, increasingly torn between its roles of government department and independent black parliament.'[8]

Problems of management continued to plague ATSIC during 1995. On 20 June *The Age* published an editorial titled 'More strife in Koori Inc.', referring to 'fraud and mismanagement' in the Aboriginal services sector in which 'the Aboriginal Legal Service alone lost $728 000'. New directors had been appointed to the service and, as no suitable Aborigine could be found, a white chief executive was appointed. He was 'unanimously recommended by an Aboriginal dominated committee'. However, the new board subsequently refused to work with him and proposed to pay him out. Said *The Age*:

> At the heart of this trouble is the conflict between two principles: accountability and self-determination ... Accountability is not simply a white principle. Aboriginal organisations must be accountable to their own people, since their failure is primarily to their detriment.9

Aboriginal management issues were not the only matters to claim the attention of the media. Aboriginal health continued to be the subject of regular news releases. They had been lifted to considerable prominence when the federal Minister for Health, Senator Graham Richardson, made a five-day trip to remote Aboriginal communities. In an *Age* article on 21 January 1995, headed 'Senator vows to help blacks' health', Richardson was reported to have said:

> I saw [conditions] yesterday that would barely be tolerated in a war-ravaged African nation, let alone here ... the conditions are just appalling, the showers, the toilets are not fit for use by humans. The thought of seven, eight, ten people sleeping in one room is appalling.

Richardson made an emotional commitment to improve these conditions. The director of an Aboriginal health service in one of the communities he visited said she was confident 'things were going to happen and happen quickly' as a result of the minister's visit.

The next day, however, *The Age* reported that one of Richardson's ministerial colleagues had other ideas: 'The Minister for Aboriginal Affairs, Mr Tickner, has rejected calls by the Minister for Health, Senator Graham Richardson, for the Government's post-Mabo package to focus on health needs.'[10]

Behind this conflict of ministerial opinions was a more serious agenda. Responsibility for Aboriginal health had a chequered history in which the control of health programmes had been handed over to ATSIC as part of the self-determination and self-management policy. In the opinion of many experts, including the powerful Australian Medical Association (AMA), this had not been a success, and the AMA was behind Richardson in urging ATSIC to give up control. In its editorial of 22 January 1995, headed 'Black health crisis', *The Age* said: 'Part of the problem lies with ATSIC which has had nominal responsibility for health programmes since 1990. As a recent *Age* investigation showed, the commission has been extraordinarily wasteful.'[11]

Having made his emotional commitment to improve Aboriginal health, Senator Richardson resigned from the ministry and shortly afterward from parliament. His successor, Dr Carmen Lawrence, continued to maintain pressure for the transfer of the control of Aboriginal health from ATSIC back to the federal Health Department. Adding to the confusion, the Labor government some years earlier had launched a National Aboriginal Health Strategy, which a more recent evaluation had found was failing to provide adequate commitment to vital health care. The findings of this evaluation were reinforced by the publication of a study on Aboriginal morbidity and mortality, which showed that between 1979 and 1991, the health of Aboriginal women had deteriorated rapidly. Disease rates for cancer, diabetes, heart disease, lung disease and pneumonia were among those recorded as worsening. Lung cancer attributed to chronic smoking had increased by 250 per cent in women and 60 per cent in men. It was estimated that 80 per cent of all

Aborigines smoked. The survey questioned whether the policy of giving funding directly to Aboriginal communities really helped.

The battle for control of Aboriginal health services continued. On 11 February 1995, another cabinet minister, Brian Howe, was reported as opposing Dr Lawrence's proposal to take control of Aboriginal health funding from ATSIC. The health problems of Aboriginal people had bedevilled successive federal governments almost from the time they assumed responsibility for the Northern Territory in 1910. Eighty-five years later it appeared that the incumbent Labor government was still struggling with the problem, despite massive injections of funding. 'Aboriginal health not just a matter of money,' trumpeted *Age* columnist Padraic McGuiness on 11 February. 'The present government has had twelve years to come to grips with the problem.' But McGuiness could provide no answer except to say that moving the problem around the bureaucracy was no answer.[12]

A probe of suspected fraud at the Victorian Aboriginal Health Service, involving funds totalling $650 000, false Medicare claims and the alleged misuse of a large bequest from a former Supreme Court Justice, only added fuel to the fire raging around the administration of Aboriginal health. *The Age* reported: 'The medical services fraud comes after the discovery of $300 000 of suspected fraud and $240 000 losses from mismanagement at the Victorian Aboriginal Legal Service, which is also in the hands of a State Government appointed administrator.'[13]

By the middle of February 1995, ATSIC found itself under attack from several directions and tentatively agreed to relinquish the administration of health to Dr Lawrence's department, placing conditions on the transfer. In the meantime the flow of reports on the state of Aboriginal health continued unabated. One report, based on data from Central Australia collected over a five-year period, described the Aboriginal disease rate as 'huge' and called for a major overhaul of health care delivery: 'The authors said crowding and a lack of washing facilities allowed secretion swapping in places where most young children had a discharge from the ears. Also alcohol abuse and petrol sniffing were contributing factors.'[14]

While Prime Minister Keating had been vociferously supportive of Aboriginal people, he had been conspicuously delinquent in his failure to visit remote communities. In late February he made a lightning visit to north Queensland and appealed to communities there to work with the government in tackling health problems. 'The head of the Cape York Land Council, Mr Noel Pearson, told the meeting that while land was being returned to Aborigines it would be empty of people if health concerns were not addressed.'[15]

The battle for control of Aboriginal health services was not yet over. On 1 March 1995, *The Age* reported that ATSIC was refusing to relinquish its role to the Health Department because it feared this would undermine the policy of self-determination. However, other newspaper reports said that some outback Aboriginal communities supported the move and wanted the Health Department to take back control of health services. Dr Lawrence eventually won the battle and on 6 April 1995 it was announced that the government had endorsed her bid to assume responsibility for primary health care service to Aborigines. ATSIC, however, would be allowed to keep its health funding, much of which was be devoted to housing and infrastructure. The subsequent Federal Budget included a $200 million lift over a four-year period for Aboriginal health.

The multiplicity of laws and statutory bodies now surrounding Aboriginal affairs inevitably led to confusion and dispute. This became apparent when a Federal Court judge in South Australia overturned Tickner's 1994 decision to place a 25-year ban on the construction of a bridge to Hindmarsh Island. The bridge had been designed to foster a tourist project on the island and had progressed a considerable distance before objections were lodged. The objections were related to the existence of sacred sites, whose nature couldn't be disclosed because they were 'secret women's business'. Tickner called in Professor Cheryl Saunders, who was allowed to view the documents and gave it as her opinion that there were sufficient grounds for stopping the project. Tickner placed a 25-year ban on the building of the bridge. In the federal court case which later overturned Tickner's decision, it was revealed that he hadn't seen the documents on which his decision was based. The judge said that Tickner should have acquainted himself with the contents of the so-called 'women's business' before making his decision. Tickner's response was that the judge was 'morally wrong'. *The Age* commented: 'Yesterday's ruling was the second time this month Mr Tickner has been overruled in the use of federal Aboriginal heritage powers. Two weeks ago the Federal Court found he had erred in blocking development at a WA crocodile farm.'[16]

But just as the Hindmarsh Bridge affair seemed to be disappearing from the media horizon the issue was re-ignited. This time it was the Melbourne *Herald-Sun* which broke the news, in a front-page article titled 'Women Koori hoax claim: tell of bridge row plot'.[17] The article was followed up a few days later by a huge two-page spread titled, 'Bridge rift takes a bitter turn'.[18] The substance of the reports was that five Aboriginal women were now saying that the 'women's business' secrets which stopped the building of a $6 million bridge to Hindmarsh Island were a hoax. The five women, one of whom took part in the original claim that stopped the building of the bridge, said that neither their grandmothers not their aunts had entrusted them with the island's secrets which had since been dubbed 'women's business'. Four of the five women signed a document saying they were 'deeply grieved' at the appalling claims made by another group of Aboriginal women regarding the so-called 'women's business'.

The next day *The Age* had a smaller article headed '$47m claim for bridge hoax compo', which was the amount the developers said they would claim for their financial loss over the project. Tickner was reported as playing down the women's allegations, saying 'some people have particular spiritual beliefs and some don't'.[19] In the days that followed, the two Melbourne papers continued to view the Hindmarsh Island affair from different perspectives, with the *Herald-Sun* claiming:

> Aboriginal Affairs Minister Robert Tickner was told that Hindmarsh Island was of doubtful heritage and archaeological value before he placed

a ministerial ban on the $6m bridge last year. It is also alleged that a group of anti-bridge activists had told the women to find a reason to stop the project.[20]

The Age countered with a report that the Prime Minister had ruled out an inquiry into the Hindmarsh Bridge affair and that the Attorney-General, Mr Lavarch, had said the matter was subject to an appeal to the Federal Court. In an *Age* feature article on 25 May, Brad Collis, an Aborigine, said:

> The Hindmarsh Island bridge affair is not just about development versus heritage or about tawdry politics or even about a dispute between two Aboriginal groups over the veracity of a spiritual belief. It is a test case for whether 'white' Australians are prepared to accept our pre-European history as a meaningful part of our contemporary heritage.[21]

Pressure continued to mount for an inquiry into the allegations that the claims which stopped the building of the bridge were based on a hoax. Thirty landowners living on Hindmarsh Island asked for a legal inquiry because they were 'sick and tired of trying to run our businesses only to have our efforts disrupted by outsiders'.[22] In response to this and other requests, the Premier of South Australia, Dean Brown, announced on 8 June that a Royal Commission into the Hindmarsh Island bridge affair would be held. What happened subsequently is best described by the editorial in *The Age* on the following day:

> Until yesterday, both the Prime Minister and the Minister for Aboriginal Affairs Mr Tickner were resisting calls for a fresh inquiry into the Hindmarsh bridge affair. But yesterday Mr Tickner swallowed his pride and ordered a new independent review. It may be that his hand was forced by the South Australian Government which earlier in the day had announced a royal commission of its own. Whatever the reason Mr Tickner had very little choice—not after the latest round of allegations by an Aboriginal husband and wife at the centre of the affair ... enough was said to cast further doubts on the 'secret women's business' story that led Mr Tickner to stop construction of the proposed bridge.b

In 1995 the Royal Commission found that there was no substance to the 'secret women's business', and thus cleared the way for the Hindmarsh Island bridge to be built. The Hindmarsh Bridge affair was a clear indication that despite parliament's having passed both the *Native Title Act* and the *Indigenous Land Corporation and Land Fund Act,* land rights issues were by no means settled. In another and equally contentious issue airing at much the same time, the Premier of Western Australia, Richard Court, had challenged the validity of the *Native Title Act* in the High Court, claiming it was a violation of states' rights. On 16 March the High Court brought down a unanimous judgment which rejected the Western Australian challenge. In essence the decision was based on the High Court's conclusion that the legislation Western Australia had introduced as a counter to the *Native Title Act* breached the federal *Racial Discrimination Act.* Under the Constitution, a state law is deemed unlawful if it is inconsistent with Commonwealth legislation. Once again the significance and centrality of the *Racial Discrimination Act* to Aboriginal affairs was demonstrated.

There had been a general belief that the Western Australian challenge wouldn't succeed because the High Court was not likely to turn its back on its own Mabo judgment. But Richard Court was still defiant: 'We do not accept the Federal Government's Native Title legislation with its interference in state land and resource management and we will fight politically to have a change as all legal avenues have now been exhausted.'[24]

In another news item on the same day, John Howard, now Leader of the Opposition in federal parliament, produced what *The Age* called a 'softer line on Mabo', saying that if elected to government the Opposition wouldn't repeal the *Native Title Act* but would reserve the right to amend the legislation in the future: 'The Act may be valid but it also has to be workable.'[25] Prime Minister Keating kept the land rights debate alive when he received the Council for Aboriginal Reconciliation's recommendations. These included official recognition of the Aboriginal flag, the inclusion of a preamble to the Constitution which acknowledged Aboriginal dispossession, and the provision of designated seats for Aborigines in the federal parliament. In receiving the recommendations, Keating took the opportunity to warn Howard about his attitude to native title.

The recommendations of the Council for Aboriginal

Reconciliation were endorsed by ATSIC on 28 March. Knowing that the government was now preparing the third stage of its response to the Mabo decision, ATSIC called on it to empower Aborigines in a number of ways. They wanted parliamentary representation, compensation, a treaty, constitutional recognition, protection of Aboriginal culture, endorsement of the Aboriginal flag and regional autonomy.

Historian Professor Geoffrey Blainey entered into the debate on Aboriginal rights again and in a speech warned of a nation divided. Strongly criticising the *Native Title Act*, Blainey said that land tenure should not be based on race: 'Most Australians have no idea of the [*Native Title*] Act and its far-reaching implications ... A handful of Aborigines could own more land than the rest of Australia put together.'[26]

Professor Henry Reynolds, whose views didn't exactly coincide with Blainey's, wrote an article published in *The Age* on 21 March, titled, 'WA land rights challenge invites a greater defeat', which said in part:

> In linking land rights with opposition to native title, Richard Court runs the risk of encouraging Aboriginal communities to challenge the whole idea of state sovereignty and to seek a form of regional autonomy that will allow them to deal directly with Canberra.[27]

Reynolds was airing the possibility that for some Aborigines the ultimate form of land rights would be a separate sovereign state.

In addition to the political wrangles, relationships between Aborigines and mining companies were still subject to dispute. On 22 March *The Age* carried an item headed 'Aborigines plan UN appeal over land decision'. The Native Title Tribunal had turned down an application from an Aboriginal group for title to land on which a big zinc mine in north-west Queensland was to be developed. The basis of the tribunal's decision was that pastoral leases which were held over the land had extinguished native title and that the mining company, Century Zinc, a subsidiary of CRA, controlled the land. In announcing the decision, Justice French, chairman of the Native Title Tribunal acknowledged that there were some problems about the *Native Title Act*.[28]

The land rights issue had first emerged in 1966, when Aborigines on Wave Hill, a remote cattle station in the Northern Territory, walked out in an industrial dispute and subsequently laid 'moral if not legal claim' to the land. For the next 26 years land rights issues continued to dominate Aboriginal affairs, until in 1992 the High Court Mabo judgment put a legal seal of approval on what it called 'native title', and the government of the time enacted legislation to make native title a workable possibility. But such was the complexity of the bureaucratic machinery created by the legislation that any hope of the land rights issue now being resolved quickly faded. As Justice French foreshadowed in handing down the Native Title Tribunal decision on the Century Zinc project, land rights would continue be a matter of disputation for some time to come.

14

Racial Discrimination: from Separation to Sport

If the Australian public didn't understand the complexities surrounding Mabo and the *Native Title Act*, it was certainly aware of the implications of the *Racial Discrimination Act*. Not only did this legislation affect land rights issues but, more prominently and publicly, it was the law that covered allegations of racial abuse or discrimination against individual Aboriginal people. Nowhere was this more obviously demonstrated than in the field of sport. In 1994, outstanding Aboriginal athlete Cathy Freeman scored a convincing victory in the 400 metres event at the Commonwealth Games in Toronto. She celebrated her win by doing a lap of honour around the packed arena carrying the Aboriginal flag. For this action she was taken to task by the team's 'boss', Arthur Tunstall, on the grounds that she represented Australia and therefore should have been carrying the Australian flag. The incident aroused a furore in the Australian media. In a subsequent event at the Games which she also won, Freeman carried both the Australian and the Aboriginal flags. The incident was all but forgotten when in 1995 it erupted again. This time, according to *The Age* of 9 May, Tunstall told a joke to a few people during a meal break at a conference. The joke, alleged to have contained references to Freeman and the famous Aboriginal boxer Lionel Rose, was described as a racist slur. Both Aborigines reacted angrily to the incident and there were widespread calls for Tunstall's resignation. Tunstall later apologised.

Allegations of racist slurs then began to emerge in the prestigious arena of Australian Rules football. On 10 March 1995, *The Age* carried a lengthy front-page article headed 'AFL code of conduct aims to clean up the game's act'. In a back-page article several Aboriginal footballers expressed their views on racial abuse. The AFL (Australian Football League), the peak body of Australian Rules football, promised that it would introduce a code of conduct to deal with a range of issues, including racial abuse. They didn't have to wait long for their new code to be tested. On 28 April a leading Aboriginal footballer, Michael Long, claimed he had been subjected to 'shocking abuse' by another player. The 'Long incident' raged in the media for almost a month, despite efforts by AFL administrators to resolve it quietly. Long and the footballer alleged to have uttered the racial abuse were persuaded to settle their differences behind closed doors, but this only added fuel to the media fire, with the federal Minister for Ethnic Affairs saying that the AFL was trying to hide the issue. On 8 May *The Age* carried the headline, 'Racism row flares again', with another Aboriginal footballer claiming they were 'still copping taunts'. Michael McLean, who played for the Brisbane Lions, was reported to have said that the AFL was out of step in its attempt to solve the race row and that after the supposed settlement of his incident Michael Long said he had been made a fool of. This was reiterated in *The Age* the following day when Long was quoted as saying the other player involved had not apologised to him in the secret discussions. The other player, Damien Monkhurst, eventually made a public apology. *The Age* pronounced, 'Fiasco has lessons for all in football. Why the AFL's moves on racism need real teeth.'[2] Still the issue wasn't settled, and a week later a further claim was made, that six leading AFL footballers repeatedly abused Aboriginal players.[3] Football crowds were also accused of racial abuse.

Other racism issues cropped up in the most unexpected places. The Chief Minister of the Northern Territory, Marshall Perron, had flagged his intention to introduce a Euthanasia Bill into his parliament, largely as a response to a tragic personal experience of lingering and painful death in his family. The announcement sparked a huge debate across Australia, including a criticism from the Territory's Opposition spokesman Neil Bell, who said the Bill made no acknowledgment of Aboriginal understanding of life and death: 'For Aborigines, Mr Perron's concentration on euthanasia was an "obscenity". They basically don't live long enough for it to be an issue.'[4]

Another racial discrimination issue came to prominence early in 1995 when supporters of a state-run Aboriginal school in Melbourne won a long-running legal battle to have it reopened. In a full-page story *The Age* said, 'School with a future. It was a David and Goliath struggle but the supporters of Northland Secondary College finally won their fight.'[5]

Northland, which focused on the specific needs of Aboriginal children, had been closed in 1992 because of falling enrolments. Supporters fought to have the decision overturned and some of the students took their case to the Equal Opportunity Board, which ordered the school to be reopened. The Victorian Government appealed to the Supreme Court and the judge reversed the board's decision. Northland supporters then appealed to the full bench of the Supreme Court, which referred the matter back to the Equal Opportunity Board, but before it had time to reconsider the matter the state government decided to drop the case and the Northland school reopened with about 150 students. Legal costs to the government were estimated in the vicinity of $3 million. In another incident, which revealed racial discrimination from a different perspective, a regional commissioner of ATSIC resigned over allegations about the authenticity of his Koori heritage. *The Age* reported that the commissioner had 'failed on key criteria of having blood lineage.'[6] The resignation raised again the whole question of the definition of an Aborigine.

Racial discrimination was further highlighted by a judgment of the High Court holding that decisions of federal tribunals and commissions were not enforceable because the judicial powers given to them were only enforceable by a court. This threw the decisions of the Native Title Tribunal under a cloud, with its president Justice French saying that 'it may be that a legislative response was necessary to ensure that native title determinations by the tribunal were secure'.[7] Attempts to solve the problems of native title and racial discrimination thus fell in a heap despite or because of the efforts of parliament. The more laws passed by parliament the more complex and ineffectual became problem solving in the area of Aboriginal affairs.

Other Aboriginal matters to receive media attention during 1995 included attempts by Aborigines to preserve their culture and rebuild their lives. An article in *The Age* told the story of Framlingham, a community of about 70 people in the Western District of Victoria. Said one of the Framlingham leaders, Geoff Clark:

> We are not descendants of the [original local tribes]. We're not bits and pieces. We have survived as a collective. What is special about Framlingham is that a group of Aboriginal people, who were completely dispossessed, showed how they could rebuild their ties to the land through the power of the community.[8]

The article said that the 30 children of Framlingham went to school in Warrnambool and had homework classes twice a week. Yet most of them failed primary school. 'What goes wrong?' asked *The Age*.

> 'Because of the collective nature of how we are here,' explained Clark, 'you can run pretty wild; you can make a lot of noise. We don't hit our kids. Kids have got to be kids and they have to learn from other methods. So they get away with more then than what they probably would in a white society'.[9]

Any thoughts that the media focus on Aboriginal affairs might moderate in the second half of 1995 were quickly dispelled by an *Age* article on 10 May. Under the heading 'A life kept away from home and family', it told the story of an Aboriginal woman who was taken away from her family in 1928 and didn't return until the early 1970s. The report said that the woman was one of six plaintiffs who would be lodging a High Court writ claiming that the policy of removing Aboriginal children from their families was not only cruel but constitutionally invalid.[10] Another article in the same newspaper, headed 'Blacks to act on removal of children', said that some Aborigines were claiming the assimilation policy had been constitutionally invalid and involved 'cultural genocide'. On 15 May, the paper reported that

Sir Ronald Wilson, former High Court judge and chairman of the national human rights body, had been appointed to examine the legality of compulsorily separating Aboriginal children from their parents, a practice that had been common during the first half of the twentieth century.

Once again the Aborigines seized the initiative in soliciting public sympathy for their plight and reinforced their right to demand recognition and compensation for what had been done to them. In the face of this rapidly rising tide of Aboriginal activism and especially the claims of racial discrimination, there were few people courageous or foolish enough to raise questions about the validity of their claims. One person who did stand against the tide was Professor Geoffrey Blainey. As reported in *The Age* of 20 May, he warned of the dangers of reverse racism, saying that Aborigines were becoming 'quiet exponents of racism'. The *Herald-Sun* on 25 May gave a more detailed account of Blainey's concerns. Referring to the proposal of the federal government to set up an inquiry into the separation of Aboriginal children from their parents, Blainey said:

> We are about to see another kangaroo court—a new inquiry into the adoption of Aboriginal children by white foster parents and institutions ... If all grievances of the near and far past are to be investigated by judges, will there be a royal commission into those infants who have died through near-criminal neglect in Aboriginal homes? Such inquiries are self-defeating. To rake up the past using a radioactive rake, is to multiply the damage. Likewise we are treated to loud denunciations of white Australian history, some of them justified and some of them false. Will the nation—and the goal of reconciliation—gain if the same standards are applied to ancient Aboriginal history where there was also much to be regretted?[11]

But as often happens, the hue and cry created by the media did not necessarily reflect what the general public was thinking. That is often only disclosed when an election is held. As 1995 drew to a close, Australia faced a federal election early in 1996. Judging from the way the Labor government and the Opposition had pronounced on Aboriginal affairs during the twelve years since Labor first assumed office, it seemed apparent that if Labor were defeated there would be a significant change of direction. But that could also have been said 20 years earlier, when Fraser defeated Whitlam. On that occasion Whitlam's radical land rights and racial discrimination Bills were not thrown out the parliamentary window but were adopted by Fraser.

By this time nearly 30 years had passed since the referendum of 1967 gave the Commonwealth powers to legislate for the Aboriginal people. There had been valiant attempts to use those powers to improve the conditions and the status of the Aboriginal people but there had been considerable frustration and disappointment in key areas such as health, education and employment. There had also been an incredible mishmash of political and legal determinations that only served to widen the gap between Canberra and remote Aboriginal communities. With an election pending, the question was whether the general Australian community was prepared to continue with this extraordinary social experiment or, with a change of government, to put an end to it. But perhaps an even more important question was whether Aborigines themselves were beginning to lose heart.

15

How Do You Say 'I'm Sorry'?

By 1997 the origins of Aboriginal land rights had all but been buried under an avalanche of parliamentary legislation, court cases, bureaucratic red tape and political rhetoric. It may therefore be useful to review briefly the history of the land rights movement from the first public statement on the matter made in June 1966. It spoke of the desire of a group of Aboriginal people

> to regain tenure of our tribal lands, of which we were forcibly dispossessed in times past and for which we have received no recompense. This land belonged to our forefathers from time immemorial—we feel that morally if not legally, the land is ours and should be returned to us. We are not a degraded people and if given our rightful heritage, we would show the rest of Australia and the world that we are capable of working and planning our own destiny as free citizens.[1]

This statement was made when 80 members of the Gurinji tribe walked off the job at Wave Hill pastoral station in the Northern Territory as a protest against their wages and working conditions. How an industrial dispute was converted into a land rights claim is uncertain, but the Wave Hill incident was certainly the catalyst for all the land rights claims that followed. The next and in many ways the most notable was the case of *Milirrpum and Others v. Nabalco Pty Ltd and the Commonwealth of Australia 1971*, in which Mr Justice Blackburn ruled against an Aboriginal claim for land rights. Twenty years of political and legal turbulence followed that decision, culminating in the High

Court case of *Mabo v. Queensland 2*. On this occasion the High Court heard a land rights claim from Torres Strait Islanders and ruled that native title existed not only for them but also for Aboriginal people who lived on the Australian mainland. The Keating Labor government subsequently enacted the *Native Title Act 1993* in an attempt to give legislative teeth to the High Court findings. But despite the good intentions of the Labor government, the *Native Title Act* proved substantially unworkable and the Coalition government under Prime Minister John Howard, which assumed office in 1996, set about amending it. One important component of the *Native Title Act* which stemmed from the High Court declaration was that valid existing leases extinguished native title. This provided some solace for pastoralists and others. However, in 1993 a group of Queensland Aborigines, notably the Wik Peoples, went to the Federal Court claiming native title to certain lands initially held under a valid pastoral lease but later re-assigned to a mining company. The claim was rejected by the Federal Court but was then appealed to the High Court, which in 1997 ruled in what is now called the Wik judgment that in certain cases native title could coexist with a pastoral lease. To put it mildly, the issue of native title was now a case of confusion become confounded. It was subsequently pointed out in an article by John Forbes in *The Adelaide Review*, December 1997, titled 'The Prime Minister's Ten Point Plan', that the Wik judgment gave no answer to several critical questions:

1. What is native title?

2. How difficult or easy is it to prove?

3. How does one distinguish an 'exclusive' Crown lease (immune from native title) from a 'non-exclusive' one?

4. On leases of the latter sort, where do the lessee's rights end and Aborigines' rights begin?

5. How are demarcation disputes to be settled, at what expense, and at whose expense?[2]

Faced with the additional complexities created by the Wik judgment, the Howard government had to reshape its amendments to the *Native Title Act 1993*. Its proposals were published in a 'Ten Point Plan' which came before parliament in September 1997. The ten points were:

1. Validation of some 1994–96 Crown grants. [This was to protect people who had taken out a lease after the passing of the *Native Title Act* of 1993 on the assumption that the Act extinguished native title.]

2. A declaration of 'exclusive possession' tenures.

3. Protection of government services (roads, pipelines, etc.).

4. Extension of 'non-exclusive' leases to other forms of 'primary production.'

5. Interim access rights for registered native title claimants.

6. Improved access for miners to land under native title claim.

7. Protection of infrastructure developments.

8. Clearer Commonwealth and Statecontrol of water resources and air space.

9. A stricter 'threshold test' for registration of claims.

10. Improved facilities for settlements out of court.[3]

The objectives of the Ten Point Plan were to ensure that the confusions created by the original *Native Title Act* and the High Court Wik judgment were so dealt with that all parties concerned could proceed without being beset by uncertainty. In introducing the Native Title Amendment Bill, Attorney-General Daryl Williams said:

> After almost four years and over 600 claims lodged under the [original *Native Title*] Act, there has been only one determination of native title in Australia ... The Act has placed a burden on resource development without yet delivering benefits to indigenous peoples ... The government is determined to reduce these uncertainties, simplify native title processes, improve the workability of the Act and increase community understanding and acceptance of native title issues and processes.[4]

When parliament rose at the end of 1997 for its long break, the Native Title Act 1993 Amendment Bill was still in the process of debate. The Labor Opposition together with the minority parties and Independents held control of the Senate and, with the Labor Party in particular fiercely opposed to the Bill, the likelihood of its passing was extremely doubtful. However, it only required a change of heart on the part of one member of the Senate to turn the situation upside down. And there was one Independent senator whose position on many issues was the subject of considerable unease on both sides of parliament. The senator in question was Brian Harradine from Tasmania, who used his position to gain concessions from the government on several issues. On 3 July 1998 Prime Minister Howard made a statement to the House of Representatives:

> As the House will be aware an agreement was made yesterday between the government and Senator Brian Harradine to give effect to certain amendments to the *Native Title Act*. If that new amended Bill passes through parliament it will after a delay of almost five years, bring to an end an enormous amount of doubt that has hung over native title management ...[5]

With Senator Harradine's vote assured, the *Native Title Amendment Act 1998* was passed by both Houses and became law. An indication of its importance can be gauged by the fact that about 120 agreements and permits which had been placed under a cloud by the Wik judgment were now assured of validity. The other significant factor associated with the passing of the Act was that it avoided the possibility of an election, which Howard had threatened if the Act was not passed. Predictions had been made that if an election were to be fought on issues of racism, it would be difficult to second-guess how the Australian electorate would vote.

The passing of the *Native Title Amendment Act 1998* wasn't the end of the story, however. Another sensitive matter frequently associated with native title was the recognition of sacred sites and similar matters of Aboriginal heritage. The protection of sacred sites was a key factor in the oil drilling incident at Noonkanbah in 1978, and often cropped up in similar mining exploration projects. Of course, the concept of heritage protection is not limited to Aboriginal affairs, as property developers in urban areas are well aware. The difference is that heritage preservation in urban areas is generally related to specific objects such as buildings which can be dated and identified as representative of certain architectural styles or periods of history. Heritage issues in Aboriginal affairs are not so easy to identify. An example of this was the 'secret women's business' at the heart of the Hindmarsh Island bridge affair. In 1984 the Labor government had passed the *Aboriginal Heritage Protection Act* that expanded the understanding of 'heritage' to include land, and then to land which had an association with Aboriginal tradition. Aboriginal heritage was defined in terms of 'traditions, observances, customs and beliefs', a definition so broad and vague that it led to a number of frivolous claims which tied up development projects for years while the validity of the claims was argued. To overcome the obstacles and confusions which the 1984 *Aboriginal Heritage Act* had created, the Howard government introduced the Aboriginal and Torres Strait Islander Heritage Protection Bill 1998, designed to clarify matters, in particular the delineation of powers between the Commonwealth and the states.

Ironically, in the midst of all the parliamentary heat and fury over native title, there was a great deal of unanimity on another matter which stemmed from the very heart of the issue on which native title was first determined. Eddie Mabo, after whom the famous High Court Mabo case is named, was a Torres Strait Islander. In validating his claim to native title rights on one of a small group of islands off the coast of Queensland, the High Court extended the concept of native title to cover Aboriginal people living on the Australian mainland. All the legislation and the administrative procedures that followed Mabo linked the two together, the most notable being the creation of the Aboriginal and Torres Strait Islander Commission (ATSIC). Numerically, the Torres Strait Islanders were much fewer than the Aborigines. In August 1997 the Aboriginal and Torres Strait Islanders Affairs (ATSI) Committee of parliament reported that the Torres Strait Islanders were burdened with 'excessive layers of bureaucracy':

> Aside from services provided in the region by mainstream Commonwealth and Queensland government agencies, there are 17 island local government councils, the Torres Shire Council, a state-based indigenous-specific

organisation, a Commonwealth specific indigenous organisation and the involvement of ATSIC itself. These are providing services to just 8,600 people ... The sheer number of separate institutions diverts scarce resources away from service delivery and leads to a lack of clarity about which services are delivered by which agency.[6]

The ATSI Affairs Committee, which included representatives from both sides of parliament, recommended that a new body should be established which gave the Torres Strait Islanders political autonomy. Thus, from being the launching pad for the rights of Australian Aborigines, the Torres Strait Islanders eventually decided that they wanted to be seen as a distinctive people.

A cynic could be excused for wondering if the Torres Strait Islanders had been used to obtain land rights for Aborigines and then restored to their own separate identity. It was also apparent from the debate in parliament that the Torres Strait Islanders felt they were being forgotten in the turmoil created by Aboriginal demands. In summing up debate on the Bill to give additional status to the Torres Strait Islander Authority, the Minister for Aboriginal Affairs acknowledged the reality of much of what had been said:

> The fact is that the *Native Title Act* is of very little relevance to Torres Strait Islanders. As they see it they won the epic battle in the High Court. [But] instead of seeking recourse to the native title legislation they have a very different agenda.[7]

The truth is that the Torres Strait Islanders were a distinctive ethnic and culturally unique people whose relationship with the land was more social and economic than spiritual. They were communal cultivators different from the mainland Aborigines who were nomadic hunter-gatherers. In essence the Mabo case was totally concerned about the rights or otherwise of the Torres Strait Islanders and at no stage in the course of the proceedings had the status of the mainland Aborigines been brought into question. History will judge whether the High Court made a bad if well-meant decision.

It's worth noting at this stage that references to Aboriginal people in parliamentary debates and other sources mentioned in this book have been generally negative and related to incidents or conditions that displayed them in a piteous and poor state. There are very few references to Aboriginal successes. An example of this negativity can be seen in a speech given by Warren Snowdon, Labor member for the Northern Territory, on 11 November 1998. He referred to the practice of petrol sniffing, which was (and still is) prevalent among young Aboriginal people all over Australia. One of the places he mentioned, the Warburton community in Western Australia, is known to me as it has a hospital for which I was once responsible. Even a high Cyclone wire fence which I had had erected around the hospital precinct didn't prevent Aboriginal youths from scaling it to obtain petrol. The prevalence of domestic violence in Aboriginal communities, another subject displaying Aborigines in a negative light, was raised by Kay Elson, government member for the seat of Forde:

> There has been much discussion in recent weeks on how this problem should be fixed ... Two things are very clear. Something must be done to protect these women and children, and just about everyone agrees that alcoholism is the root cause of these violent attacks.[8]

But the key issue dominating debates on Aboriginal affairs through the 1970s to the 1990s was that much of the Aborigines' present suffering and deprivation could be attributed to the way they had been treated in the past. It was certainly the catalyst that triggered and fuelled the land rights debates, the Aborigines claiming that separation from their land had destroyed their cultural, spiritual and economic bases. Only by restoring their land, they said, could they begin to rebuild their lives and restore their dignity. Many non-Aboriginal Australian people agreed with these assertions and supported them in the claims that led to the Mabo and Wik High Court cases. But the matter which most aroused the emotions of the Australian public was the so-called 'Stolen Generation' report, which emerged as a result of a commission of inquiry into the forceful removal of children from their families.

The report, 'Bringing Them Home', produced a wide range of recommendations, including the payment of compensation to the victims of the policies that resulted in children being taken away from their families and communities. The recommendation that aroused the greatest emotional reaction was that the present Australian community and its various governments should issue a formal apology to the 'stolen generation' victims and to the Aboriginal people in general. It gave rise to heated debate over whether the present generation of Australians should apologise for abuses they had not committed. One side argued that in some cases the removal of Aboriginal children from their families was justifiable in terms of the abuse or neglect they had been suffering at the time, but 'Bringing Them Home' contained so many appalling personal testimonies to the ill-treatment which the 'stolen ones' had suffered as children, and the continuing effects of that treatment on their lives, that it became very difficult to justify the practice. Eventually there was general agreement on both sides of parliament that the policies which led to the removal of Aboriginal children from their families were harsh and cruel and constituted a dark stain on Australia's history.

What remained in contention, however, was the kind of response that was appropriate to this tragedy, which was said to have affected thousands of Aboriginal people. 'Bringing Them Home' recommended that there should be a National 'Sorry Day', a day on which the rest of the Australian population should not only express their sorrow but also apologise to the Aboriginal people. This was seen by the Aborigines as an important step along the road to 'reconciliation', which by now had become the keynote word in Aboriginal policy. A National Stolen Generation Working Group was established by the Aborigines, who invited non-indigenous people to join with them in setting up a National Sorry Day committee. The first of what was to become an annual event was to be held on 26 May 1998, exactly one year from the day that the report was tabled in federal parliament. State committees began planning a wide range of events and thousands of non-indigenous Australians signed Sorry Books, offering their 'personal apology for the hurt and harm' caused by the removal policies. Carol Kendall, co-chair of the National Sorry Day Committee, said, 'The ceremony will validate the experiences of removed people and celebrate the strength, resilience and determination of those who survived these policies.'[9]

Hopes that federal parliament would issue a formal apology were expressed on that first national Sorry Day when Kim Beazley junior, then Leader of the Opposition, moved in parliament that:

> Members of this House ... place on record their concern for the policies enforced by earlier governments that separated Aboriginal children from their parents producing a fundamental denial of their human rights and causing untold human suffering. Notwithstanding that in some instances these policies were well motivated, they nevertheless had the effect of separating children from their parents and deprived them of their right to be reared within their own families denying them knowledge of their culture and traditions.
>
> For that we members of this parliament apologise and express their deepest regret for the pain and suffering caused to our fellow Aboriginal citizens. We apologise for the mistakes of the past believing such an apology is the first step to effective reconciliation.[10]

The proposal that parliament should apologise to the Aboriginal people did not, however, win the support of the government. Speakers on the government side who responded to Beazley's motion pointed out that the National Sorry Day had been privately organised, and that while many people might want to support it and identify themselves with it by signing the Sorry Books, there were others who didn't see it that way—therefore the government couldn't make a formal apology on behalf of all Australians. The government fully supported the concept of reconciliation and expressed regret for what had happened in the past but felt its most appropriate response was to develop programmes that would both help to right the wrongs of the past and address the key issues of health, education and employment. At the heart of this matter was the question of whether present-day Australians, including those who were relatively recent arrivals in the country, should apologise for what had been done decades before. Quoting anthropologist Kenneth Maddock, government member Tony Abbott said:

> What we are seeing is a struggle for the high moral ground, using the politics of embarrassment. The aim is to soften up your opponents by making them feel bad about themselves or their ancestors. I feel deeply and personally sorry ... for

the pain and suffering of my Aboriginal fellow Australians. But ... I have always thought that repentance was better judged by deeds than words.[11]

One of the concerns about parliament formally apologising was the possibility that its members collectively and individually could be held legally accountable for what happened to Aboriginal people in the past. In moving his motion, Beazley said that the Labor Party had removed from it anything that could be inferred as accepting legal responsibility. He went on to list other amendments to his motion that he hoped would soften the government's opposition to it. Despite this the motion was defeated. But it was not the last that would be heard about Australia saying 'sorry' to its Aboriginal people.

In August 1999, Prime Minister Howard sought to grasp the initiative in the matter of reconciliation by introducing a motion reaffirming parliament's commitment to this objective. As Bob Hawke had done in 1988 when Australia celebrated the 200th anniversary of the first arrival of white settlers, so John Howard, on the eve of the celebration of 100 years of federation, sought to avert a hostile demonstration by the Aborigines and their followers. Nevertheless Howard's statement on reconciliation included acknowledgements such as this:

[Parliament] acknowledges that the mistreatment of many indigenous Australians over a significant period represents the most blemished chapter in our international [sic] history [and] expresses its deep and sincere regret that indigenous Australians suffered injustices under the practices of past generations and for the hurt and trauma that many indigenous people continue to feel as a consequence of those practices ... Present generations of Australians cannot be held accountable ... for the errors and misdeeds of earlier generations ... The Australian people do not want to embroil themselves in an exercise of shame and guilt.[12]

Saying 'sorry' was not the only symbolic act playing an important part in keeping the plight of Aboriginal people before the Australian public. Another, which had been a continuing source of interest for over 30 years, was the Aboriginal Tent Embassy, first erected in 1972 outside the old parliament house. Initially the tent embassy had created some scenes of violence as attempts were made to remove it. Later, the opening of the new parliament house some distance away diminished its visual prominence. Nevertheless in 1992, on the occasion of the twentieth anniversary of the first tent embassy, it was re-erected outside the old parliament house. This time however, only a small number of people attended. Then, much to the surprise of many people and the anger of others, the site of the embassy was placed on the National Heritage List. The embassy continued to be active in promoting claims for sovereignty and was also the base from which deputations to Parliament and to Government House stemmed. There was even a wedding conducted there for a couple who had an early association with it. In 1998 the embassy issued warrants of arrest for John Howard and other members of the government for crimes of genocide. Despite being served with a notice urging it to remove illegal structures and seek an alternative site, it survived. In 2000 a second embassy was established in Sydney during the Olympic Games, and in 2002 the Canberra embassy celebrated its thirtieth anniversary. In a way it had become an icon of Aboriginal activism.

Another battle centred on symbolism took place when the nation began to consider altering the Constitution to make Australia a republic. It was proposed that the new Constitution would have a Preamble containing the fundamental values which undergirded the nation. The validity of several of the clauses was debated, but the one that aroused the ire of many Aboriginal people was: 'Honouring Aborigines and Torres Strait Islanders, the nation's first people, for their deep kinship with their lands and for the ancient and continuing cultures which enrich the life of our country.'[13]

There was an immediate reaction from Aboriginal leaders to the phrase 'kinship with their lands'. The clause should speak about 'custodianship', they said. This in itself was a commentary on the semantics of Aboriginal land rights, which had moved from 'tenure' to 'ownership' to 'native title' and so on. However, argument proved fruitless, for the 'republic' referendum held in November 2000 resulted in a 'no' vote. The move to create a republic was defeated and the contentious Preamble slipped into oblivion. A further issue of symbolism concerned a request to the Speaker of the House of Representatives, asking that the Aboriginal flag be placed along with the Australian flag during National Reconciliation Week in May 1999. There was some talk about it remaining there permanently but the Speaker's decision was to have it installed only for the week in question.

If it's possible to speak of a human symbol, the death of Neville Bonner on 5 February 1999 marked the end of the life of a remarkable symbol to the Aboriginal people. Bonner, who served as a senator from Queensland from 1971 to 1983, was the first Aborigine to be elected to federal parliament. In his message of condolence in parliament, Prime Minister Howard spoke of Bonner's early life:

> He was born under a tree as his mother being an Aborigine had to be out of the town before sunset and could not return until sunrise the next day. Orphaned at the age of nine Neville was raised by his grandmother in what he referred to as 'a blacks' camp' under the lantana bushes ... He first worked as a dairy hand, stockman and carpenter.
>
> In his maiden speech to parliament Neville Bonner said, 'Aborigines of Australia are most certainly not looking for handouts. They have suffered enough from the stigma of paternalism however well-intentioned it may have been. I am sure they will respond to efforts being made to enhance their self-esteem.'
>
> That an Aborigine from humble beginnings rose to become a Senator of the federal parliament was a living symbol of the dignity and respect he achieved and which other Aboriginal people are still seeking to be afforded.[14]

In 1999 the legislative processes of parliament continued to lumber along with their customary lethargy. The ATSI Heritage Bill had not been passed before the federal election at the end of 1998 and needed to be re-introduced when the Howard government was returned to power early in 1999. It was December of that year before agreement was reached that led to the Bill being passed. There were two contentious issues that prolonged the Heritage debate, especially in the Senate. One was the need to strike an appropriate balance between heritage concerns and development concerns. The second was to strike a balance between Commonwealth and states' responsibilities, especially in land management. In this latter matter the

Opposition went back to the referendum of 1967 which had given the Commonwealth powers to legislate in Aboriginal affairs. However, unlike Gough Whitlam, who maintained that the Commonwealth powers overrode those of the states, the Labor Opposition in 1999 seemed to have softened its stance and spoke more of partnership between the Commonwealth, the states and indigenous interests.

Amending Acts that related to Aboriginal affairs became a regular feature of parliament. Another to come under amendment was the original *Aboriginal Land Rights (N.T.) Act, 1974*, with a change arising out of a move to excise stockyards in the small Northern Territory town of Elliott which had inadvertently been included in an Aboriginal land claim. Similarly, there were amendments to eliminate stock routes from the land claim. There were passionate speeches about taking away from Aborigines land that had already been given to them, but in reality the amendments related to small practical matters.

A matter of considerable interest was the report of the committee commissioned to oversee the operations of the Native Title Tribunal, established under the *Native Title Act* in 1993. The committee raised three matters of concern. First, in the five years since its appointment there had only been eight determinations of native title—and there were more than 700 applications still awaiting determination. Second was the effect of the *Native Title Act*, the Wik judgment and other legal determinations on the meaning and application of the word 'extinguishment'. Third was the High Court's determination that native title could exist over the sea and the sea bed. With masterly understatement the committee's report said: 'The actual extent of extinguishment and impairment of native title rights is still being established as a result of these cases and it may be some time before all aspects of this issue are settled.'[15]

Despite all this legislative housekeeping in Aboriginal affairs, little change had taken place in basic areas such as health and education, and they were still matters of deep concern. For example, it was reported to parliament that approximately 75 per cent of young Aborigines could neither read nor write.

Perhaps the most realistic comment was made by Dr Michael Wooldridge, Minister for Health, on 4 June 1997:

> Looking at specific strategies, we have an Aboriginal sexual health strategy after a year of tough and difficult negotiation and consultation with Aboriginal people. We have a mental health action plan that, again, does not promise the world but does promise incremental improvements and has taken Aboriginal people on board to be part of it. We have new services starting up—18 that we have been able to announce in the last six months; 17 we are still trying to negotiate the location of with states and territories and Aboriginal people on the basis of need. In places like Balgo in Western Australia, up to a thousand people have no access to health services whatsoever. On the broader issues, Aboriginal people are now getting their fair share in mainstream programs as well—diabetes, public health, HIV and AIDS.
>
> Not all things of course happen because of government. In three shires in the Kimberley over the last 10 years—only three shires—STD [sexually transmitted diseases] rates amongst men have dropped by two-thirds. The only thing those three shires have in common is that they are the only three shires in the Kimberley to have an Aboriginal medical service.[16]

Referring to a statement by Patrick Dodson, a leading member of the Aboriginal community, Wooldridge said:

> Mr Dodson is obviously frustrated. I can understand his frustration. Aboriginal people get frustrated when they see $400 million spent by the Commonwealth and states on a royal commission into Aboriginal deaths in custody and Aboriginal death rates go up. Aboriginal people are frustrated when there is a national Aboriginal health strategy that spends $500 million and they can find only traces of it in some places. Australians are generous, and that generosity does extend to improving Aboriginal wellbeing. But their generosity will be severely tested if only one side of the argument is put. Their generosity will be severely tested if the view is put around and believed that only bad things are happening, because in many places in the country there are some wonderful, exciting things happening. If the view that everything we do is hopeless does become current, then I am sure the Australian public's generosity will be severely tested.[17]

Later events would prove that this statement was prophetically close to the mark.

16

Exposing the Real Agony

By the end of 1999 the political and legal battles for land rights appeared to be coming to an end. Amendments to the *Aboriginal Land Rights (N.T.) Act* had been accepted by both sides of parliament, largely due to the work of John Reeves, QC, a resident of the Northern Territory and former Labor member of federal parliament. In a report to parliament Reeves said:

> Land rights have been achieved. Aboriginal people have won their land. There is a much more serious issue or at least as serious an issue in the welfare of the Aboriginal people; their education, their employment and their extreme poverty. We must move from this period of quite activist land rights approach in political terms to a time when we must think about the genuine welfare and wellbeing of Aboriginal people as human beings.[1]

However, the political and public agenda for Aboriginal affairs had other items of unfinished business. Both in parliament and in the public arena, the demand for a proper response to the report on the 'Stolen Generation' continued to generate heat. Words such as 'guilt', shame', 'sorry', 'regret', 'reconciliation', 'apology', 'forgiveness', 'repentance', 'healing' and 'atonement' all had strong moral and even religious overtones. Sir Ronald Wilson, chairman of the commission that produced the 'Stolen Generation' report, was at one time President of the Uniting Church in Australia and was therefore accustomed to such terminology. And many other mainstream Christian churches in the forefront of the move to achieve a formal apology from the federal government used the same words.

Agitation to achieve a formal recognition of and apology for the sufferings of the Aboriginal people had actually begun with the Deaths in Custody inquiry, which ran from 1987 to 1990. That inquiry had not been able to prove that the death rate for Aboriginal prisoners was significantly different from that for the total prison population. But because it revealed that many of the Aborigines who died in custody had been taken from their parents at an early age, the agitation moved to the 'Stolen Generation' inquiry, where the evidence gathered was far more conclusive. In all these inquiries the Aboriginal people and their supporters seemed to be seeking a rewriting of Australian history so that the injustices and ill-treatment they had suffered would be acknowledged and included. Increasingly members of parliament of all persuasions came to acknowledge the facts openly. A speech by Dr John Stone, parliamentary secretary in the Howard government, is an example. Speaking about the removal of Aboriginal children Dr Stone said:

> The legacy of such policies—now gone for more than 40 years—continues to hurt indigenous communities, from my electorate of Murray to the top of Northern Australia. We see adults searching for family, language and cultures that they lost before they were old enough to remember. It leaves boys and men who never had a role model father, or grandfather, or brother or uncle; daughters whose mothers and grandmothers also saw their children taken away because they were too poor or too sick or because it was official policy.[2]

Like many others at the time, Dr Stone advocated a 'shared history', implying that the history of Australia was incomplete without recognition of the Aboriginal people both before and since white settlement. While people on the government benches, like Dr Stone, were prepared to speak openly about the 'dark stain on the Australia's history', the Opposition increasingly focused its attack on the Prime Minister and his unwillingness to make a formal apology. On 3 April 2000 Kim Beazley, Leader of the Opposition, confronted the Prime Minister in the House: 'Prime Minister, do you believe there was a stolen generation or not?'

Howard's reply was couched in typically cautious language:

It is clear that large numbers of children were taken away in circumstances that could only be described as forcible removal ... As to the use of a particular term [stolen generation] to collectively describe the practice, different people have different terms ... The reality is that large numbers of children were taken in circumstances where they should not have been taken. Those practices as I have often acknowledged in the past represent the most blemished chapter in the history of this country. I have never walked away from that ... We do not achieve anything on this issue by arguing the toss about a particular expression on either side.[3]

But the matter of making an apology wouldn't go away. Indeed, it was to reach its greatest height a month later on the occasion of the annual National Sorry Day held on 26 May 2000. Organisers had arranged what they called Corroboree 2000, in which the main event would be a 'walk across the Sydney Harbour Bridge'. It is estimated that 250 000 people took part in the march, which the media described as an informal but orderly event. Similar walks were held in other towns and cities across the nation. The weather was kind and the atmosphere convivial. Many members of parliament from all parties took part in the walk as part of the crowd. Among other things the marches were intended to send a strong message to Howard and the federal government that parliament should say 'sorry' to the stolen generation and all those affected by the policies of removing children from their families. But the Prime Minister was conspicuously absent from the walk and remained adamant that while he regretted deeply the injustices committed he would not issue a formal apology. This led to accusations from the media. 'Walk of hope leaves PM out of step', was the headline in *The Australian*. The nation seemed to be divided between those who believed that a formal apology was a necessary precursor to the 'healing' process of reconciliation and those who believed it unnecessary because such an apology assumed the present generation should accept guilt for crimes they didn't commit.

While the push for an apology reached a high-water mark with the 'walk across the Sydney Harbour Bridge', there were other things happening in the realm of Aboriginal affairs which indicated the beginning of a significant change of opinion. Noel Pearson, a north Queensland Aborigine, had begun to make his presence felt and his views were not necessarily coincidental with those of ATSIC. On 7 December, the last parliamentary sitting day in 2000, there was a debate on the ATSIC Amendment Bill. In the course of that debate Peter Lindsay, Coalition member for Herbert in north Queensland, said:

> In relation to welfare dependency, it is probably timely to introduce into the debate this morning an article that appeared in *The Australian* last week. It was a précis of an article titled 'Beyond Dependency', written by Noel Pearson. Noel Pearson has not always been known as a fierce supporter of the government, but the article poses the question: 'All is not well or fair; why is the Labor Party silent on welfare?' I quote from the first two paragraphs: 'There are mainly two groups talking about welfare reform in this country: the federal Coalition Government, and Aborigines who are suffering most from the social problems that passive welfare dependence has caused. Apart from isolated commentaries and backbencher Mark Latham, the federal Labor Party has largely left welfare reform policy to be articulated by the Coalition.' … The [income] safety net as a permanent solution for able-bodied people is not just undesirable, it is destructive. The experience of Aboriginal Australians disengaged from the real economy tells us this plainly.[4]

It was becoming increasingly apparent that dependency on welfare payments was endemic among Aboriginal people and was one of the major obstacles to enhancing their self-esteem. The Community Development Employment Programme (CDEP), begun in 1997, had been designed to remove the 'dependency syndrome' by offering people employment in a variety of community services. The trouble was that many of these services had been created just for the sake of giving people work. Referring to this, Lindsay said:

> On Palm Island, there is a strong CDEP, but I guess the frustration for everybody, including the Aboriginal members of that CDEP, is not that there might be criticism of Aboriginals going into it; it is that the program never seems to achieve anything. I know that there are very many good Aboriginal people who want to do some decent work. They want to be seen to be valued, and to be able to contribute to their community. But, for some reason or other, which nobody seems to be able to get to the bottom of, the CDEP works every week, but at the end of the week you cannot actually see any result from it, and that is sad.[5]

The purpose of the ATSIC Amendment Bill, at that time before the House, was to establish a new body known as Indigenous

Business Australia (IBA). It would operate as an entity distinct from ATSIC and was designed to encourage the development of business opportunities for Aboriginal people. Concern about the existing process for the allocation of enterprise funding was voiced by Barry Haase, Labor member for Kalgoorlie:

> I rise today to highlight a major impediment to Aboriginal advancement. Too many projects are being set up to fail—so well meaning, but so misguided. In the mid-90s, an operating citrus orchard in Wiluna in Western Australia, known as Desert Gold, was handed over to Aboriginal interests. With 20 000 prime trees, all necessary infrastructure, eight accommodation units and both grid power and emergency generators, the orchard, worth millions of dollars and producing in excess of 1000 tonnes of fruit per year, is now in ruins, abandoned.
>
> I ask: Who gains in such an exercise? Is it mainstream bureaucrats, entrepreneurs, infrastructure providers? It is certainly not the Aboriginal people. They are left humiliated and further accused of waste. They continue to be dependent. The welfare mentality is not helping. Highlighting this in yesterday's *Australian*, Tracker Tilmouth, the former Director of the Central Land Council, says that the Northern Territory Labor Party treats its Aboriginal electorate like 'pet niggers' and will pay dearly for it at the polls. He says that Labor's two Aboriginal politicians, John Ah Kit and Maurice Rioli, had been ineffective because Labor's party machine ensured they remained ineffective. [Tilmouth] went on to say: 'For the past 20 years, we've all voted Labor—to our detriment. They just expect us to vote Labor. It's a plantation mentality. Education, and the teaching of the importance of education, is the future for Aboriginal people. Education is the long-term answer. Communities have a collective responsibility to recognise the value of education. It is not the sole responsibility of educators to turn schools into a circus to attract children to attend. Parents must encourage their children to take advantage of all facilities, high quality and expensive facilities, both primary and secondary, to equip them for the future. Of the funded projects that fail, too often the cause is through lack of management skills or maladministration. Too often, control is given to the most influential, not to the most capable.'[6]

The first sitting of parliament in 2001 was highlighted by a statement announcing that the Hindmarsh Island bridge had been officially opened on 4 March that year. It brought to an end a decade of controversy marked with some extremely damaging dents in the Aboriginal cause. The bridge had been designed to replace a ferry service which was causing delays of over two hours to cross a couple of hundred metres of water.

The project had been approved by the state planning authorities after consultation with the local Aboriginal people. Then, on the basis of some so-called 'secret women's business', the then federal minister for Aboriginal Affairs, Robert Tickner, placed a 25-year moratorium on the building of the bridge. After a number of commissions and court cases, culminating in an appeal to the High Court, the objections to the construction of the bridge were rejected and it was able to proceed. At the official opening several thousand people walked over it as a symbol of reconciliation. The key to the resolution of the matter had been the revelation by a group of Aboriginal women that the 'secret women's business' had been a fabrication.

Early in 2001 another issue arose in parliament that began to reshape public thinking about Aboriginal affairs. The Queensland Government had set up an Aboriginal and Torres Strait Islander Women's Task Force on Violence to investigate alarming reports about violence to women and children in Aboriginal communities. The task force consisted of fifteen Aboriginal women, led by Associate Professor Boni Robertson of Griffith University. On 21 June 2001 Barry Wakelin, Coalition member for Grey, spoke about the problem of violence against Aboriginal women:

> This is an issue that has been there for a very long time. It is an issue that, in more politically correct times, it was very difficult to discuss, because it was subjugated by issues around racism. As Joseph Elu said in the media this week, it is all very well to talk about reconciliation, but it is far more important to have food on the table, an economic structure, education, stronger health and stronger infrastructure than it is for more academic types to debate these issues around reconciliation.[7]

On 26 June, Danna Vale, Coalition member for Hughes, also spoke about the report of the Women's Task Force on Violence:

> The women [members of the task force] travelled Queensland, the state with the most Aborigines, listening to their people talk of the mayhem engulfing them. Page after page of their report to the Queensland Government describes scenes of a nightmare like this one: A three-year-old child in [one] community was sexually assaulted by three males and about ten days later another male returned, and after sexually assaulting her, assaulted her again using a mangrove root.

Or: A 10-year-old had been caring for his siblings, a one- and a two-year-old, for three weeks after being abandoned by their mother. They were reported to have no money or food, and the 10-year-old was apprehended stealing food in a supermarket.

The report tells of children being punched, kicked, neglected, abandoned, raped or left so hungry by drinking parents that they sniff petrol to dull the pangs. It tells of elders bashed by their grandsons for cash for booze or drugs; of drunken men and horrific attacks on women, and of local nurses being often frightened to help.[8]

Vale then referred to a report in the *Herald-Sun* of 2 March 2000, written by Andrew Bolt:

Appalling acts of physical brutality and sexual violence are being perpetrated within some families and across communities to a degree before unknown in indigenous life. Murders, bashings and rapes, including sexual violence against children, have reached epidemic proportions.

Recently a sad Aboriginal boy hanged himself in a Darwin jail. The media and rights activists have been in uproar since over our 'racism'.

Well, the Robertson task force found one Aboriginal town in which 17 youngsters killed themselves in a single year, three children died of neglect, and at least two males were murdered.

Where was the anger then? The speeches in Geneva? The protests?

'Something has gone desperately wrong,' the Robertson report says in anguish.

ATSIC spends $12 million a year just on conferences, and a staggering $15 million on public affairs, communications and publications. But until last year, it spent barely a cent in three years to curb the family violence so starkly described by Boni Robertson's team ...[9]

Another example of the shift in parliament's perception of the needs of Aboriginal people occurred in September 2001. It was the report from the ATSI Standing Committee titled 'The Needs of Urban Dwelling ATSI People'. Presenting the report, Harry Quick said:

One little appreciated fact is that the majority of Aboriginal and Torres Strait Islander people live in capital cities and regional centres. Sadly, these people are likely to be poorer, less healthy and less well formally educated than their non-indigenous neighbours. They are also more likely to be unemployed and [to] have had greater contact with the criminal justice system. Against this backdrop, the committee investigated the special needs of indigenous people living in urban areas.[10]

Thirty years of emphasis on land rights and native title had created an impression in peoples' minds that most Aborigines lived in remote areas where a relationship with the land was important in day-to-day life. The standing committee's report shifted attention to those Aborigines, the majority, who live in close proximity to 'their non-indigenous neighbours' in urban areas. For them land rights may be an important ideological issue but their real needs, as expressed by the committee report, are the alleviation of poverty, ill-health, poor education and the lack of employment.

In seconding the report, Wakelin made the focus on urbanised Aborigines even sharper:

> I will take this opportunity to highlight two issues the committee addressed in its report; namely, the particular needs of transient Aboriginals living on the fringes of urban centres in town camps, and the importance of providing training and employment for indigenous people in country areas. These issues were raised in each state the committee visited and in many of the submissions. The committee found that there is a need for local councils and public housing authorities to consider the provision of suitable living space and facilities for transient Aboriginals living on the fringes of towns and capital cities. These people may stay in camps on a semi-permanent basis or only during short visits to the town. Many have health and substance abuse problems. Unfortunately, their presence can sometimes lead to tension with town residents.[11]

It should not be assumed from this statement that Wakelin was describing a static situation similar to the fringe-dwellers' camps of previous decades. These new fringe camps were used by Aboriginal people as 'half-way houses', where they lived before moving on to more permanent accommodation in the towns. Other Aborigines came to the fringe camps from desert communities and stayed for a short time before going back. But the general drift was towards permanent settlement in the towns.

In addition to the need for urban housing, both Quick and Wakelin went on to speak about employment, Wakelin saying:

> The other issue I wish to highlight today is the importance of providing training and employment opportunities for indigenous people in rural areas. These opportunities are vital if indigenous people are to gain economic independence and a greater sense of integration into the wider community. To this end, the committee has recommended that the government assist CDEPs to develop closer links with major employers, both public and private, in urban areas.[12]

It is to be noted that Wakelin referred to a 'greater sense of integration into the wider community'. But it is also important to note that the transition to a situation where the majority of Aboriginal people are now living in urban areas has been a gradual process, not something that happened overnight. Those who have studied the demographic changes in the location of Aboriginal people will have observed that their ambivalence towards living in urban areas dates back to the earliest days of white settlement. For example, when George Langhorn set up a mission station on the Yarra River in 1840, he found to his disappointment that it became a kind of transit station for Aborigines who were attracted to the fleshpots of the nearby settlement of Melbourne. If he attempted to settle them in the mission station they quickly retreated into the bush.

Slowly but inexorably the movement of Aboriginal people towards towns and cities had gathered momentum. But the contrast between the two lifestyles was stark and led to a view that the Aboriginal people living in close proximity to urban areas were second class citizens whose presence was either an embarrassment or a cause for 'doing something'. Now in 2001, the ATSI Standing Committee could express the opinion that urbanised Aboriginal people were here to stay and that therefore matters of housing, health, education and employment must be addressed because they were fundamental to urban living.

It would be easy to say that 'integration' was really 'assimilation' under a different guise and that eventually Aboriginal people would be as much part of the Australian community as any other race. The big question was whether the movement of Aboriginal people from remote communities to urban centres would continue until the former ceased to exist ... and how long the process would take.

17

ATSIC:
the Beginning of the End

The year 2002 marked the tenth anniversary of the historic Mabo decision which overturned the basis of property ownership in Australia and gave legal recognition to native title. Strangely, the anniversary created little comment in federal parliament, with only two or three relevant speeches recorded in the House of Representatives' *Hansard*. However, one speech, made by Philip Ruddock, then Minister for Aboriginal Affairs, was noteworthy because it traced the history of Aboriginal affairs since the High Court Mabo decision:

> Like the 1967 referendum, the Mabo decision was a turning point in relations between indigenous and non-indigenous Australians. It rewrote our property law and recognised indigenous rights to land as part of our common law. But, without a statutory reinforcement in the form of native title, the potential for Mabo could have been quite quickly eroded. Parliament enacted the *Native Title Act* in response to that decision, and in 1998 significant amendments to that original legislation were enacted to reflect developments in the law, particularly as a result of the Wik decision.
>
> In 1998, those amendments paved the way for greater certainty and improved workability of the native title process. The steps that we took then are now bearing fruit. As at 29 May, there have been 41 determinations of native title across Australia. In addition, there have been 48 indigenous land use agreements that have been registered, with a further 24, as I understand it, in the pipeline at this time. As well, we have seen some 2700 agreements with developers and native title parties relating to future development activity.
>
> Prior to 1998, progress was painstakingly slow. There had only been

three determinations in a period of four years. So we have shifted the focus away from litigation to negotiation and agreement, which would not have been possible without those 1998 amendments. And, of course, combined with land purchases and the various statutory rights schemes, over 15 per cent of Australia and almost half of the Northern Territory is now owned or controlled by indigenous people.

Of course the more important question, which all of us ought to focus on is why, as a result of all these significant changes, we have not seen, in relation to those who have acquired interest in land, significant changes in their situation and circumstances. I think, as a number of leading articles have said over the weekend, there is a need for an effort to ensure that landownership adds to the social and economic wellbeing of indigenous people. I note particularly some comments of Noel Pearson, where he said the so-called 'rights agenda' had little to offer in comparison to new policy directions. He said: '... a much more important starting point for any national government is to recognise that substance abuse epidemics are today not merely symptoms of Aboriginal disadvantage ... but self-perpetuating disasters in their own right ...'[1]

The inescapable fact was that despite the acquisition of large areas of land and the application of considerable sums of money, the deep-seated problems of the Aboriginal people still impacted negatively on their lives. Incidents of community and domestic violence continued to be reported in parliament during 2002.

How Aboriginal children were faring in schools was another matter of deep concern. On 14 November 2002 Jenny Macklin, Labor member for Jagajaga, made this statement:

Last year almost two-thirds of indigenous children dropped out of school before year 12 ... By year 5 most children should be able to read newspapers, magazines, junior novels and book chapters—skills that are pretty basic to continuing their education. But in 2000 less than two-thirds of indigenous students at year 5 level reached the basic reading benchmark. For a substantial number of indigenous communities [44 per cent], the closest year 12 school was more than 100 kilometres away. So the scale of odds stacked against indigenous students is incredible.[2]

Surprisingly, Aboriginal health issues received little Parliamentary attention during 2002. The only identifiable speech was made by Warren Snowdon, Opposition spokesman on Aboriginal Affairs. He began by quoting from a speech made by Ruddock many years earlier, in 1979:

> When innumerable reports on Aboriginal health are released there are
> expressions of shock or surprise and outraged calls for immediate action.
> However, the report appears to have no real impact and the appalling state
> of Aboriginal health is soon forgotten until another report is released.[3]

Snowdon said that the history of indigenous health was littered with report after report each decrying the poverty in which indigenous people lived and calling on the government of the day to solve both the underlying causes and the symptoms of what was a tragic situation. Referring specifically to the widespread abuse of petrol sniffing, Snowdon went on:

> I am ashamed, and I am even more ashamed that people in this place
> have not been shamed into action. The coroner's report [into deaths in the
> Northern Territory] concludes that the wider Australian population and
> this parliament must take responsibility to assist indigenous people address
> the problem of petrol sniffing, for which there is no precedent in traditional
> culture.[4]

This lone exercise in breast-beating was the only indication that parliament might be deeply concerned about Aboriginal health, or perhaps had simply run out of ideas as to how the problem might be fixed.

The only positive suggestion about Aboriginal affairs that seemed to emanate from parliament in 2002 was the initiation of what was called a 'whole of government' approach. Federal and state governments agreed to trial an experiment in which a selected Aboriginal community in each state would negotiate with the all the state and federal departments concerned as to how best to deliver services. It was hoped that this would overcome duplication and confusion.

The beginning of 2003 found parliament so deeply engaged in debate over Australia's role in the Iraq war (35 speeches in one day) that Aboriginal affairs were receiving scant attention. Outside parliament, however, rumblings of dissatisfaction concerning ATSIC's performance gained enough strength to penetrate parliamentary awareness. In June 2003 Minister Ruddock reacted, announcing that some immediate changes would be made to ATSIC and that a wide-ranging review of all its activities was being undertaken. The thrust of the immediate changes was the removal from ATSIC of the administration of its programmes and its decision-making powers over the allocation of grants. These functions would now be administered by a new independent agency called Aboriginal and Torres Strait Islander Services (ATSIS). The changes, said Ruddock, were designed to promote good governance and improve accountability in Australia's peak indigenous body.[5]

Ruddock's announcement came in the wake of months of damaging news stories alleging misuse of taxpayer-funded moneys and misappropriation of funds by top-ranking ATSIC officials. Against the organisation itself, the main criticism seemed to be that despite ever-increasing allocations of funds its activities in terms of service delivery to Aboriginal communities had been ineffectual, to say the least. Leading Aboriginal figure Noel Pearson was especially critical of ATSIC, maintaining that it was hamstrung by a centralised bureaucratic structure.

Ruddock's statement received a different reception from other prominent Aboriginal leaders, however, ATSIC chairman Geoff Clark saying that the criticism was more a matter of public perception than of reality. He hoped that the transfer of financial responsibility to another body would signal an end to the 'scapegoating' of ATSIC. Other Aboriginal leaders were more vehement in their criticism of Ruddock's move, asserting that this was the beginning of the dismantling of ATSIC and the return of the control of Aboriginal affairs to the white bureaucracy.

Unlike most other democratically-based organisations, ATSIC's constitution didn't separate powers of policy making from powers of policy execution. For example, parliaments make laws and the public service administers them. Critics of ATSIC asserted that where the two powers were held by one body there was greater potential for abuse and corruption. Likewise, policy makers were not necessarily endowed with the skills or the objectivity needed for good administration. Tragically, ATSIC's history had been riddled with examples of the breakdown of effective service delivery. Of particular concern was the field of hospital and health services, traditionally operated by the states. When the 1967 referendum gave the Commonwealth power to legislate for Aboriginal people, vast sums of money were injected directly into hospital and health services in regions with predominantly Aboriginal communities. To give an example, in 1967 I was responsible for a number of hospitals and community health services in remote areas, staffed by one or two valiant nurses working and living in primitive, ill-equipped buildings. With the injection of Commonwealth money these were replaced with larger, better-equipped buildings staffed with six to eight nurses. Later, when ATSIC began to find its feet, it moved to take control of Aboriginal health services. So ineffective was its administration that in 1995 the Keating Labor government reassumed control of the money and the states reassumed their role of providers and administrators of hospitals and health services to everyone.

The immediate changes to ATSIC outlined by Ruddock and the proposed review of all its activities was the subject of a background paper produced by the Department of Information Analysis and Advice to Parliament in May 2003. Largely defensive of ATSIC, the paper adopted the theme that ATSIC had been made the scapegoat for things that were the responsibility of others. Among other things:

> ATSIC's role as advocate of indigenous peoples' rights has been the source of some tension with the present Commonwealth Government, particularly since Geoff Clark's election to the ATSIC Chair in 1999 which heralded a discernable increase in ATSIC's activities in this area. Clark's pursuit of the concept of a treaty, for example, has sometimes been at odds with the present government's 'practical reconciliation' focus on Aboriginal health, education and employment. These sorts of conflicts highlight the potential that has always existed for tensions between ATSIC's advocacy and service delivery roles: while ATSIC is accountable to the government, particularly in its role as deliverer and overseer of some indigenous-specific government programs, it is also accountable to its indigenous constituency for its performance in advocating the recognition of indigenous rights.[6]

The paper also contained a suggestion as to why public perception of ATSIC was so negative:

> Criticism of ATSIC was reflected by Christopher Pyne in his speech to the Victorian Liberal Speakers Group in March 2003. He said that most Australians would have some level of awareness that ATSIC is 'inefficient', that it is 'not held to account in the same way as non-Indigenous government bodies', and that its culture is one of 'waste, corruption and nepotism'.

Recent media reports about ATSIC Chairman Geoff Clark's wife going on a taxpayer-funded trip to Ireland in 2002, and allegations about fraud and corruption in Queensland Aboriginal organisations associated with ATSIC Deputy Chair Ray Robinson, have helped to reinforce these perceptions.[7]

On 16 June 2003 Ruddock was questioned on the current status of the review of indigenous participation in government policy making. In his reply the minister said the (discussion) paper observed that ATSIC had reached a crisis point in respect of its public credibility and with the indigenous constituency, that it lacked vision and strategy and that it did not have the requisite skills and understanding of government policy to drive a policy agenda.[8]

Most alarming, however, were the continued reports to parliament about conditions in remote Aboriginal communities. On 15 September 2003 Harry Quick, member for Franklin, made a statement about conditions in the Aboriginal community on Mornington Island in the Gulf of Carpentaria, based on an article in the Brisbane *Courier-Mail*:

> Mornington Island, in the Gulf of Carpentaria almost 1900 km north of Brisbane, is one of 20 remote indigenous communities crippled by alcohol-fuelled violence. A 13-month-old, called Jarvin, was sent to Townsville's Stuart Creek prison on Thursday to share a cell with his mother. She was jailed in April for 15 months for attacking another islander with a chair. Jarvin's father is also in jail and his extended family is already overburdened with caring for other children. Little Jarvin was handed from family to family before the Justice Group decided to send him to join his mother. Jarvin briefly stayed with the only accredited foster carers on the island, Michael and Helen Rosser, but they already have 13 children in their three-bedroom house—10 of them foster children. Do Queenslanders know that we have 'lamp post children'—an expression I have never heard before—children as young as three sleeping under lit areas so that they are not sexually abused or beaten? Almost 10 per cent of Mornington Island's population is in jail or on community service orders. And here is the bit that really stumped me: The population of around 1000 spends almost $5 million a year on beer at the council-owned canteen. A staggering 20 000 cans of beer are delivered each week.
>
> The continuing poor state of Indigenous health, and the many efforts of successive governments to address the issue, has seemingly left a nation at a loss to know what to do for the best on this issue. I do not wish to cast aspersions on the people of Mornington Island. But, surely to goodness, we

have to look at this issue and come up with some serious recommendations to be implemented right now—not in three or five years down the track.[9]

Against this rising tide of gloom and despair there were occasional reports of positive results. On 15 September Kevin Andrews, Minister for Employment and Workplace Relations, reported:

> I am pleased to inform the House that, from 1999 until August this year [2003], the partnership between the Australian government and business has seen more than 75 000 Indigenous job seekers helped by the Job Network and nearly 40 000 being placed in jobs. In addition, more than 30 000 Aboriginal and Torres Strait Islander people have been assisted under the Indigenous Employment Policy ...[10]

The final item in Aboriginal affairs for 2003 was the report of the Native Title and the Aboriginal and Torres Strait Islander Land Fund Committee, presented by Patrick Secker. In the course of his presentation Secker said:

> In relation to the work of the tribunal, there were views offered that the tribunal represented a duplication of functions that were more efficiently performed by others in the process and that the tribunal was over-funded. The committee examined these concerns and concluded that the under-spend evident in the tribunal's financial statements over the previous years is exactly that. The tribunal did not deliver the anticipated or expected outcomes.[11]

In the eyes of the general public an organisation is often judged by the quality and character of its leaders, and ATSIC is no exception. ATSIC chairpersons such as Charles Perkins, Lowitja (Lois) O'Donohue and Gatjil Djerruka, though often controversial, bore themselves with a certain degree of dignity. Geoff Clark, however, presented himself in another light. An article in the *Guardian* described him thus:

> With his brooding intensity, pugilist's nose and wiry beard, there is more than a touch of Ned Kelly about Geoff Clark, the Aboriginal leader. Like the 19th century bushranger, the chairman of the Aboriginal and Torres Strait Islander Commission (ATSIC) has a tendency to present himself as a rebel hero. And, like Kelly, others regard him as little better than a criminal.[12]

Clark came from Framlingham, a small community near Warrnambool in Victoria. In 1865 it was handed over to the

Anglican Church Missionary Society, which set about gathering together all the Aborigines in the Western District of Victoria with a view to creating a segregated community—at a time when the policy of 'civilisation by segregation' was popular. No longer an Anglican-controlled institution, Framlingham has retained its identity as an Aboriginal community. Clark developed a rough and tumble kind of leadership style and in 1992 was elected to the board of ATSIC as a commissioner from Victoria. In 1999 he became chairman. Clark's policy position was made clear in a number of addresses he gave shortly afterward. In his address to Corroboree 2000 on 27 May 2000, for example, he said:

> True reconciliation means recognising we possess distinct rights. They arise from our status as first peoples, our relationships with our territories and waters, and our own systems of law and governance. Our right to self-determination is a core principle. The reconciliation process must lead us into a new era of constitutional consent. There has been no treaties, no formal settlements; no compacts. There now needs to be. A commitment from Government to negotiate a treaty is essential.[13]

This assertion, repeated several times in other addresses, demonstrated that Clark was on a collision course with a government whose policy had been described as 'practical reconciliation'—to be achieved by concentrating on improving health, education and employment. Despite Clark's vigorous advocacy for the rights of Aboriginal people, his personal power and credibility and that of ATSIC began to crumble during 2003. First, 'Sugar' Ray Robinson, deputy chairman of ATSIC, resigned in the face of allegations and investigations into his misuse of the organisation's funds. On August 19 former deputy chairman Robinson was asked to explain 21 instances of using taxpayers' funds for private purposes amounting to $700 000.

On 12 August 2003, an article in the *Australian* said:

> Indigenous Affairs Minister Philip Ruddock has asked Mr Clark to show cause why he should not be dismissed from the nation's most senior indigenous leadership position. He received Mr Clark's response almost three weeks ago. Mr Ruddock raised two issues as possible justification for sacking Mr Clark; an overseas trip and his conviction on charges arising from a fight in a hotel. Mr Clark has vigorously denied misleading Mr Ruddock

on the nature of the trip, which was to address a human rights conference in Ireland. He has appealed against his conviction in March on charges of 'obstructing police and behaving in a riotous manner.'[14]

Shortly after this challenge to his position as chairman of ATSIC, Clark faced further charges. The *Guardian* reported:

> He was in court again yesterday, this time over rape allegations 'dating back more than 20 years. His cousin Joanne McGuiness [Mr Clark, like Kelly, has Irish blood] claims that the commissioner raped her in 1981, when she was just 16 years old. Carol Stingel was the same age when she claims to have been gang-raped by Mr Clark and six other men in his hometown, Warrnambool, in 1971. A previous criminal trial collapsed due to lack of evidence, and Mr Clark denies both claims. Such sensational allegations against a major public figure would normally guarantee blanket media coverage. Mr Clark's position as ATSIC chair means that he is the putative representative of 427 000 indigenous Australians. Until a fortnight ago, he was also responsible for administering A$1.1 billion in government funds. However, the hearing, and another trial last month in which he was found guilty of brawling in a Warrnambool pub (he is appealing against the decision), have been greeted with something much more like raised eyebrows.
>
> People are no longer surprised when he is faced with such cases. To some, they are evidence of his continued battle against a hostile white Australia but, to the vast majority, the trials add to the feeling that ATSIC's leader and leadership are irrevocably tarnished.[15]

The court case arose as the result of the investigative journalism of Andrew Rule of the Melbourne *Age*. Rule's article aroused huge media interest and evoked comments from people such as Prime Minister Howard that a person is innocent until found guilty. But the damage had been done. Public perception of Clark's credibility, and the public's attitude towards Aboriginal people in general, were at all-time lows. Support for ATSIC dived even further as more evidence of corruption appeared. A news item on March 10 stated that a taxpayer-funded organisation formerly chaired by Robinson had handed out more than $1 million in a single year in cash cheques without a trace. Normally the Labor Party was supportive of its 'love child', but on 25 March Mark Latham, Leader of the Opposition, asked of the Prime Minister:

> I refer him to my public statements declaring no confidence in Geoff Clark's leadership of ATSIC. Why has it taken the government so long to sack Mr

Clark and enable Indigenous Australians to have the leadership they need for a better future?[16]

To which Howard replied:

There are certain legal processes involved, and whatever my personal view or, indeed, the view of the Leader of the Opposition—he does not have executive responsibility; I do—I am constrained from expressing those views. The minister is handling the matter very competently. The proper legal processes will be followed, and I am not going to make statements that might undermine the efficacy of those procedures.[17]

Five days later, on 30 March, Latham went a step further and washed Labor's hands completely of any taint of association with ATSIC:

My question is to the Prime Minister. Does the Prime Minister support Labor's policy to abolish the Aboriginal and Torres Strait Islander Commission and the executive agency ATSIS and replace them with a new system of governance based on regional and community partnerships? Will the government now join with Labor in a new approach to Indigenous policy?[18]

To which Howard replied:

I thank the Leader of the Opposition for his question. On 12 March I expressed my views about ATSIC in the following terms: I don't think ATSIC has been a body that overall has been of assistance to Indigenous people and I have all the reservations in the world now about the whole notion of having a separate body like ATSIC.[19]

Behind Howard's statements lay a series of law cases that were best summarised in the findings delivered in the Federal Court of Australia by Mr Justice Gray in the case of *Clark v. the Honourable Amanda Vanstone* (in her capacity as Minister for Immigration and Multicultural and Indigenous Affairs) on 27 August 2004:

On 28 March 2003, the Magistrates' Court at Warrnambool convicted Mr Clark of two offences, obstructing police and behaving in a riotous manner in a public place. Mr Clark appealed to the County Court. On 3 December 2003, the County Court allowed the appeal against the conviction for behaving in a riotous manner in a public place and dismissed that charge. On the charge of obstructing police, Mr Clark was convicted and fined $750.

By letter of 23 December 2003, the Minister gave notice to Mr Clark to show cause why he should not be suspended on the ground of misbehaviour.

Mr Clark responded. By letter dated 22 January 2004, the Minister advised Mr Clark that she was suspending him from office as a Commissioner:

> In this proceeding, Mr Clark has challenged the validity of the decision to give him notice, and the decision to suspend him, on several grounds. He has succeeded in establishing that the decision to suspend him should be quashed, substantially on the ground that 'misbehaviour' in the ATSIC Act has a more limited meaning than that applied by the Minister. Mr Clark has failed to set aside the decision to give him notice, requiring him to show cause why he should not be suspended.[20]

In brief, the Federal Court judge overturned the determination of Minister Vanstone to suspend Clark but still required him to reply to the minister to show cause why he should not be suspended. The judge's reasons for overturning the minister's decision were primarily on the grounds that Clark's 'misbehaviour' was not of sufficient magnitude as to prevent him from carrying out his duties as a commissioner of ATSIC effectively. Another ground given by the judge was to the effect that the standards required by the ATSIC constitution are higher than those in any other institution and that therefore they could constitute a breach of the racial discrimination laws. But it mattered little. On 16 April 2004 headlines in the *Australian* announced: 'The experiment has failed. Howard announces abolition of ATSIC after 15 years saying indigenous communities have lost their direct say in running their own affairs.'[21]

Clark remained defiant, saying he was confident of hanging on, but the bad news continued to accumulate. Finally, the government announced it would replace ATSIC with a new entity called the National Indigenous Council. A number of the Aboriginal leaders invited to become members of the new body refused, but ALP deputy president Warren Mundine said that the crisis in Aboriginal communities 'imploding' from violence and health problems forced him to go beyond politics and accept the position. The abolition of ATSIC was initially supported by the Opposition, but under pressure from representatives of the Aboriginal community Labor referred the enabling legislation to a Senate committee. The committee was scheduled to report back on 30 October 2004, but the timeline was extended to March 2005, which meant the legislation would not pass through both houses of parliament before August. 'Given that timeframe, the total cost to taxpayers to keep the 18 ATSIC commissioners in offices doing nothing will be almost $4 million,' said a spokesperson for Minister Vanstone.

Clark continued to receive a salary package of $280 000 a year, including a $257 000 wage. The other seventeen commissioners were each being paid a salary of $136 240. Clark and others threatened to challenge the government's decision to abolish ATSIC, declaring they would sell heritage items and property to pay for the legal costs. But such was the hostile reaction from Aboriginal communities to this idea, it was doubtful whether a challenge would occur. Predictably, with no real support from any party in parliament, the future of ATSIC appeared doomed.

Meanwhile, violence continued to erupt in Aboriginal communities, the most notorious incident taking place on Palm Island, off the coast of north Queensland. Tourist advertisements had once included it among the 'tropical paradise' venues, but by 1999 the *Guinness Book of Records* had listed the island as 'the most violent place in the world outside a combat zone'. Palm Island is home to the largest indigenous community in Australia, with more than 2000 residents. Like many similar communities it was used to resettle Aborigines from all over Queensland in the days of the 'civilisation by separation' policy. In recent times Palm Island has had a sad history of violence, alcoholism and unemployment. On 26 November 2004 it was once again the scene of violence as the community erupted in anger. The reason was outlined in the Kerry O'Brien *7.30 Report* on ABC TV:

> Tempers flared on Friday when the Coroner found 36-year-old Cameron Doomadgee died from a fall while in the custody of a senior police sergeant. Hundreds marched on the police station, pelting it with rocks and eventually setting it on fire, as police officers feared for their lives. Sales of alcohol had stopped three days earlier because of Cameron Doomadgee's death, so this rioting was fuelled purely by emotions of anger and frustration. [The police station barracks and court house were burned to the ground.][22]

Riot police were sent to the island to quell the disturbance; in the process they arrested eighteen men and took them back to Townsville in custody. This further inflamed emotions in the community, although no more disturbances occurred, largely due to the presence of 80 police patrolling the streets. Aboriginal people claimed that Cameron Doomadgee had died as a result of police brutality, an opinion based more on suspicion than fact. The police maintained it was Cameron Doomadgee who began a scuffle and sustained a fatal injury when he fell on concrete steps. The Premier of Queensland visited the community in an attempt to hose down the situation, but the nature and extent of the violence had caught everyone by surprise. Many white workers, teachers and health professionals left the island in fear of their lives. The Premier promised that the government would make every effort to address the underlying issues, but as ABC reporter Peter McCutcheon observed, 'Rebuilding the police station is relatively easy compared to tackling the community's problems of violence, alcohol abuse and unemployment.'[23]

In an article in *The Age* on 1 December 2004, former senator and chairman of Reconciliation Australia, Fred Chaney, was quoted as saying that the frustration of people on Palm Island was understandable. 'I'm not excusing unlawful behaviour,' he said, 'but I think it's not hard to understand why people become immensely frustrated.' Chaney said the government needed to work with representative bodies that gave Aboriginal people a voice. A failure to engage would lead to a continuation of 'these terrible blots on our national life'. Once again it was a passionate articulation of the problem but no real answer.

The decline in public and parliamentary interest in Aboriginal affairs in this period can be attributed to many things. Several events of international magnitude had taken Australia's focus of attention in other directions. Suicide bomber attacks on high profile targets in New York and Washington brought home sharply the fact that terrorism was a far more organised and potent threat to the security of the world than hitherto realised. Closer to home, the Bali bombing outrage claimed the lives of many Australia citizens. Other issues such as the liberation of East Timor, wars in Afghanistan and Iraq, and the sustained attempts of illegal immigrants to enter Australia, dominated the headlines and occupied much parliamentary time.

It seemed that a tumultuous era in Aboriginal affairs that had lasted almost 40 years might be coming to a close.

18

Aboriginal Health: So Much Effort, So Little Progress

The *Medical Journal of Australia* is a prestigious publication that jealously guards the professional standards of its contents. It came as a surprise therefore when an editorial in 2004 began with the following statement:

> Not so long ago, we at the *Medical Journal of Australia* realised that, when it came to Indigenous health, we were great at publicising the problems. Most of the articles we publish are observational studies confirming that, yes, in health, as well as in almost every other area, Indigenous Australians are worse off than other Australians and, indeed, Indigenous populations worldwide. We also realised that the *Journal* was missing an important 'voice', telling us the story of Indigenous health. The human reality of statistics like those mentioned above is that Indigenous Australians inhabit a world of sickness, death and tragedy. Many of the seeds of future ill health are present from before birth. Many doctors, when they look into the eyes of an Indigenous child, get a glimpse of a world they never knew existed; when we look into the eyes of that child, we see ourselves, and are reminded of the toll taken by unending stress and anxiety, and cycles of grief.[1]

In response to this 'vision on the road to Damascus', the MJA set up an annual essay competition in honour of Dr Ross Ingram, an indigenous doctor who died at an all too early age. The purpose of the competition is to provide indigenous health workers with the opportunity to tell their stories and share their ideas on how indigenous health can be improved. It seems strange that after nearly half a century of intensive effort to improve the health of indigenous people the medical profession should only now turn to what is fundamental to the practice of medicine, namely listening. But they are to be applauded for their honesty.

In trying to make sense out of the complex and confusing

farrago of legislation, legal determinations, policies and practices that has engulfed Aboriginal affairs since the referendum of 1967, it would be wrong to single out one factor as the major contributor to the failure to find a solution to the problem. What is certain is that poor health and high mortality rates have consistently been the most alarming and serious symptoms of the situation. So the question must be asked: Has the health of Aboriginal people improved significantly since the Commonwealth entered the picture in 1967? Has it changed little? Or, worst-case scenario: Has it deteriorated?

In answer, it's worth starting with a few simple statistics. Firstly: How many Aboriginal people are there in Australia? In 1966 the official estimate was around 80 000. Five years later, in 1971, when Aborigines were first included in the national Census count, their number was calculated at 106 000, a 35 per cent increase in five years. In the Census counts since 1971, the numbers of Aborigines and Torres Strait Islanders have increased at an astonishing rate. This extract from a publication of the Human Rights and Equal Opportunity Commission describes what has happened:

> Aboriginal and Torres Strait Islanders were first counted as citizens in the 1971 Census. Since then, censuses have shown a significant increase in people identifying as Aborigines and/or Torres Strait Islanders. Between the 1991 and 1996 Census there was a 33% increase recorded in Australia's Aboriginal and Torres Strait Islander population, while between the 1996 and 2001 Census there was a 16% increase. In contrast, the total population in Australia increased by five per cent between 1991 and 1996 and four per cent from 1996–2001.[2]

To give these figures greater clarity; in 1966 the number of Aborigines was reckoned to be 80 000 while the total population of Australia was estimated at 10 million. Since then the total population of Australia has doubled to 20 million but the Aboriginal population has increased fivefold, to over 400 000. The Australian Bureau of Statistics commented that this cannot be accounted for by the birth rate alone, and attributes the increase to 'a growing propensity of people to identify as Aboriginal and/or Torres Strait Islander, and [to] the greater efforts made to record Aboriginal and Torres Strait Islander people in the censuses.'[3] Nevertheless, Aborigines and Torres Strait Islanders still constitute only 2 per cent of the total population.

A second helpful statistic relates to where these 400 000 people live. Most non-indigenous Australians probably still believe that the majority of Aborigines live in very remote communities, but they are greatly mistaken. The following table reveals that 75 per cent live in major cities or regional towns; only 25 per cent live in remote or very remote locations.

Aboriginal and Torres Strait Islander

Major cities	30.2%
Inner regional	20.3%
Outer regional	23.1%
Remote	8.8%
Very remote	17.7%

Source: Australian Bureau of Statistics, *Population Distribution, Indigenous Australians*, 1997

That is, only about 100 000 Aboriginal people live in remote or very remote regions. It's important to keep this fact in mind— while urban Aborigines also experience health problems, they don't always have the same causes as the problems suffered in remote communities where distance, environment, and the absence of essential infrastructure such as water supplies, exacerbate the situation.

Concern for the health of Aboriginal people was one of the key factors driving the push for equal rights that led to the 1967 referendum. Prior to this, the belief that Aborigines would eventually be an extinct race led to an attitude that was once described as 'smoothing the dying pillow' or, as would be said today, 'providing palliative care'. Lack of interest led to lack of information and consequently to lack of understanding. It wasn't until the 1960s and 1970s that the systematic collection of data pertaining to Aboriginal health began, and when it did the results were horrifying, to say the least. A vivid account of the conditions under which Aboriginal people lived was given by Sister Pat McPherson, who worked for many years in north-west Australia. In 1971 McPherson conducted a survey of Aboriginal people in the Pilbara, and found that of the 1000 people she contacted most had one or more serious diseases, including leprosy, venereal disease, roundworms and trachoma. McPherson managed to reduce the prevalence of disease but the levels were still unacceptably high.

In 1966 the late Sir Douglas Nicholls, one of the finest representatives of the Aboriginal people, who at one time held the office of Governor of South Australia, visited a remote Aboriginal community in Western Australia known as Warburton Range. He reported that the Aborigines lived mainly in humpys, had no employment and no incentive for education. They were not even encouraged to engage in food production. Their health problems were alarming, with a high prevalence of chest and respiratory diseases, poor nutrition and substantial malnutrition. Children suffered from persistent discharge from the ears and gastrointestinal problems. Conditions in the homelands communities, said Sir Douglas, were if anything worse, with an 80 per cent prevalence of eye diseases.[4] There were equally horrific stories and statistics from other Aboriginal communities in the 1960s and 1970s. The fact that many communities, such as Warburton Range, received only one visit a month from the Royal Flying Doctor Service didn't help.

The question is whether, nearly half a century later, the situation has improved. In a speech to federal parliament on 24 March 2004, Mr Griffin, member for Bruce, gave an address based substantially on information he'd taken from the Austr— alian Bureau of Statistics *Yearbook* for 2004

> Indigenous Australians tend to die younger, smoke more and earn less than the national average. The average life expectancy of Indigenous men is 56 years versus 77 years for those in general society, and for women it is 63 years versus 82 years. We are also looking at a situation where only three per cent of Indigenous Australians are aged over 65 years, against the national average of 13 per cent. Indigenous Australians were more than twice as likely to smoke and were significantly more prone to being overweight or obese. On the other hand, heavy drinking and lack of exercise were around the national average, which, again—certainly on the heavy drinking aspect— tends to fly in the face of popular perceptions.[5]

A few days later, on 30 March, the BBC News website contained an item about Aboriginal health titled 'Aborigine health "getting worse". It was based on a report from the Fred Hollows Foundation, which said that the health of many indigenous Australians was worse than that of people in the developing world. Fred Hollows was a charismatic doctor who in the late 1960s began to examine and treat outback Aborigines for eye diseases. He said the diseases he encountered were like something out of a medical history book, and had not been seen in Western society for generations. More than three decades later, the aid organisation he founded claimed that indigenous health standards were still going backwards.6

In considering these depressing statements it's important to look at the causes of Aboriginal ill health and in particular the causes of death. The six main causes of death are:

- Diseases of the circulatory system (inc. heart disease)

- External causes (inc. accidents, suicide etc)

- Neoplasm (inc. cancers)

- Diseases of the respiratory system

- Endocrine, nutritional and metabolic diseases (inc. diabetes)

- Diseases of the digestive system.[7]

It will be apparent that a lot of these causes of death can be attributed to the adoption by Aborigines of lifestyle practices common to Western societies. A doctor of longstanding experience and expertise in treating Aboriginal patients once ruefully remarked to me that as fast as a disease such as leprosy was eliminated it was replaced with a rapidly mounting increase in another, such as heart disease—the product of stress, alcohol consumption and smoking.

The government's response to the criticisms of the Fred Hollows Foundation was to point out that positive results are being achieved in certain areas; for example, death rates from infectious and parasitic diseases have fallen significantly. But Aboriginal leader Linda Burney, while acknowledging some improvements had been made, said that progress had been excruciatingly slow. 'I don't think things have changed very much,' she said in a news interview, pointing out, for example, that Aboriginal women are dying at an increasingly younger age. Domestic violence is partly to blame for this, fuelled by a brutal mix of alcohol abuse, boredom, and a lack of education and opportunity.[8]

The tragic, depressing but inescapable fact is that standards of health and mortality rates among Aboriginal people are still at a level far below those for the rest of the Australian community. Male life expectancy is 56 years compared with 77 for the rest of the community, and children die at a rate four times that for the rest of the community. Since the referendum of 1967 Australia as a nation has tried to fix the problems of the Aboriginal people by devising a variety of policies and programmes and injecting huge amounts of money into these systems. It has to be admitted that despite all these efforts, very little improvement has occurred.

That the ideologies underlying the Aboriginal Affairs policies of the various Labor and Coalition governments have been radically different has not helped the situation. Distinguished Aboriginal academic Margaret Valadian has described the difference this way: Labor's policy was 'laissez faire', that is to say, to give Aboriginal people the right to self-determination and prevent others from interfering with their decisions. Coalition policies were more 'government driven', which meant that having identified what the problems were, the government set out to solve them.[9] The evidence presented in this book and elsewhere suggests that not only have both these policies failed but they were flawed in concept in the first place.

The simple explanation for both the failures and the flaws is the gulf that exists between Western culture and the culture of the Aboriginal people, particularly those living in very remote areas, is the difference between a development-driven culture and a culture in which survival depends on adherence to rituals and practices that haven't changed over thousands of years. The two are by nature incompatible and constitute a classic example of the 'science versus religion' contest in which developing scientific knowledge challenges every precept of traditional religion. Governments of both sides of the political spectrum speak earnestly about the need to respect and preserve Aboriginal culture, but there are forces at work which undermine any chance of achieving those objectives. There are Aboriginal communities in very remote parts of Australia where the whitefella is only welcome for a short term and for a specific purpose, such as providing medical treatment, so that the people can go about living their lives in their traditional fashion. But in almost every one of these communities satellite television discs can be found. Aborigines can erect fences and gates to control land traffic but there are no fences or gates to control what comes out of the sky. Aborigines can claim sacred and special sites such as Uluru and Kakadu, but tourists crawl over them like ants.

The fundamental flaw in the policies of both political parties was the belief that they could stop the clock so far as history was concerned, or even, as happened in the Mabo and Wik cases, turn the clock back. But history has a habit of moving on and taking the world with it. To paraphrase something that former US President Bill Clinton once said, 'the rising tide of development will float some into the waters that lead to the future but will leave others stranded on yesterday's shores.'

19

'Shared Responsibility': a Policy of Pragmatism

The demise of ATSIC brought to an end a lengthy but ultimately unsuccessful experiment in Aboriginal self-determination. In scrapping the commission the federal government had the support of many people and organisations, including some from the Aboriginal community. The most trenchant criticism of past policies came from the Centre for Independent Studies in a paper titled 'New Deal for Aborigines and Torres Strait Islanders in Remote Communities'. Commenting on the paper, the *Weekend Australian* of 4–5 March 2005 said, 'It makes out a compelling case that the existing deal is a disaster and that the main beneficiaries of the present arrangement are a parasitic and incompetent class of whites in the so-called caring professions.'

The removal of ATSIC left a big vacuum in Aboriginal/federal government relations, one that the government needed to fill quickly. In December 2004 Prime Minister Howard unveiled a new approach to Aboriginal Affairs with the theme of 'shared responsibility'. Howard said that ATSIC had been too preoccupied with symbolic issues and had not addressed the serious day-to-day problems confronting Aboriginal people. In place of ATSIC the government proposed to appoint an advisory body called the National Indigenous Council, whose fourteen members were to be selected to represent various aspects of the wider Aboriginal community rather than geographical regions, and whose task would be to give the government expert advice rather than to make and administer policy. Chair of the new body, Sue Gordon, a magistrate from South Australia, said that NIC would take as its priority issues domestic violence and the reduction of widespread dependence on welfare. There was much work to be done, she said, as violence within Aboriginal families had become monstrous.

Aboriginal reaction to the proposed NIC was surprisingly mixed. Leading activist Pat Dodson angrily condemned the plan. 'This is not reform—this is social engineering at its worst,' he said. But Lowitja O'Donohue, former chairwoman of ATSIC, backed the idea: 'Radical measures really need to be taken to get communities viable once again.'

The second part of the 'shared responsibility' programme was announced in February 2005. The government now proposed to negotiate directly with individual communities and families to allocate funding. Examples of this approach included financial sanctions for parents who did not send their children to school, and an expansion of the 'no school/no pool' system—which prevented children from attending the local swimming pool if they didn't attend school—a policy already implemented by some communities in the Northern Territory. It was further reported that under its new policy the government had made an offer to the Mulan People, a remote community in Western Australia, whereby it offered to provide petrol bowsers and new health programmes if the community met certain health conditions. These included ensuring children showered every day, emptying household rubbish bins twice a week and treating houses for pests four times a year. The proposal was warmly received by the Mulan People, who said that saving their children's lives was more important than fighting over political issues. The Labor Party said the new policy was 'paternalistic' and opposed it, but was embarrassed when one of its federal vice presidents, Warren Mundine, also a member of the newly formed NIC, said that he supported the notion of shared responsibility arrangements:

> A lot of people have been saying for many, many years that Aboriginal people have all these rights, and we need to give them all these rights, which was

correct, but at the same time we need to have responsibilities back. I'm in favour in regard to that people need to sign on board in regard to improving their communities and making changes within their communities—in regard to community safety, in regard to people who are committing crimes, need to stop committing crimes against Aboriginal people and need to sign up with their community and sign up with the elders to make sure that they change their behaviour, and also that we need to look at economic developments for our communities, and that's why my push is for community safety and economic development in our communities.[1]

Aboriginal activist Mick Dodson disagreed:

> What we need to do is think about creative ways. The problem isn't with the land ownership; the problem is with the lack of imagination and creative thinking on behalf of financial institutions and governments. In some instances in this country, Aboriginal people are prohibited from using their land as collateral in a lease title way without threatening the underlying title. For example, the national parks in the Northern Territory—controlled by the Commonwealth. I'd love to see how much they'd be worth on the open market, but I'm not allowed to do that, Commonwealth law prevents them from doing that.[2]

Despite the variety of reactions to the proposed National Indigenous Council and the concept of 'shared responsibility', there was a high level of agreement that ATSIC no longer served the interests of the Aboriginal people. Gary Foley, a veteran Aboriginal activist and historian whose brother Cliff had sat on the ATSIC board, said that the problem lay with the institution as a whole. 'It's the structure that's flawed,' he said. 'It's not the personalities that matter. [ATSIC] was created out of political expediency: it wasn't created to do good things for us. It was to solve a problem that existed for the government.'[3]

One Aborigine who reflected the new mood which existed among many of his people, especially the younger ones, was Noel Pearson. He grew up in the Hope Vale Aboriginal community on Cape York, which had once been a Lutheran mission. Pearson won a scholarship to St Peter's Lutheran secondary college in Brisbane and went on to study law and history at the University of Sydney. He became a prominent and influential figure in Aboriginal affairs, partly because he wasn't identified with the ATSIC structure and partly because he developed an independence of thinking. Pearson's philosophy was expressed during a 2004 interview with the ABC:

> There are a lot of people who share my sense of question about what has happened ... that we've got to get out of this dependency, because the dependency has killed the will to live really, the will to work. You know, it sounds terribly conservative and terribly old-fashioned to talk about the fact that we've got to restore work, and work was part of our traditional life, a huge part of our traditional life. It was harder work than it is living in this modern society, and yet we tend to think that Aboriginal people and work are somehow foreign to each other.[4]

Speaking about the future, he went on:

> The people who are having success are these entrepreneurs. You don't send a bureaucrat in, you send a social entrepreneur into a situation. And those entrepreneurs don't have some kind of preconceived program; [they see] opportunities, they're people who can actually see that [there are] not just problems here on the ground, there's opportunities, there's talents, there's people, and if only we went in, not just with a kind of needs list, we actually go in and compile an assets list.

Pearson described how two people went into the Lockhart community on Cape York, which he described as 'pretty dismal', and discovered great artistic talent among the young women. Within four years an art 'industry' was thriving in the community:

> Who would have thought that there was this talent at Lockhart? If you'd walked the streets of Lockhart four or five years ago, who would have thought that within that social disaster there's this amazing talent, amazing pool of talent? Six or seven hundred people and there's about nine world-class artists amongst them.

Pearson developed an enterprise called Cape York Partnerships, designed to arrest the fiasco created by fifteen different government departments coming into one little Aboriginal community, each with its own agenda and resources. He proposed a collective approach, whereby the various departments in consultation with the community pooled their resources and ideas and reached agreement on what were the priorities for that community. Other ideas developed by Cape York Partnerships included assisting people with the management of their finances. Pearson said that the whitefellas allow banks to deduct mortgage payments, telephone bills and so on from their accounts; his plan was to assist Aborigines in similar ways. Predictably, there was hostility towards his ideas. Some right-wing elements claimed that the company that ran Cape York Partnerships was controlled by Pearson and a colleague and that he was using it as a 'milking cow' for his own benefit. Left-wing opponents were equally critical, claiming that Pearson was betraying his social welfare ideology. Queensland's Premier Beattie was dismissive of these criticisms, however, being so impressed with Pearson's blueprint for reform that he provided him with financial support, an office and staff.

Whether Pearson is right or wrong, whether his projects will last five months of five years, the situation in the Cape York Aboriginal communities is such that any new approach is worth a try. Tony Koch, a journalist with the Brisbane *Courier-Mail*, summed up the situation in a series of articles written after visiting some of the communities. In a discussion on ABC Radio's *Background Briefing* programme, he said:

> The articles actually challenged indigenous men to do something about looking after their women and kids. It's all right to stomp round with land rights placards and stomp the world stage and go to Geneva and all that, but I can tell you now I was at Kowanyama [a community on Cape York] on Thursday afternoon; there were 300 people there fighting, there was a woman getting her brains bashed out by a bloke with a tree branch and no-one was helping. This particular woman ran off into this apology for a Women's Shelter there. I went over the Shelter later on, the bloody place is full of bullet holes, and is just appalling. And I made an acquaintanceship later on with a lawyer who looks after victims of crime up there, he's got 800 clients on his books, and it's just a dreadful situation.[5]

Speaking of another Cape York community, he commented:

> I mean Aurukun, a community of fewer than 1000 people, in a six-week period this year had four murders. Four domestic murders. So this sort of thing has to be controlled, looked at; somebody has to do something about it; it's up to the men to do something about it. They're the leaders of the community; the women are desperate for something to be done, and the women are doing great things. And it's taken someone like Pearson, with his intellect and his responsibility, to confront it.

It's important to note that the concept of 'shared responsibility' between government and indigenous people has been part of the official policy in Canada since about 1990. Recognition of the special needs of urban indigenous people has also been part of government policies in Canada and the United States for some time.

It's now transparently and depressingly obvious that the ideologies which have driven the politics of Aboriginal Affairs since the referendum of 1967 are no longer relevant or realistic, if they ever were. The position was summed up in an article in a *Weekend Australian* in late 2004:

> The Coalition has entered a new phase with its own positive agenda free of Labor's reconciliation paradigm. This represents probably the most sweeping rethink since the 1967 referendum and it embodies the application of Howard's values to indigenous affairs. Within the Government it is described as a revolution.
>
> The aim is to terminate passive welfare delivery and substitute instead 'shared responsibility agreements' between local communities and government. It is about changing individual behaviour and community culture around the concept of mutual responsibility.[6]

The logic behind the government's new approach was articulated about a decade ago by a doctor friend of mine who has spent many years working with remote Aboriginal communities. He said that it was useless pouring more and more money and other resources into health and other programmes for Aboriginal people. The fundamental problems were personal hygiene and domestic hygiene. 'Self-determination' begins with 'self', and the initiative and the commitment to tackle health problems therefore lies with individuals and with families. Trying to remedy the situation by turning back the clock has been tried and has failed. Trying to isolate and preserve cultural capsules in the form of isolated communities has also failed, as witness the tragedies in the Cape York region and elsewhere. Contact with Western culture is inevitable and will increase.

But let it not be thought that all the ideals and efforts of the past 40 years have been a waste of time and effort. On the wider canvas the courageous fight to eliminate racial discrimination has largely been fought and won. True, there remain pockets of resistance, but a walk around the campus of any university will demonstrate that the future is in safe hands in this respect. The tragedy is that the Aboriginal people are not sharing in the fullness of this new multicultural Australia as they should. For most Australians they are not visible except through occasional media outbursts and the odd display of ceremonial rites. It's time for all Aboriginal people to share the benefits of this wonderfully diverse country.

20

The Way Ahead: from Dreaming to Visioning

One of the less appealing aspects of contemporary society is its use of words whereby they lose their precision of meaning. A good or rather bad example of this is the abuse of the word 'culture', its most degenerate form being found in the populist term 'multiculturalism'. 'Culture' can be applied to the assisted growth of all living things such as plants and trees, or specifically to human beings, where it means development or improvement by education or training. More recently, however, 'culture' has become identified with groups of people who share a common heritage of knowledge, belief, art, morals, law, customs, etcetera. A multicultural society therefore is one which contains a number of groups of people, generally minorities, each of which has a distinctive cultural character. The problems with the concept of multiculturalism are first, that it assumes all cultures are fixed and immutable, and second, that it is possible to retain cultural distinctions in the context of a wider society. The reality is that the dynamic of growth and development, the real 'culture', is played out in the wider society and not in the various 'cultures' within it—and the result is that the specific identification of these minority cultures is gradually reduced to symbols such as dress and dance. Nor is this confined to the cultural characteristics of more recent arrivals to Australia. Over the past two centuries Scottish tartans and highland dancing have survived the inevitable diminution of Scottish ancestry, and the strict lines of delineation and hatred between Catholics and Protestants has been reduced by such things as 'mixed marriages.'

Which brings us to what is called 'Aboriginal culture' or, to use another example of a recent populist twist in the use of language, 'indigenous culture.' If I had to describe the difference between Aboriginal culture and Western culture in very simple terms, I would exemplify Aboriginal culture in terms of ancient ceremonies and tribal practices, and Western culture in terms of science fiction films and video games. Each in its own way delves into the realms of fantasy but the difference is that the former delves into the past while the latter launches into the future. This is an important distinction to make when dealing with the issue of reconciliation. For it's not simply a question of whether present-day Aborigines and present-day 'Western culture' people can get along with each other. It's also a question of whether the respective cultures are reconcilable. Attempts at reconciliation between Aborigines and the rest of the Australian population are often based on the fallacious belief that two or more dramatically different cultures can actually stand side by side in the community without one, generally the more dominant, ultimately absorbing the other.

What has kept Aboriginal culture alive for so long has been the vast, empty, geographical and demographic character of the Australian continent that has allowed some Aborigines to remain relatively free of Western influence. However, their isolation is becoming increasingly difficult to sustain. Satellite television, for example, has the capacity to direct a vertical invasion of Western culture into every remote community even if horizontal invasion is blocked by a high wire fence. In any case, the acquisition of four-wheel-drive vehicles has increased the capacity of people in remote communities to travel to larger regional centres such as Alice Springs where their indigenous customs inevitably come under assault by Western ways.

There is a real fear, held by a number of Aboriginal leaders, that their culture will inevitably atrophy until it is nothing more than a museum collection of legends and ritual practices. The question is whether the Aboriginal dreams of the past can find a common ground with Western visions of the future. Some Aboriginal leaders hope this might yet be achieved. In a meeting of Aboriginal leaders at Port Douglas in 2004, organised by Noel Pearson, the most significant statement was made by Pat Dodson, known as a fierce critic of government policy:

> 'We want to reopen the dialogue with the Prime Minister,' Dodson told [the *Weekend Australian*]. 'Such a dialogue would be about clarification and trying to find common ground with him in the social arena. We are prepared to move beyond the past. We want to put our people first, not ourselves.'[1]

The decisive point of the meeting was Dodson's declaration that the prime minister's concept of mutual obligation was embedded in Aboriginal culture through their tradition of kinship. This meant 'it had grounding within our culture and society' and that 'it is not just a Western concept'.

But, as with past policies in Aboriginal affairs, while the concept of mutual obligation is good in theory it has to be grounded in the harsh reality of who Aboriginal people are and where they live. Stories about the continuum of violence, poverty, disease and the 'passive welfare' mentality in remote Aboriginal communities make it hard to believe that the discovery of a common ground between the cultures of Aboriginal and Western societies will in itself create a foundation for the future. One Aboriginal leader commented sadly that these terrible conditions are now so endemic in many communities they can no longer be treated solely by 'cultural therapy'.

In finding a solution to these tragic circumstances we have to accept the fact that Aboriginal people have been perceived by Australian governments as 'a problem' for a long time. The term, indeed the term 'Aboriginal problem', has been used over the years by many members of parliament, even by Paul Hasluck from the Liberal Party and Kim Beazley senior and Gordon Bryant from the Labor Party, who while politically opposed were all equally passionate in their advocacy of the rights of Aboriginal people. In 1950 Hasluck presented a private member's Bill that won the approval of both sides of the House. The substance of his address was a condemnation of the past treatment of the Aboriginal people and a plea for the exercise of national responsibility, in the course of which he said, 'The problem is so small as to be manageable.'[2]

In 1958 Bryant, who like Hasluck became Minister for Aboriginal Affairs, made a statement mirroring Hasluck's: 'The problem is quite small. There are only about 60 000 Aborigines and I suppose that half of them will make out quite well given reasonable opportunities.'[3]

This problem-solving approach to Aboriginal affairs has stemmed from our reaction to the stark contrast between what we regard as reasonable living conditions and the conditions in which we see Aboriginal people living. Most often our concerns have been health, housing, education, employment and, more recently, domestic violence. To a large extent these conditions were created when our predecessors removed Aboriginal people from their traditional hunter-gatherer lifestyle and herded them into compounds. It was inevitable that, living in the resulting ghetto-like conditions, hope and opportunity would gradually wither and eventually die. The enforced changes which the Aborigines experienced traumatised them and all but extinguished their life spirit.

The historical turning point for Aborigines, as for many colonised peoples around the world, came at the conclusion of World War II, when the human rights movement began to gather strength. In many countries the movement was linked to the end of colonialism and the achievement of independent nationhood. In a few countries, such as Australia, the indigenous community was only a very small percentage of the total population, and government policy was directed towards assimilating their indigenous peoples into the whole community as free, equal and respected members. Not everyone agreed with this, and a strong and growing movement developed that believed indigenous peoples should be treated and respected as having a separate identity and the right to determine their own future.

One of the most ardent advocates of this belief in Australia was Dr H. C. Coombs, a man of considerable influence and power. A noted economist and long-serving governor of the Reserve Bank, 'Nugget' Coombs played a leading role in postwar reconstruction and was a key adviser to both sides of politics. His interest in Aboriginal affairs began after his retirement from the governorship of the Reserve Bank in 1967, when he was appointed to the newly formed Aboriginal Affairs Council. Coombs played a big part in determining the policies that were adopted by Prime Minister Gough Whitlam in 1973, policies reflecting his own underlying philosophy of self-determination. Initially, Coombs conceived self-determination as a way of enabling Aboriginal people to adjust to the 'Australian way of life' at their own pace and in their own way. He also believed that Aboriginal political practices in their various communities possessed a self-regulating legitimacy that made public accountability requirements unduly disciplinary, a belief that turned out to be somewhat idealistic.

It's possible that Coombs believed that the period of self-determination for Aboriginal people would last until such time as they comfortably embraced the 'Australian way of life'. As a biography published in 1994 said:

> 'Aboriginal autonomy' is not a blueprint for political or cultural separatism. Despite an inglorious past, Coombs retains hope that Australians can avoid the endlessly retold 'historical' animosities of Ireland, Bosnia and the Middle East. Nor is he, like some environmentalists, guilty of Eurocentrism in reverse, for he makes no attempt to imprison Aborigines in a bucolic past. He understands that indigenous societies are not museums but organisms that constantly evolve and change.[4]

Somewhere along the way Coombs' Utopian ideal was refashioned by certain Aboriginal activists into a demand for separate sovereignty. A letter to *The Age* on 27 March 1993, from K. J. Everett, Aboriginal Provisional Government, South Hobart, was headlined 'Conciliation out until blacks have own state'. Everett wrote:

> Until we are free, a separate people with our own nation recognised as a state in the United Nations, until the Australian people can agree to that notion and be humble in handing control back to the legal owners of this land, until they can rid themselves of the notion that we must all be Australians, any hope of conciliation is beyond reach of all of us.

That kind of separatist philosophy has now all but disappeared but there still remains the unresolved matter of how Aboriginal people can participate in the decision-making processes involving the things that affect them. The ATSIC structure of federal and regional bodies that was designed to address this matter failed, and has been put to rest. In its place the federal government has sought to eradicate what has been called the 'middle man' of bureaucratic engagement and put in its place direct engagement between government and Aboriginal communities. (Examples of this were described in the previous chapter.) Some Aboriginal leaders, however, believe that 'rogue' bureaucrats are unwilling to let go of their involvement and in insidious ways are seeking to retain their grip on Aboriginal affairs.

Another impediment to the success of the new approach is that every so often the media spotlight focuses fiercely on some unsuspecting remote Aboriginal community in the Australian outback. It generally coincides with the visit of a prominent politician or journalist, or the published findings of a 'research study' that reaches alarming conclusions. In *The Age* in April 2005, for example, considerable space was devoted to a community with the Aboriginal name of Wadeye, more generally known to Australians as Port Keats. Two hundred and seventy kilometres south-west of Darwin, Wadeye has a population of over 2000. In addition there are 20 outstations (outlying communities of 15 to 30 people located on the traditional land of the clan concerned). In rhetoric reminiscent of media outbursts in the past, the conditions in Wadeye were described as being akin to those in Third World countries:

> An average of seventeen people live in each [three-bedroom] sweltering graffiti-covered house.
>   In 2003 only 45 Aborigines in an adult population of 1100 had a 'normal' job.
>   Some houses had no windows, filthy rooms and broken air-conditioners.[5]

Reaction to this information was expressed in customary shock/horror tones. And, as in the past, the response was to send consultants and researchers—who produce statistical data, make recommendations, and depart. Opinions about the future of Wadeye ranged from its being a 'basket case' to optimism about a viable economic future.

Bureaucrats now bear the brunt of criticism for what has happened. Ted Egan, Administrator of the Northern Territory, condemns a system 'whose best interests lie in further extensions of the problem [that word again] whereby more funds will be available to enable more jobs for concerned whitefellas to conduct more surveys, formulate new programs, extract more millions of taxpayers funds'.[6]

The one positive and hopeful sign that emerges from Wadeye and other communities swamped by the failures of bureaucracy is that Aborigines themselves are declaring they are fed up with this kind of treatment. They are expressing a desire for change, a change that engages more and more of the practices of Western culture. In addition to the usual desire for better health, better housing, education and employment, there's a desire to develop commercial projects using the land they have acquired through native title or grants. To achieve this will, however, require transferring land leases to individuals or companies that are free to carry out such developments—which, of course, will create conflict with traditional landowners and traditional land use. But there is a rising tide of desperation in what Aboriginal people are saying, especially the women, who see what is happening to their children.

So land once more becomes a crucial factor in the future of Aboriginal people. Not this time because of their spiritual connection with it, but because it is possibly the only resource that can provide them with a sound economic base for their future.

How can their land be utilised? Land is a necessary resource for pastoral, agricultural, mining and tourist opportunities. In the kind of country where most remote Aboriginals live, effective pastoral activities now require large landholdings and sophisticated corporate management geared to the market forces that determine the sale prices of stock. It's not the kind of activity that a small Aboriginal community could manage, and in any case it's questionable whether it would provide great employment opportunities. There was a time when Aboriginal stockmen sat tall in the saddle—but not now. It's all motor bikes and helicopters—and far fewer stockmen.

Agricultural activities require good supplies of water and sophisticated growing, cropping and marketing techniques. Interestingly, there's an increasing trend to grow genetically modified crops such as cotton in regions like the Kimberley where Aborigines often hold large tracts of land. Unfortunately, the development costs of such projects are very high and cash returns are not available for several years.

Tourism, coupled as it often is with arts and crafts, is another source of income for Aboriginal people. Here again there's a conflict between traditional culture and economic benefit. The best example of this is the insatiable desire of tourists to climb the monolith in Central Australia called Uluru. This practice is said to be painful for the local Aboriginal people in terms of what Uluru means to them traditionally. But it's unquestionably a good milking cow for the tourist dollar. The development of an arts and crafts market raises the question of the possible prostitution of Aboriginal culture and is also a risky business proposition. It's one thing to sell didgeridoos at the Alice Springs airport, but quite another to market hand-painted scarves in city retailing centres. Distance, and the lack of capacity to introduce new product lines every season, as fashion demands, militate against a thriving market for arts and crafts. And while some Aboriginal artists have earned huge sums of money for their paintings, we see their impoverished brothers and sisters trudging the streets of Alice Springs trying to sell their wares to contemptuous art dealers.

Mining, probably more than any other single factor, has been the catalyst for land rights battles. Miners and Aborigines have not exactly been the best of friends but, after government funding, mining royalties have been the greatest source of income for Aboriginal people. If Aboriginal people want to use their land as a source of economic benefit, the most likely way would be to encourage mining exploration and development.

The greatest barrier to the successful development of economic enterprises by Aboriginal people in remote communities is the fact that they are so small, so widely scattered across the continent and so far from the major population centres. There are over 1000 such communities spread across the outback, averaging in size between 15 and 50 people. It's unrealistic to expect that they can have the same facilities as larger communities. Organisations such as the Royal Flying Doctor Service, for example, experience great difficulty in servicing small remote outstation communities, some of which have no landing facilities.

While all these issues need to be addressed, by far the major problem today is the demolition of the myth that most Aborigines live in remote regions. The hard fact is that the vast majority of Aboriginal people now lives, and will increasingly live, in major cities and regional towns. By and large Aboriginal people are urbanised and no longer live on land with which they have a spiritual association. If Australia wants to assist its Aboriginal people we must begin by discarding the concept of a single 'problem'. Urban Aborigines and remote Aborigines should no longer be treated as one. There was a link between them when urban Aborigines took up the battle for remote Aborigines' land rights. With that battle won, urban Aborigines now have to look at the issues that specifically affect them. To do this requires discarding another myth—that most urban Aborigines live in the suburb of Redfern in Sydney. Actually, in 1998 only 236 lived in Redfern, compared with 2000 in Liverpool, 1200 in Fairfield, 1100 in Parramatta, 1000 in Marrickville and 1000 in Bankstown.[7] (That's only 6536 of the approximately 120 800 Aborigines who live in Australia's major towns and cities; see table on page XX.)

Another factor that must be taken into consideration is that in 54 per cent of urban households, an Aboriginal adult was married to, or cohabiting with, a non-Aboriginal person. When asked about their religion in the 1996 Census, 71 per cent of all Aborigines professed Christianity. A mere 2.5 per cent professed to be adherents of traditional Aboriginal religion, amounting to only 7952 individuals. As writer Keith Windschuttle commented, 'The beliefs of these 7900 people form the basis of the current "romantic movement" for the restitution of Aboriginal culture, despite the fact that 98 per cent of Aborigines do not own them.'[8]

Australia is not the only country grappling with the problems of an increasingly urban indigenous population. In Canada, the federal government introduced an Urban Aboriginal Strategy in 1998 to address the serious socio-economic needs of the nation's urban indigenous people. The results of that programme have been described as 'successful'. Part of the success is attributed to a policy of concentrating on specific pilot projects where people are working to provide local solutions to local priorities. In the city of Regina, for example, community priorities were housing improvement, crime reduction and employment, while in Winnipeg the focus was on education, housing, poverty and economic development, and in Thunder Bay, child poverty.

Aborigines in remote regions may be smaller in number than in urban areas but meeting their needs is far more difficult. The key question seems to be: How much individual initiative and responsibility is possible in a culture that has been traditionally corporate or tribal? Nowhere is the difficulty of finding an answer more apparent than in the issue of land ownership. Government policies stemming from the various land rights acts established land trusts and land councils which were based on the principle of corporate ownership. Now, however, it appears that an increasing number of Aboriginal communities and individuals want to own their homes or businesses individually. They believe this can be achieved by leasing, which will not threaten the underlying traditional ownership of land as set out in the *Native Title Act*. There's a belief among some Aborigines, which the federal government shares, that private ownership of homes will be an incentive to the better care of houses, and private ownership of businesses a better incentive to work. The better care of houses is also seen by some experienced medical professionals to be fundamental to the achievement of better health. They say that the root causes of bad health stem from poor personal and domestic hygiene. Others go deeper and say that this in turn is the product of lack of motivation stemming from no work or educational opportunities. It's also been suggested that the breakdown of traditional authority in Aboriginal communities has led to practices such as petrol sniffing running rampant. Whatever the cause, it would seem there's a change of mood becoming apparent in Aboriginal communities, and a desire to participate in a change for the better.

Another challenge is to tackle the health problems in remote communities head on. If it's possible for a voluntary organisation such as Rotary International to practically eliminate poliomyelitis worldwide, in a vaccination programme involving millions of people, then surely it must be possible for an Australian government to eliminate at least some of the health problems of a comparatively minute number of Aboriginal people living in small communities. The concept of mutual responsibility seems to be the most constructive approach presently being offered. There are three parties whose involvement is essential to the success of such a proposal. Two are, of course, the Aborigines themselves and the government. The third is the people who facilitate the process. And this may be where the real problem lies. As indicated earlier, bureaucrats are under the hammer because some are seen to be putting self-interest before work achievement—and that includes both government and Aboriginal bureaucrats.

In the 'protection' era, Aboriginal people had little or no say in matters that affected them. In the 'self-determination' era they, or their leaders and advisers, sometimes had too much say. Coupled with an unrealistic commitment to preserve their culture at all costs, this inevitably separated them from the Australian community as a whole. When the hiatus was recognised it led to a plea for reconciliation, both from the Aboriginal side and from government.

Reconciliation, though, requires more than the healing of past hurts. The situation will not be resolved simply by Australia paying for its past sins. There are certain aspects of Aboriginal culture that constitute blocks to a permanent improvement in living conditions. Some of these, such as the authority structure, are already eroding. Others, such as a spiritual relationship with a certain tract of land, will inevitably lose their strength as young people move away. The equation of human rights balanced with human responsibility must assume its rightful place, as it should in any community.

My fear is that the Australian people as a whole will gradually lose interest in the Aborigines, partly because efforts to assist them seem to have failed and partly because other ethnic groups are now far more prominent in the community and are competing for their place in the sun. The image of Aboriginal people for the average Australian is tied to either impoverished living conditions in the outback or riots in Redfern. That has to change.

Aboriginal people want to keep their identity as the original inhabitants of Australia. The question is whether it is possible to lose a culture and still retain an identity. Many years ago I visited Native American reservations in the United States. My travelling companions were the late Gatjil Djerruka, former ATSIC chairman, and his wife Jenny. I was impressed with how easily they and the Native Americans related to each other and were able to exchange views of the respective challenges they faced. One of the fine young men and women whom we met impressed me greatly, a young man who was a lawyer by profession. Speaking to us of his Indian heritage, he said, 'We have lost our language and that is sad. We have lost our tribal law and that too is sad. We have lost most of our cultural heritage and that too is sad. But we have not lost our identity. We know who we are.'

I hope that Australia's indigenous peoples never lose their identity and certainty as to who they are. To do this, however, they must win the respect not only of the Australian community but of the whole world. I'd like to see some of them participating in relief work among people whose plight is even worse than theirs. Let's face it, there are such people, in refugee camps in Africa and among the teeming millions of India, for example.

It was the famous Mahatma Gandhi of India who said, 'No culture can live if it attempts to be exclusive.' Recent events in the realm of terrorism have taught us that there is no room in Australia for exclusive cultures.

Postscript

At the time of writing, petrol was very much in the headlines—for two dramatically different reasons. The first was the soaring price of petrol being experienced globally, with prices unheard of a few years ago now commonplace. Talk of the impact of high petrol prices on the economies of industrialised countries, including Australia, suggested a fall in living standards. The second factor putting petrol in the headlines was the staggering revelations of the extent to which petrol sniffing was wreaking havoc in Aboriginal communities, especially among children. The two provided a stark contrast: a global problem affecting hundreds of millions of people, and a local problem which by comparison was affecting a relative handful.

In many ways the epidemic of petrol sniffing in remote communities epitomises the fundamental tragedy that has afflicted the Aboriginal people since Europeans first settled here. In the beginning the contrast in cultures was a matter of curiosity for both sides, but in the 200 years that followed, the contrast became a conflict and brought with it pain and suffering for the Aboriginal people. Nothing could be more tragic than the sight of young children destroying themselves through the abuse of a substance which in other respects has become almost the lifeblood of the Australian economy and way of life.

I first encountered the practice in 1974 when the Australian Inland Mission, of which I was superintendent, took over the responsibility for the hospital and health care of the Aboriginal community of Warburton Range. Located near the point where the Western Australian, South Australian and Northern Territory borders abut each other, Warburton Range was the most remote Aboriginal community on the face of the continent. Its origins stemmed from the days when it was the practice of Christian missionaries to hand out food and clothing to nomadic Aborigines at a central spot called a 'ration point'. Eventually people from four tribes settled there and allowed themselves to come under the care of the missionaries. I don't think it could ever have been a really happy place because it was a bit like putting four large families under one roof. I'm not sure how petrol sniffing came to be practised there, but I do know that it was mainly confined to youngsters who siphoned it from the vehicles our nurses used. Not even the erection of a high Cyclone wire perimeter fence deterred them. I also know that it gravely worried the nurses because of its effects, including brain damage.

The reasons the youngsters sniffed petrol were all too obvious. Warburton had a school and so from the age of about five to the age of twelve the children were confined to a classroom, having their minds expanded. Once they left school there was literally nothing on which they could employ their brains or bodies constructively. In brief, they were bored beyond belief, and natural curiosity and a sense of adventure led them to experiment with things that would give them a buzz. Coupled with this was the sad fact that the traditional sources of tribal and parental authority had weakened to the point where elders and parents felt powerless to take corrective action. At that time I knew of a few other remote communities where petrol sniffing was practised, and there was a sense of deep concern about it. But along with other damaging practices such as domestic violence, it wasn't given a very high profile by Aboriginal Affairs because intervention from outside would be seen as contrary to the policy of self-determination.

The devastating truth about the disastrous effects of petrol sniffing inevitably emerged. An article by Lindsay Murdoch in *The Age* in 2005 was headed 'The epidemic we cannot stop'. It was a heart-rending account of the effects of petrol sniffing in some remote Northern Territory Aboriginal communities where it had reached epidemic proportions. Said Murdoch:

> Forty-seven registered petrol sniffers are running rampant in Ngukurr, one of Australia's most remote indigenous communities ... Day and night sniffers wander aimlessly inhaling petrol fumes. Many have their faces stuck in a bottle for hours, making them oblivious to everything else in the town.

Murdoch wrote of a Central Australian community called Mutitjulu, where deaths caused by petrol sniffing resulted in the Alice Springs coroner reporting that brain-injured sniffers in wheelchairs were a common sight in the community, and that many sniffers continued the practice despite their disabilities. Even the introduction of 'non-sniffable' petrol didn't deter the sniffers, who resorted to stealing the old fuel. 'They even burgled the local police station,' said Murdoch.

An associated article in the same issue, written by Karen Michelmore, was titled 'Sniffing is a "lifestyle choice" for the young'. Michelmore reported that 'a sense of helplessness and a lack of money, jobs and education are driving young men particularly to slowly kill themselves with petrol sniffing'.

Reactions to these dramatic statements were as predictable as was to be expected. In most cases government copped the blame:

> Governments cannot expect Aboriginal communities gripped by petrol sniffing and other addictions to solve those crises [said the Alice Springs coroner]. The suggestion that the problems can be solved by the Aboriginal community in terms of simply saying in effect, just give us some money and we'll do it, has been tried and doesn't work. We know the men aren't doing it [taking responsibility for the problem]. It may be the men can't help; the men have got their own problem. The start of any solution must be the recognition of the really horrible circumstances that pertain at Mutitjulu. Honest recognition, complete recognition [is needed] and if that's going to upset the sensibilities of politicians, then too bad in my view.[2]

Blair Macfarland, a youth worker in the Mutitjulu community, told the inquest the sniffing crisis was resulting in serious violence. 'We have got a list of petrol sniffers back in the office, killing, raping, maiming,' he said. 'The list is appalling—that's the cost of neglect.'[3]

Vicki Gillick, from the Ngaanyatjarra, Pitjantjatyyara, Yankunytjatjara (NPY) Women's Council, blamed a hospital for releasing a teenage sniffer with brain damage who had tried to kill herself. Gillick said young female sniffers were particularly vulnerable, with some men buying petrol and swapping it for sex. 'Some of them [the female sniffers] are incoherent,' she said. 'They are preyed upon, not just in Mutitjulu, but in other parts of our region.'[4]

Inevitably academics, especially those who had espoused the land rights and self-determination causes, weighed into the battle with heavy criticism of governments. Peter D'Abbs, of James Cook University, said the inaction of various governments over time had contributed to the sniffing crisis:

> The result had been fragmented policies, short-term funding and no efforts to evaluate which programs were working. I think one of the main factors up until very recently has been a position that governments ... have adopted. They have said this is really a community problem and the community has to take ownership. For communities to be left to themselves to meet these needs ... that's simply untenable.[5]

The Australian community as a whole doesn't need to be reminded of the tragedies resulting from young people engaging in wholesale acts of self-destruction. From drug addiction to reckless driving to anorexia, almost daily the community is made aware of cases where young peoples' lives end in death or permanent disability. The Australian community is also increasingly aware that while therapeutic programmes can sometimes help to overcome drug or alcohol addiction, the root causes of these problems lie deeper, having to do with a person's lack of self-esteem or purpose in life.

This brings us to the question as to whether remote Aboriginal communities, in which traditional ways of life and authority structures are rapidly diminishing and opportunities for employment and development minimal, can really provide young people with a sense of hope and purpose for the future. The fact that three-quarters of the Aboriginal population now lives in cities and major regional centres would seem to suggest that without any formal government policies of assimilation or integration, Aboriginal people of their own volition are choosing to move into the future. As for those who choose to remain in the remote communities, it is questionable whether the community in general will be prepared to continue to pour money into such places without the assurance of some positive outcome. In any case it's doubtful whether problems such as petrol sniffing are capable of resolution in that kind of environment.

It's also important not to fall victim to the shock/horror reaction that so often accompanies sporadic visits to their communities by outsiders. Someone once said that one person's chaos is another person's comfort. If you can tear your eyes away from the environment in which Aborigines live and look at the people themselves, especially their eyes, you will gain another impression entirely. You will discover people with whom you share a common humanity and who therefore are deserving of your compassion and respect.

Bibliography

Primary sources (available on the Internet)
A chronological listing
Australian Referendum 1967 (Aboriginals)
1967 Referendum, the Official 'Yes' Case
Milirrpum v. Nabalco Pty Ltd and the Commonwealth (1971) 17 FLR 141
Aboriginal Land Rights Commission, First Report, AGPS July 1973;
    Second Report, AGPS April 1974
Racial Discrimination Act 1975
Environmental Protection (Impact of Proposals) Act 1976, Acts of
    Parliament
Aboriginal Land Rights (N.T.) 1976, No. 191 of 1976
Aboriginal Councils and Associations Act 1976
*Aboriginal and Torres Strait Islander (Queensland Discriminatory) Act
    1975*
Hawke Government (first) policy statement on Aboriginal Affairs,
    Hansard, 1983, vols 134–135
Aboriginal and Torres Strait Islander Heritage Act 1984
Hawke Government (second) policy statement on Aboriginal Affairs,
    Hansard, 1985, vol. 140
Hawke Government (third) policy statement ('Foundations for the
    Future'), *Hansard*, vol. 158
Aboriginal and Torres Strait Islander Commission Act 1989
Royal Commission on Aboriginal Deaths in Custody, Parliamentary Papers
    126–130, 1991
Resources Assessment Commission: Justice Stewart, Parliamentary Papers
    110–111, 1991
Council for Reconciliation Act 1991
Australia Act 1986
Mabo v. Queensland 1, 166 CLR 186, 1998

Mabo v. Queensland 2, 175 CLR 1, 1992
Native Title Act 1994
Royal Commission on Aboriginal Deaths in Custody Report, 1994
    (findings)
ATSIC (Amendment) Indigenous Corporations and Land Fund Act 1995
The Wik Peoples v. the State of Queensland and Others, www.isis.aust.com.
    wik
Native Title Amendment Act 1998
ATSI Heritage Protection Act 1999
'Bringing them Home', Report of the National Inquiry into the Separation
    of Aboriginal Children from their Families, December 2005
Indigenous Australians, 'Opportunity and Responsibility', Howard
    Government 'shared responsibility' policy, 2005
Australia Bureau of Statistics, *Australian Social Trends 1998*,
Population—Population Growth: Growth and distribution of Indigenous
    people
Aboriginal Social Justice Commission, *A Statistical Overview of Aboriginal
    and Torres Strait Islander Peoples in Australia*, 2005

Books
Broome, Richard. *Aboriginal Australians*, Allen & Unwin, 1995
Butt, Peter, and Eggleston, Robert. *Mabo: What the High Court Said*,
    Federation Press, 1993
Durack, Mary. *Kings in Grass Castles*, Corgi Books, 1974
Hasluck, Paul. *Shades of Darkness: Aboriginal Affairs 1925–1965*,
    Melbourne University Press, 1988
Hawke, Steve. *Noonkanbah: Whose Land? Whose Law?* Freemantle Arts
    Centre Press, 1989
Idriess, Ion. *Our Living Stone Age*, Angus & Robertson, 1963
Partington, Geoffrey. *The Australian History of Henry Reynolds*, AMEC,
    1994
Reynolds, Henry. *The Other Side of the Frontier*, Penguin, 1983
Weller, Patrick. *Malcolm Fraser PM*, Penguin Books, 1989
Windschuttle, Keith. *The Fabrication of Aboriginal History*, Macleay Press,
    2003

Endnotes

Introduction

1 *Encyclopaedia Britannica.* CD-ROM, 2001.
2 Idriess, Ion L. *Our Living Stone Age*, Angus & Robertson, Sydney 1963, author's note, p. xii.

Chapter 1

1 *Hansard*, 1963, vol. 39, p. 934.
2 Blackburn judgment, p. 147.
3 ibid., p. 151.
4 ibid., p. 150.
5 ibid., p. 164.
6 ibid., p. 193.
7 ibid., p. 198.
8 ibid., p. 270.

Chapter 2

1 Durack, Mary. *Kings in Grass Castles*, Constable & Co., London, 1959, reprinted Corgi, London, 1974, p. 304.
2 *Hansard*, 1966, vol. 53, p. 2359.
3 Robinson, Scott. 'The Aboriginal Embassy 1972', unpublished master's thesis, Australian National University, 1993, pp. 22–3.
4 ibid., p. 99.
5 *Hansard*, 1970, vol. 69, pp. 1968–70.
6 *Hansard*, 1970, vol. 70, p. 2214.

7 ibid., p. 2686.

8 *Hansard*, 1971, vol. 74, p. 2498.

9 Coombs, H. C. *Trial Balance*, Macmillan, 1981, p. 28.

10 *Hansard*, 1972, vol. 75, pp. 122–48.

11 Robinson, op cit, p. 117.

Chapter 3

1 *Hansard*, 1973, vol. 82, p. 14.

2 ibid., p. 540.

3 *Hansard*, 1973, vol. 86, p. 2365.

4 Aboriginal Land Rights Commission Second Report, April
    1974.

5 ibid., Main Principles, Item 50, p. 10.

6 ibid., Items 62, 64, 65, p. 11.

7 Borchart, D. H. *Checklist of Royal Commissions*, 1974, p. 81.

8 Aboriginal Land Rights Commission Report, Appendix E.6.

Chapter 4

1 1976 Acts of Parliament, p. 1617.

2 *Hansard*, 1975, vol. 95, p. 222.

3 ibid., p. 224.

4 Ranger Uranium Environment Inquiry Report, p. 319.

5 ibid., p. 323.

6 ibid., p. 33.

7 ibid., Conclusion.

Chapter 5

1 *Hansard*, 1975, vol. 93, p. 42.

2 *Hansard*, 1975, vol. 94, p. 1416.

3 ibid.

4 ibid., p. 1426.

5 *Hansard*, 1975, vol. 93, p. 285.

6 Racial Discrimination Bill 1975, Section 9.

7 *Hansard*, 1975, vol. 93, p. 1396.

8 ibid., p. 1414.

9 Weller, Patrick, *Malcolm Fraser PM*, Penguin Books, 1989,
    p. 283.

10 *Hansard*, 1976, vol. 99, p. 2551.

Chapter 6
1 Discussion with author, 2004.
2 *Hansard*, 1977, vol. 100, p. 533.
3 *Hansard*, 1976, vol. 101, p. 1641.
4 ibid., p. 1642.
5 *Hansard*, 1977, vol. 106, pp. 1013–5.
6 *Hansard*, 1978, vol. 110, p. 964.
7 *Hansard*, 1978, vol. 113, p. 1588.
8 Weller, Patrick, *Malcolm Fraser PM*, Penguin Books, 1989, p. 292.

Chapter 7
1 Hawke, S. *Noonkanbah: Whose Land? Whose Law?*, Fremantle Arts Centre Press, 1989, p. 47.
2 ibid., p. 178.
3 ibid., p. 210.
4 *Hansard*, 1980, vol. 117, p. 873.
5 ibid., p. 873.
6 ibid., p. 945.
7 *Hansard*, 1980, vol. 119, p. 38.

Chapter 8
1 *Hansard*, 1983, vol. 134, p. 3488.
2 ibid., p. 3489.
3 *Hansard*, 1983, vol. 135, p. 450.
4 *Hansard*, 1984, vol. 137, p. 2715.
5 *Hansard*, 1984, vol. 138, p. 778.
6 *Hansard*, 1985, vol. 140, p. 10.
7 ibid., p. 427.
8 ibid., p. 1265.
9 ibid.
10 *Hansard*, 1985, vol. 142, p. 2243.
11 ibid.
12 ibid., p. 2228.
13 *Hansard*, 1986, vol. 147, p. 1480.

14 *Hansard*, 1987, vol. 158, p. 3152–63.
15 ibid., vol. 156, p. 1041.
16 *Hansard*, 1988, vol. 160, p. 1327.
17 ibid., p. 1801.
18 *Hansard*, 1988, vol. 162, p. 251.
19 *Hansard*, 1988, vol. 160, p. 253.
20 *Hansard*, 1988, vol. 162, pp. 876–85.
21 ibid., pp. 891–2.
22 ibid., p. 903.
23 *Hansard*, 1988, vol. 164, p. 2555.
24 ibid., p. 2555ff.
25 *Hansard*, 1989, vol. 165, p. 1141.
26 ibid., p. 1146.
27 ibid., p. 1323.
28 ibid., p. 1331.
29 ibid.
30 ibid., p. 1338.
31 ibid., p. 1340–2.
32 *Hansard*, 1988, vol. 167, p. 2459.
33 ibid., p. 2464.
34 *Hansard*, 1988, vol. 168, p. 14.
35 *Hansard*, 1988, vol. 169, p. 16.
36 ibid., p. 17.

Chapter 9
1 *Hansard*, 1989, vol. 168, p. 201.
2 ibid., p. 857.
3 *Hansard*, 1990, vol. 168, p. 859.
4 ibid., p. 3412.
5 ibid., p. 3413, p. 3414.
6 ibid., p. 3568, p. 3659.
7 Stewart Report, p. 155.
8 *Hansard*, 1991, vol. 178, p. 5109.
9 *Hansard*, 1991, vol. 176, p. 1485 ff., p. 1487.
10 *Hansard*, 1991, vol. 177, p. 4498.
11 ibid., p. 4827.
12 *Hansard*, 1991, vol. 179, p. 507, p. 3088.

Chapter 10

1 Address to Samuel Griffith Society, November 1992.
2 *Arena*, April 1991.
3 Partington, G. *The Australian History of Henry Reynolds*, AMEC, 1994, p. 2.
4 ibid.
5 ibid., p. 3.
6 High Court of Australia, *Mabo and Others v. State of Queensland 1*, 1988, 166 CLR 186.
7 ibid.
8 Butt, P. and Eagleson, R. *Mabo: What the High Court Said*, Federation Press, 1993, pp. 8, 9.
9 High Court of Australia, *Mabo and Others v. State of Queensland 2*, 1992, 175 CLR 1.
10 ibid.
11 ibid.
12 ibid.
13 ibid.
14 ibid.
15 ibid.
16 ibid.
17 ibid.
18 ibid., p. 3586.
19 ibid.

Chapter 11

1 Hulme QC, S. E. K. 'Aspects of the High Court Handling of Mabo', *Mabo and After*, Association of Mining & Exploration Companies Inc., 1993.
2 *The Age*, 10 November 1993.
3 Address to Rotary Club of Hawthorn, 7 July 1992.
4 *Hansard*, 1993, vol. 189, p. 417. 5 ibid., p. 1489.
6 ibid., p. 2877, p. 2878.
7 ibid., p. 2883.
8 *Hansard*, 1993, vol. 191, p. 3406. 9 ibid., p. 4549.
10 *Native Title Act*, 1993, p. 2.
11 ibid., Definitions.

12 ibid., p. 3.
13 ibid. p. 122, p. 126.
14 Ewing, Geoffrey. Address delivered at Law Council of Australia Conference, 24 August 1994, p. 2.
15 *Hansard*, 1994, vol. 192, p. 261, p. 267.

Chapter 12
1 *Hansard*, 1994, vol. 192, p. 1489.
2 Hansard, 1994, vol. 194, p. 885.
3 ibid., pp. 18–19.
4 ibid., vol. 194, p. 409.
5 ibid., p. 815.
6 *Hansard*, 1994, vol. 196, p. 587.
7 ibid., p. 590.
8 ibid., p. 590, p. 592.
9 *Hansard*, 1994, vol. 198, p. 3731.
10 ibid. p. 3843.
11 ibid, p. 4613.
12 *The Age*, 3 March 1995.
13 ibid.
14 *The Age*, 4 March 1995.
15 ibid.

Chapter 13
1 *The Age*, 21 April 1994.
2 ibid.
3 ibid.
4 *The Age*, 11 March 1995.
5 *The Age*, 14 March 1995.
6 *The Age*, 17 February 1995.
7 *The Age*, 22 February 1995.
8 *The Age*, 2 March 1995.
9 *The Age*, 20 June 1995.
10 *The Age*, 22 January 1995.
11 ibid.
12 *The Age*, 11 February 1995.
13 ibid.

14 *The Age*, 18 February 1995.
15 *The Age*, 25 February 1995.
16 *The Age*, 16 February 1995.
17 *Herald-Sun*, 20 May 1995.
18 *Herald-Sun*, 24 May 1995.
19 *The Age*, 21 May1995.
20 *Herald-Sun*, 22 May 1995.
21 *The Age*, 25 May 1995.
22 *Herald-Sun*, 26 May 1995.
23 *The Age*, 9 June 1995.
24 *The Age*, 17 March 1995.
25 ibid.
26 *The Age*, 21 March 1995.
27 ibid.
28 *The Age*, 18 April 1995.

Chapter 14
1 *The Age*, 28 April 1995.
2 *The Age*, 10 May 1995.
3 *The Age*, 17 May 1995.
4 *The Age*, 22 February 1995.
5 *The Age*, 25 February 1995.
6 *The Age*, 19 May 1995.
7 *The Age*, 25 February 1995.
8 *The Age*, 27 February 1995.
9 ibid.
10 *The Age*, 10 May 1995.
11 *Herald-Sun*, 25 May 1995.

Chapter 15
1 *Hansard*, 1966, vol. 35, p. 2359.
2 Forbes, John. 'Prime Minister's Ten Point Plan', *The Adelaide Review*, December 1997.
NB Hereafter all references to *Hansard* from www.aph.gov.au//hansard/-
3 *Hansard*, 2 June 1997.
4 *Hansard*, 4 September 1997, speech on Native Title

Amendment Bill.
5 *Hansard*, 3 July 1998.
6 *Hansard*, 26 August 1997, Report of ATSI Affairs
   Committee.
7 *Hansard*, 27 June 1997.
8 *Hansard*, 12 December 1998, Kay Elson.
9 Carol Kendall.
10 *Hansard*, 26 May 1998, Kim Beazley.
11 *Hansard*, 28 May 1998, Tony Abbott.
12 *Hansard*, 26 August 1998, John Howard.
13 *Hansard*, 24 March 1999, Kim Beazley.
14 *Hansard*, 8 February 1999, John Howard.
15 *Hansard*, 30 March 1999, Philip Ruddock.
16 *Hansard*, 4 June 1997, Dr Michael Wooldridge.
17 ibid.

Chapter 16
1 *Hansard*, 27 August 1999, report of ATSI Committee,
   'Unlocking the Future'.
2 *Hansard*, 10 April 2000, Grievance Debate.
3 *Hansard*, 3 April 2000.
4 *Hansard*, 7 December 2000, ATSIC Amendment Bill.
5 ibid.
6 *Hansard*, 9 November 2000.
7 *Hansard*, 21 June 2001.
8 *Hansard*, 25 June 2001.
9 ibid.
10 *Hansard*, 24 September 2001, ATSI Affairs Committee
   report on Urban Aborigines.
11 ibid.
12 ibid.

Chapter 17
1 *Hansard*, 3 June 2002.
2 *Hansard*, 14 November 2002, National Report to
   Parliament on Indigenous Education and Training, 2001.
3 *Hansard*, 23 September 2002.

4 ibid.
5 *Hansard*, 2–5 and 16–19 June 2003, speeches re crisis in ATSIC.
6 *'Make or Break?' A Background to the ATSIC Changes and the ATSIC Review*, Information and Research Services to Commonwealth Parliament, Current Issues Brief No. 29, 2002–03.
7 ibid.
8 *Hansard*, 16 June 2003.
9 *Hansard*, 15 September 2003, Grievance Debate.
10 ibid.
11 *Hansard*, 4 December 2003, Committee on Native Title and the ATSI Land Fund.
12 *Guardian Unlimited World Despatch*, 29 April 2003.
13 LRQ, June 2000; www.faira.org.au/lrq/archives/2000
14 *The Australian*, 12 August 2003.
15 *Guardian Unlimited World Despatch*, 29 April 2003.
16 *Hansard*, 25 March 2003.
17 ibid.
18 *Hansard*, 30 March 2003.
19 ibid.
20 2004 211 ALR 412.
21 *The Australian*, 16 April 2004.
22 ABC TV, *7.30 Report*, programme transcript, 29 November 2004.
23 ibid.

Chapter 18

1 *Medical Journal of Australia*, 2004, 180(10), 492.
2 Australian Human Rights and Equal Opportunity Commission, *ATSI Social Justice: Statistical Overview of ATSI People in Australia*, 1998.
3 ibid.
4 ibid.
5 *Hansard*, 24 March 2003.
6 BBC TV News, UK Edition, 30 March 2004.
7 *Australian Social Trends 2002: Health and Mortality of*

ATSI Peoples, ABS, 2002.
8 BBC TV News, UK Edition: 'Challenge to Improve Aborigines' Lot', 14 February 2005.
9 Conversation with author 2005.

Chapter 19

1 BBC News, UK Edition: 'Australia Unveils Aboriginal Body', 6 November 2004.
2 ibid.
3 ibid.
4 ABC Radio, *AM* transcript, 6 December 2004.
5 ABC Radio, *Background Briefing*, 31 December 2000.
6 *Weekend Australian*, 8 December 2004.

Chapter 20

1 *Weekend Australian*, 8 December 2004.
2 *Hansard*, 1950, vol 208, p. 3978.
3 *Hansard*, 1958, vol. 20, p. 295.
4 Rowse, T. *'Nugget' Coombs' Legacy in Indigenous Affairs*, CUP 2000 (review).
5 *The Age*, 2 April 2005.
6 Egan, Ted, *The Age*, 2 April 2005.
7 *Australian Social Trends 1998*, ABS, 1996.
7 Discussion of Gary Johns' paper, 'The Failure of Aboriginal Separatism', Keith Windschuttle Address to Bennelong Society, December 2000.

Postscript

1 *The Age*, 11 August 2005.
2 ibid.
3 ibid.
4 ibid.
5 ibid.

Index